Speed, Data, and Ecosystems

Excelling in a Software-Driven World

Chapman & Hall/CRC Innovations in Software Engineering and Software Development

Series Editor
Richard LeBlanc
Chair, Department of Computer Science and Software Engineering, Seattle University

AIMS AND SCOPE

This series covers all aspects of software engineering and software development. Books in the series will be innovative reference books, research monographs, and textbooks at the undergraduate and graduate level. Coverage will include traditional subject matter, cutting-edge research, and current industry practice, such as agile software development methods and service-oriented architectures. We also welcome proposals for books that capture the latest results on the domains and conditions in which practices are most effective.

PUBLISHED TITLES

Building Enterprise Systems with ODP: An Introduction to Open Distributed Processing
Peter F. Linington, Zoran Milosevic, Akira Tanaka, and Antonio Vallecillo

Computer Games and Software Engineering
Kendra M. L. Cooper and Walt Scacchi

Engineering Modeling Languages: Turning Domain Knowledge into Tools
Benoit Combemale, Robert B. France, Jean-Marc Jézéquel, Bernhard Rumpe, Jim Steel, and Didier Vojtisek

Evidence-Based Software Engineering and Systematic Reviews
Barbara Ann Kitchenham, David Budgen, and Pearl Brereton

Fundamentals of Dependable Computing for Software Engineers
John Knight

Introduction to Combinatorial Testing
D. Richard Kuhn, Raghu N. Kacker, and Yu Lei

Introduction to Software Engineering, Second Edition
Ronald J. Leach

Software Designers in Action: A Human-Centric Look at Design Work
André van der Hoek and Marian Petre

Software Development: An Open Source Approach
Allen Tucker, Ralph Morelli, and Chamindra de Silva

Software Engineering: The Current Practice
Václav Rajlich

Software Essentials: Design and Construction
Adair Dingle

Software Metrics: A Rigorous and Practical Approach, Third Edition
Norman Fenton and James Bieman

Software Test Attacks to Break Mobile and Embedded Devices
Jon Duncan Hagar

Speed, Data, and Ecosystems: Excelling in a Software-Driven World
Jan Bosch

REVIEWS

"This book gives you a great set of tools on how to bring business architecture and technology architecture together to drive a common set of goals and objectives."

—**Brendan Bank**,
CTO Booking.com

"SDE offers a fascinating and well-researched overview of the major trends in the software industry. If you want to survive as a software company in the 21st century, add this wonderful book to your reading list."

—**Jurgen Appelo**, author of *Management 3.0 and Managing for Happiness*

"Jan Bosch has a unique background with both leading academic expertise and a profound industry experience, and utilizing his knowledge and ideas in conjunction with digitalization will result in great improvements and export values for Swedish companies. Jan Bosch is a pioneer in how he systematically demonstrates the strength of changing the perspective for working with software. He shows how new services, products and value is created by drawing on the deep knowledge software developers have of customers, coupled with tools such as software architecture knowledge and ways of working, user feedback and data collection."

—**Ingrid Nordmark**, CEO Swedish Institute for Computer Science

"Jan Bosch has compiled a book that describes the challenges and the opportunities all industries are facing connected to the increasing importance of software. The book addresses the dynamics in the world: changing needs, technology development and also globalization where new competitors appear and existing competitors reach new markets rapidly. These challenges require speed, use of data (facts) for effective decision making and also clever use of collaborations with external organisations in s.c. eco-systems. Fortunately, the book also describes ways to meet these challenges and how to concretely achieve speed, use of data and effective use of eco-systems of partners. I really like the approach that the book takes to first describe the challenges and drivers for change, the why, in a management or strategy book manner, and then describe how and by who to meet these challenges in a way that engineers and practitioners can relate to. This means that this book is an excellent tool for a dialogue within a company between general management, middle management and senior engineers — which in fact is an imperative to survive in the future."

—**Stefan Andersson**, Director Future Aircraft Systems at Saab AB
and Chairman of Swedsoft (www.swedsoft.se)

"The excellent book of *Speed, Data and Ecosystems* by Jan Bosch captures the essence for any industry and company that is in the process of transforming into a digital future. Jan Bosch builds his knowledge based on academic research and experience from the industry combining this into a holistic approach how to work with software leveraging from the opportunities and meeting the challenges.

The practices of agility, continuous integration and how to capture and manage the value of data that will turn into services and products combined with the need for speed in a collaborative way of working is an excellent opportunity to stimulate a needed dialog on many levels within a company."

—**Mats Melander**, Director Automation Solutions at Tetra Pak

"In an ever-changing world we all need to strive for speed with accuracy. Doing so can easily drive you and your company on bad paths and this is why evidence based software development becomes so crucial. Jan Bosch's book is a great read for anyone that wants to make sure they build what actually has the intended impact on their business let alone doing it with great speed and minimal investment."

—**David Rejdemyhr**, Engineering Manager Klarna

"If you're interested in how to manage things in R&D intensive companies, this is the book for you. You get a bleeding edge overview of the latest theories and models and how it all fits together. Best of all, it's easy to read and it's full of relevant practical ideas that I can use in my daily work. One thing is sure, I will be handing out copies of the book at my company."

—**Pontus Bergendahl**, Manager FW development at Axis Communications

"A must read for any leader or professional in the software industry. Simple but insightful Stairway models provide compelling and practical guidance for both every-day challenges and extensive transformations in the realm of software development."

—**Mladen Pilipovic**, Director of Engineering, Spotify

"During my 15 years working with strategy & business development I´ve read a lot of books, attended several conferences and hired consultants within the field. Prof. Dr. ir. Jan Bosch plays in another league in comparison. His experience from business and his research makes his advice unique and invaluable for an old financial institutions struggling with digital transformation. Mr Bosch's advice on have to handle innovation in complex IT-system has been especially valuable for us. If I should recommend one person to talk to when it comes to innovation in the 21st century and one book to read it would be Mr. Bosch's."

—**Gustav Gorecki**, strategy & business development within Storebrand, founder of several startups and ex Accenture strategy manager

"The software industry has been continuously speeding up the digital transformation of our lives. Repetitious manual work gets automated, systems become more autonomous. We are at the edge of autonomous driving, our kids hunt virtual comic figures in the real world, our bookkeeping is close to being fully automated. So-called algorithmic tasks become digital, while heuristic tasks, like creativity, stay with us humans.

Applying this to software development: In software development you can and must be smart, and you need to make use of the machines, not only during final code execution but also in every step of software development: automate every task, let the machines verify your code, free us of any tedious work, produce and consume data, and close the feedback loops between creators and end users.

On the other side, digital processes bring us knowledge in form of data in unprecedented dimensions: transactions, receipts, usage data of applications, etc. Managing the risks and obeying privacy—we should apply the available technology to make responsible and positive use of the available data. Whether it is really Big Data in the sense of extremely large and complex, or not, the evaluation of that data allows the machines to learn, predict, feedback, and potentially automate, based on patterns and correlations.

Thirdly, already half of the top 10 of the most valuable companies do not sell or deal with classic goods, but are creators and owners of powerful digital ecosystems. Ecosystems that scale not linearly, like typical manufacturing or trading, but exponentially by the number of partners in and users of the ecosystem.

This book unifies those three of the most current best practices of the software-driven industry: speed, data, and ecosystems. Speed in value creation through software, namely continuous integration, continuous delivery, and continuous experimentation. Data to feedback what we did is actually the most effective and efficient to create value. Ecosystems to supersede classical business models by factors. The book explains the relationships, gives examples, and guides you with frameworks so that the application in your next project will let you harvest all the smartness and profitability that is possible in todays software development."

—**Michael Kircher**, CTO DATEV eG, Germany

"Professor Jan Bosch has written a book that relates to the most important challenge that many companies are going through these years: Becoming more and more software dependent (Digitization). In fact, he puts words on and suggest solutions on how to adapt to this. I particularly like his "Stairway to Heaven" models that relate to Speed, Data and Ecosystems. I like the BAPO-model thinking and the three layer model. All these make it possible for Leaders and Employees that are not SW-experts to understand and suggest changes in their business to overcome the challenges."

—**Jan Harding Gliemann**, Senior R&D Director, GRUNDFOS, Denmark

"Volvo Group is a company where the amount of software is increasing rapidly. A majority of the new innovations in a truck and the transport system are based on software. Our ability to efficiently develop software and to reach our customers with new innovations, are already, and will increasingly in the future be a key competitive differentiator. With this book we get methods and tools to assess our software development maturity and the steps that we need to take to keep us being a leader in commercial transport solution taking full advantages of the possibilities that software and digitalization bring."

—**Ted Kruse**, Director Electrical & Embedded Systems,
Advanced Technology & Research, Volvo Group Trucks Technology

"As an executive manager of a mid-size software product development organization, I found this book as an eye opener. The Stairway to Heaven concept in three areas (speed, data and ecosystem) is a recipe to transform not only the software development team but the whole company into an organization where all decisions are made based on facts, not opinion. New products are build much faster at much higher quality, features are determined based on data from real customers, and on top, development costs are greatly reduced. The steps are simple, the R&D organization organizes itself to deploy software much faster and get feedback from the field automatically, product management organization analyzes the feedback makes product decisions based on evidence and the company transitions from internally focused to ecosystem-centric allowing to focus on their core competencies and outsource all activities that are not strategic. Any professional involved in advanced software development must read this book."

—**Metin Ismail Taskin**, CTO AirTies

CHAPMAN & HALL/CRC INNOVATIONS IN
SOFTWARE ENGINEERING AND SOFTWARE DEVELOPMENT

Speed, Data, and Ecosystems

Excelling in a Software-Driven World

Jan Bosch

Chalmers University of Technology
Gothenburg, Sweden

CRC Press
Taylor & Francis Group
Boca Raton London New York

CRC Press is an imprint of the
Taylor & Francis Group, an **informa** business

CRC Press
Taylor & Francis Group
6000 Broken Sound Parkway NW, Suite 300
Boca Raton, FL 33487-2742

First issued in hardback 2017

ISBN-13: 978-1-1381-9818-0 (pbk)
ISBN-13: 978-1-1384-6841-2 (hbk)

This book contains information obtained from authentic and highly regarded sources. While all reasonable efforts have been made to publish reliable data and information, neither the author[s] nor the publisher can accept any legal responsibility or liability for any errors or omissions that may be made. The publishers wish to make clear that any views or opinions expressed in this book by individual editors, authors or contributors are personal to them and do not necessarily reflect the views/opinions of the publishers. The information or guidance contained in this book is intended for use by medical, scientific or health-care professionals and is provided strictly as a supplement to the medical or other professional's own judgement, their knowledge of the patient's medical history, relevant manufacturer's instructions and the appropriate best practice guidelines. Because of the rapid advances in medical science, any information or advice on dosages, procedures or diagnoses should be independently verified. The reader is strongly urged to consult the relevant national drug formulary and the drug companies' and device or material manufacturers' printed instructions, and their websites, before administering or utilizing any of the drugs, devices or materials mentioned in this book. This book does not indicate whether a particular treatment is appropriate or suitable for a particular individual. Ultimately it is the sole responsibility of the medical professional to make his or her own professional judgements, so as to advise and treat patients appropriately. The authors and publishers have also attempted to trace the copyright holders of all material reproduced in this publication and apologize to copyright holders if permission to publish in this form has not been obtained. If any copyright material has not been acknowledged please write and let us know so we may rectify in any future reprint.

Visit the Taylor & Francis Web site at
http://www.taylorandfrancis.com

and the CRC Press Web site
http://www.crcpress.com

This book is dedicated to everyone in Software Center. Researchers, engineers, architects, managers, administrators and others.
The prime technology that is making the world a better place in this time and age is software.
Thank you for contributing to the realization of the vision of a software-driven world.

Contents

SECTION III **Data**

CHAPTER 8 ▪ The Stairway to Heaven: Data 127

SECTION IV **Ecosystems**

CHAPTER 11 ▪ The Stairway to Heaven: Ecosystems   197

List of Figures

List of Tables

Foreword

Software is everywhere. Today, software fills a very critical function for humanity, society and industries, and it will continue to increase in importance as one of our most powerful tools to meet individual, business and social challenges. Software is an enabling area of knowledge available and used in all domains and sectors of society – from the internet to devices, communications, transportation, energy, manufacturing, production, banking, finance, management, health care, gaming, education and more. Software has become one of the most important industrial competitive factors, making software development a key activity today, and it is clear that software and system development is a key to future growth. Software has today become synonymous with innovation and is a main component in the ongoing digitalized transformation.

The opportunities made available through connectivity and software allow us to develop more and more advanced, complex systems. Developing, producing and managing these systems, however, is becoming increasingly challenging. We therefore need to improve how we use software for innovation and how software innovates and create new products and services, as well as how we can use it to enhance productivity and efficiency in research and development. We need to innovate and mature when it comes to creating and producing software. The importance of Speed, Data and Ecosystems to improve software and system development will increase drastically in a software driven world.

Ericsson has always been at the forefront of creating sophisticated, complex, robust, maintainable and scalable software. We have been delivering best-in-class software for communication systems for several decades, and providing our customers with quality software running on large scale of systems of systems, has always been one of our core assets. Continued leadership in this area is essential for our future success. I believe we are well positioned enough to mature further in software and system development in order to sustain our technology leadership in ICT.

This book provides a summary of the experience we have gained and the research that has been performed through the fruitful cooperation that our company and its experts together with partners in the Software Center. This cooperation focuses on large-scale software and system engineering, taking traditional software development and making it part of an innovation eco system. Our partnership in Software Center is driven by our desire to learn from others and to share what we have learned from our own experience. It is our strong belief that cooperation is vital in order to be at the forefront of research for future software and system development from which we all can benefit.

Sara Mazur
VP & Head of Ericsson Research

Preface

The world is driven by software. Virtually every part of our lives is infused with software. At work, administrative systems have automated numerous business processes. At home, we spend our time on the web using many different websites. In our interaction with the physical world, the software in our mobile phones, our cars and even our electric toothbrushes delivers the functionality that we care about. Over the last decades, the value in virtually every industry and every aspect of our lives has shifted from the "atoms" to the "bits".

One may wonder what it is that makes software such a valuable technology. There are at least three reasons. First, software allows for a much more fine-grained, customized and personalized behavior of products. Using software, one can cause a product to act in ways that are impossible to achieve using mechanics or electronics. For instance, the fuel efficiency and reduced environmental impact of modern cars and trucks would be impossible without the software in their engine control units. Second, software is infinitely more malleable and changeable than the traditional technologies. In embedded systems, the "atoms" need to be frozen at some point before the start of manufacturing but software can be deployed during manufacturing, when the system is taken in operation or at any point in time afterwards. Third, software allows for orders of magnitude shorter feedback loops between the producer of a system and the users of these systems. In "The Lean Startup" [45], Eric Ries introduces the "Build-Measure-Learn" (BML) loop as the basic feedback mechanism in innovation. The BML loop in mechanical and hardware tends to be measured in years and sometimes decades. With modern continuous deployment techniques, the BML loop for software is often measured in weeks, days or sometimes even hours. As shorter feedback loops lead to faster innovation, software allows for this faster innovation.

For organizations that traditionally identified as mechanical or hardware companies or even traditional software companies with yearly release cycles, this has major implications in the way the business needs to operate. Many companies struggle with this transition. This is clear when looking at the tenure of companies on the Fortune 500. Over the last decades, the duration of a company on this list of the largest companies in the world has decreased from more than 30 years in the 1990s to around a decade in the most recent listings. Clearly organizations are failing to adjust themselves to the increasing rate of innovation and the fundamental transition to a software-driven world.

This begs the question why companies that seemingly have all the pre-conditions for continued success still fail at such an astonishing rate. Having worked at Nokia in the mid-2000s and in my consulting with companies struggling to adjust themselves to this new reality, I have learned that it is not a lack of awareness of the relevant developments. Often the companies that I work with know even better than I what the likely implications on their business are. The main struggle is to convert that insight into action. As there are more things happening in the outside world than anyone can keep track of, all the threats to and opportunities for the organization become an unmanageable, amorphous cloud and there is a major risk of "analysis paralysis".

This book provides a simple set of priorities and a clear road map to successfully transition your organization towards the "digitalization era". We discuss the three focus areas that firms need to address: speed, data and ecosystems. Speed is concerned with shortening the feedback loops between the company and its systems deployed in the field as well the users of these systems. As virtually any software-intensive system these days is connected to the Internet, we have unprecedented possibilities to collect data. This allows organizations to shift from opinion-based decision making to data-driven decision making and to generate novel insights. Finally, ecosystems allow companies to focus their internal activities on the most differentiating aspects and to rely on partners in the ecosystem for everything else.

In the three main parts of the book, we provide systematic "stairways" for organizations to follow in order to systematically build their capabilities. Each stairway has five steps that organizations evolve through. In addition to the five-step stairways, each part offers a set of methods and techniques to help organizations develop the necessary capabilities. These range from visualization of continuous integration to management of architectural technical debt; from A/B testing to evidence-based decision making and from industry structures to ecosystem strategies.

When combined, the stairways, the methods and the techniques provide a strategic road map and the tools for companies to transition to a digitized economy. The material in the book is based on collaborative research with dozens of companies and hence has a solid empirical and validated foundation. It is intended to help you, the reader, to develop a strategic, systematic approach to driving change at your company. All the best on your journey!

Acknowledgments

This book is the result of more than 25 years of research and hands-on experience of which close to 10 were spent as vice president at great companies such as Nokia and Intuit and the remainder as a professor in Sweden and the Netherlands. The majority of the concrete frameworks, models, methods and tools presented, however, result from my last five years as director of and active research in the Software Center (www.software-center.se).

The Software Center is a collaboration between, at the time of writing, ten large software-intensive systems companies (Ericsson, Volvo Cars, AB Volvo (trucks), Saab AB, Grundfos, Jeppesen (part of Boeing), Axis Communications, Tetra Pak, Verisure and Siemens) and five universities (Chalmers University of Technology, University of Gothenburg, Malmö University, Linköping University and Mälardalen University). Over the last years, the Software Center has more than doubled its members, grown its research from three to over 20 projects and from a handful of researchers to over 30. This expansion would have been impossible without the relentless and incredible support from the companies and the universities in the center and, more specifically, the individuals at these organizations. This book would have been impossible without the support and active engagement from its steering committee, especially Anders Caspar and Anna Sandberg from Ericsson, Mladen Pilipovic from Jeppesen, Ted Kruse from AB Volvo, Pontus Bergendahl from Axis Communications, Kent Niesel from Volvo Cars, Fredrik Wising and Jonas Lindgren from Saab AB, Jan Smith from Gothenburg University and Catarina Coquand from Malmö University, as well as the task force, especially Fredrik Hugosson from Axis Communications, Mats Linden from Ericsson and Jens Svensson from AB Volvo, and the coordination team, especially Wilhelm Meding from Ericsson and Gert Frost from Grundfos. I am indebted to these individuals as well as their colleagues on the steering committee, task force and coordination team.

The frameworks, models, methods and tools discussed in this book are the result of research activities at the Software Center companies as well as numerous other ones. This research, however, was conducted in collaboration with other researchers. The first and foremost person I need to thank is Helena Holmström Olsson. We collaborated on many topics presented in this book, including the speed dimension of the Stairway to Heaven, customer-specific teams, the HYPEX and QCD models for evidence-based development as well as the TELESM framework for engaging with ecosystems. Over the last half-decade, we have formed an incredibly productive, creative and fruitful research partnership and friendship for which I am immensely grateful. Antonio Martini is the driving force behind our work on software architecture technical debt. First as my PhD student and now as a postdoctoral researcher, Antonio has blossomed into a highly recognized member of the research community as well as gained respect with the companies for his deep knowledge and experience around the topic. Few things are more satisfying in life than being part of such a journey of growth as Antonio experienced. Daniel Ståhl, in his role as industrial PhD candidate, and I have collaborated on the topic of continuous integration, especially in large-scale software engineering. Agneta Nilsson and I developed the original CIVIT model presented in this paper, later reinforced by the contributions of Christian Berger. Aleksander Fabijan, as the PhD student of Helena, has done great work on evidence-based or data-driven development that I have been blessed to be part of. Over the last years, I have also done research with, among others, Ulrik Eklund, Anna Sandberg, Michel Chaudron, Herman Hartmann, Enrico Johansson, Rafael Capilla, Miroslaw Staron, Matthias Tichy, Jan Salvador van der Ven, Torvald Mårtensson and the late Lars Pareto. Several people, including Ray Carnes from Boeing, reviewed all or part of the book and provided very valuable insights and feedback. I want to thank them for their help. I have been inspired by all these collaborations and learned so much from the perspectives brought by all and I am grateful for your gifts!

Although it is customary to end an acknowledgment by referring to family, my life partner for over 25 years, Petra, is also a researcher and we have co-authored several papers together and some of our work ended up in this book as well, including the ESAO model and the model of customer feedback techniques. The opportunity to discuss professional topics and interests in addition to the personal with one's life partner is a gift that I am incredibly thankful for. This book would not have been possible without her strong, continuous love and support.

Petra and I are the parents of three amazing boys, David, Nathan and Adam. They keep me grounded and help me realize that whatever I do at work will never be more important than what I have in them. The energy, ambition and potential that radiates from them reminds me continuously that they represent the future and that it is my job to make their future as well as the future of society as a whole the best possible one.

Finally, although the ideas presented in this book are the result of the intellectual energy of many people, all errors, mistakes and omissions are mine.

I

Introduction

CHAPTER 1

Introduction

As Marc Andreessen wrote in his Wall Street Journal op-ed [6], software is eating the world. For industry after industry, investment in software R&D is increasing and the software in products, rather than the mechanics and hardware, defines the value. Thus, software plays an increasingly central role in the modern world. In virtually any industry there are examples of software enabling new business models, novel applications and unprecedented efficiency improvements. Of course, well-known companies such as Google, Facebook and Spotify are entirely driven by software. But even for a Volvo truck, more than 70% of all innovation is now driven by software.

With the growing importance of software for the industry, the size of the software in systems has been going up accordingly. According to Ebert and Jones [26], the size of software increases with an order of magnitude (10x!) every five to ten years. This leads to several strategic challenges for the companies delivering these systems. First, we see a marked shift in R&D investment from the mechanical and hardware parts of systems to the software parts. In several of the companies that we work with, we have witnessed the investment in software R&D going up significantly (sometimes dramatically) at the expense of investments in other fields. Second, as the size of the software goes up and companies have a tendency to keep using the same development models, the cycle time of development has a tendency to slow down. For example, in one of the companies that we work with, the release cycle for their main platform slowed from once every nine months to once every 18 months until the company realized that this was unacceptable and took measures to address this. Third, part of the increase in software size is caused by the company taking in new externally developed software. This software can be commercial or open-source, but it requires integration and validation as much as any other subsystem and consequently requires R&D effort to be allocated to it. As the saying goes, quantity has a quality of its own. Another consequence of relying increasingly on externally developed software is that companies naturally shift from being internally focused to paying more attention to their business ecosystem and the partners and suppliers that are part of it.

The cloud computing and Software-as-a-Services companies have been leading the industry in these developments. By taking an experimentation-based approach and adopting short feedback loops, the traditional organizational models using functional hierarchies of product managers, architects, developers, testers and release engineers are becoming increasingly obsolete. Often referred to as DevOps, these roles can no long stay in their respective silos and instead need to become part of the same team. Each team needs all the functions required to take an innovative idea to a fully implemented and deployed feature. This includes skills around product management, software architecture, development, testing and deployment as well as other skills depending on the type of system, such as user experience, security or safety. Such teams are often referred to as cross-functional teams, but in this book we use the term multi-disciplinary teams. The reason is that the term cross-functional suggests that the team members belong to different functions (as in organizational units) and that working cross-functional is an exceptional approach. Instead, multi-disciplinary teams with a high degree of autonomy are increasingly becoming the norm in many companies, especially in the cloud computing and SaaS industries but rapidly followed by the embedded systems industries.

The notion of requirements engineering through experimentation changes the role of product management in traditional organizations. Traditionally, product managers talk to current and potential customers and listen to their wishes and desires. Subsequently, this input is turned into an elaborate requirement specification that covers all aspects of a new product or the next release of an existing product. This specification is then given to the R&D organization together with a budget. Due to the complex and frequently antagonistic relationship between product management and development, the iteration speed of the system is often low, for instance yearly or six-month cycles. Adopting multi-disciplinary teams and shifting towards continuous deployment allows organizations to overcome these challenges.

Over the last decade, the space of software start-ups as well as online companies have changed quite fundamentally along the approaches discussed above. Although cloud and SaaS provide inherent advantages, many industry observers fail to recognize that these companies work in a different way, embrace a different culture and have different norms and values. This contributes as much to the success of these companies as the underlying technology infrastructure. Traditional on-premise software companies as well as embedded systems companies have now started the transition as well. For pure software companies, this transition is challenging but in certain ways easier and consequently we see large on-premise software companies experiment with cloud and SaaS and introduce new offerings based on these technologies.

Embedded systems companies, on the other hand, have had a much more difficult time to adapt the aforementioned approaches. This is, among others, due to two factors. First, embedded systems often have safety and reliability requirements that exceed those of pure software systems. For instance, a software failure in the safety-critical parts of a car, train or airplane can result in devastating consequences. This leads to quite conservative behavior by both the producers of embedded systems as well as the certification institutes. Second, the culture at these companies has traditionally been driven by mechanics and hardware (electronics) and both of these disciplines are defined by the immutability of the product post-manufacturing. Consequently, engineering processes are focused on ease of manufacturing and the minimization of issues at the customer through rigid, milestone-based development processes.

The embedded systems industry is, however, at the verge of a fundamental shift similar to the shift from installed software to SaaS. Various metrics show that the amount of software in embedded systems follows Moore's law and doubles every couple of years, depending on the industry. This is leading to a fundamental shift in R&D resource allocation from mechanical and electronics to software. In addition to the shift of resources, we also see increasing frustration with the aforementioned rigid, milestone-driven product development process dictated by mechanics and electronics. As embedded systems are increasingly connected to the internet, the ability of performing continuous deployment of software on systems out in the field becomes a reality.

In addition to software being deployed at products out in the field, the products can also be instrumented with data collection mechanisms that can determine the use cases employed by the system, the level of quality attributes such as performance, reliability and safety as well as contextual information using sensors.

Once the products deployed in the field are constantly accessible for data and deployment of software, it becomes possible to perform A/B experiments where the installed base of products is viewed as a population. Out of this population, experiment groups can be selected and experiments performed. These experiments can consist of alternative implementations of existing functionality and features and alternative workflows as well the introduction of new functionality and features with the intent of improving some aspect of the system.

The experiments typically are small-scale changes in functionality, features or structure and hence are typically not or barely noticeable by users. In a continuous deployment context, the delta between two releases of the software is highly limited. This addresses one of the main concerns by some users who have experienced the large changes present in infrequent, e.g., yearly, releases of software.

The potential benefits of an experimentation-based approach to software development for embedded systems are even larger than in traditional SaaS software. In SaaS solutions, the experimentation is virtually exclusively directed towards the user experience. In embedded systems, all qualities of the system can be experimented with. For instance, imagine a car that gets better with every day of use as software ranging from engine control to active safety to infotainment is constantly undergoing minor changes that, as a whole, result in a superior, continuously improving system.

Achieving the potential benefits resulting from very short feedback cycles using technologies, such as continuous deployment, experimentation-based development and multi-disciplinary teams, requires a fundamentally different R&D strategy, process and ways of working, tooling, relationship to customers as well as organizational changes. However, adopting this alternative approach is complicated as it requires so many changes in so many different areas and aspects of a business and its organization. There is surprisingly little research and publications that provide a top-level, end-to-end overview including business, technology, process, tooling and organization implications. Often, the literature tends to address aspects of the above, e.g., agile development for teams or continuous integration, but fails to connect this to an integration vision of how the organization will function as a whole.

The goal of this book is to address that gap and to provide an integrated, high-level perspective while combining it with detailed, actionable and concrete methods, techniques and tools for achieving the desired outcomes in the context of an organization. As the literature that exists mostly focuses on cloud and SaaS companies, we will allocate significant space to large-scale embedded systems. However, the concepts apply to any company that has major software products in its portfolio, including products that are only used internally.

As we conducted the research that forms the basis for this book, it became clear that companies are grappling with three overall challenges, which can be summarized as speed, data and ecosystems. Speed is concerned with shortening the cycle time in R&D or, in other words, how to shorten the time from identified customer need to delivered solution in the hands of customers. The speed dimension is concerned with agile development practices, continuous integration and continuous deployment but needs to address all the relevant dimensions of large-scale software development, including system and software architecture, ways of working and organization. Data is concerned with increasing the use of and benefit from the massive amounts of data that companies are collecting from their systems deployed in the field, including data about user behavior and system performance. The data dimension is concerned with data-driven decision making in R&D and with using the fast release cycles enabled in the speed dimension for fast, evidence-based decision making about the value and viability of new features and new products. Ecosystems are addressing the transition of companies from being internally focused to being ecosystem oriented. The ecosystem dimension is concerned with analyzing what the company is uniquely good at and where it adds value and, subsequently, relying on its ecosystem of partners and suppliers to deliver everything else.

The speed dimension is concerned with increasing the efficiency of software development in the software-intensive systems industries. The data and ecosystem dimensions are concerned with increasing the effectiveness of the companies in their own way. The increased use of data during the development process allows R&D teams to decide whether a feature or product is viable and

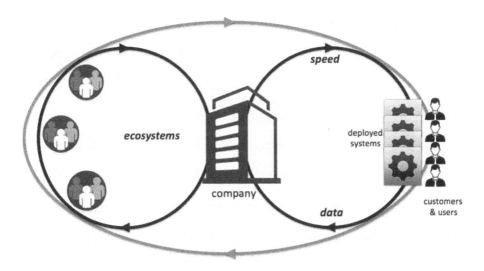

Figure 1.1 Overview of the Stairway to Heaven model

will deliver on its promise. This allows the company to stop development after investing only a fraction of the allocated resources if the data show that the potential is not realized. As research by us and others shows that more than 50% of features in systems are waste as these are not used but add to clutter and complexity, there is a major opportunity for increasing effectiveness of R&D in terms of value delivered to customers. Ecosystems focus on using the company's R&D resources on the things best done by the company itself and relying on the ecosystem for everything else. Although ecosystem partners will need to share part of the revenue generated, the company can focus on its key differentiators rather than the entire scope of system functionality. This also increases the effectiveness of R&D efforts.

We have structured our findings around speed, data and ecosystems in a model that has been christened the "Stairway to Heaven." The model has three dimensions and each dimension has five levels. The levels in each dimension are the result of extensive research with dozens of companies and capture the typical evolution paths for companies. In figure 1.1, we provide an overview of the model as well as the stakeholders involved in it.

As such, the Stairway to Heaven model provides a framework for assessing the current state of software development, modeling desired state and planning and sequencing the improvements required to reach desired state. We provide methods, techniques and tools for each of these activities for each of the dimensions and describe in detail the changes that companies go through when evolving from one level to the next in each dimension. In the next sections, we provide a short introduction into each of the dimensions of the model.

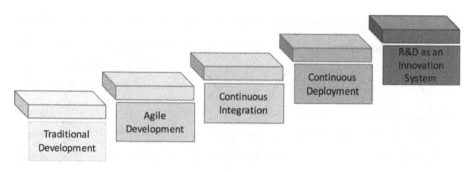

Figure 1.2 Speed dimension of the Stairway to Heaven

1.1 SPEED

Over the last decade, one of the main developments in software products is the broad adoption of continuous deployment. This development started in the cloud-based "Software as a Service" (SaaS) companies. This is due to the fact that the cost of deploying new versions of software in a SaaS environment is very low, perhaps even negligible, compared to traditional installed software. That allows for a deployment model where software is updated very frequently, in some cases many times per day.

The ability to deploy frequently brings enormous benefits to companies and, as a consequence, the software-intensive systems industry is now undergoing the transformation towards continuous deployment of software even in areas where the reliability requirements are much higher. Even without the data that come back from deployed systems, continuous deployment allows for constant adjustment of the development backlog to customer needs, allows for continuous testing of small slices of new functionality in systems in the field and provides a productive outlet for teams as the functionality that they developed is not sitting on a shelf for months at a time but in the hands of customers hours or days after it got written.

Based on studying dozens of companies, we have identified and defined the levels that companies evolve through in the speed dimension. As shown in figure 1.2, starting from traditional development, companies adopt agile development practices first. Then there is a need to build continuous integration capabilities. Once the company reaches a point where it always has a production quality version of the software, it moves to continuous deployment where software gets deployed in systems at least every agile sprint and potentially much more often. Finally, the company uses this capability to shift its development process from requirements driven to experimentation driven.

1.2 DATA

The ability to continuously deploy new versions of software to some or all customers leads to another major evolution concerning the radically changed ability of companies to measure how users are using the software. Although software companies have often used techniques to collect usage and quality data, continuous deployment demands continuous connectivity for the deployed systems. This, in turn, allows for the collection of much more detailed, timely data.

The ability to collect product data in real time leads to the possibility to significantly shorten the feedback loop of product development. Shorter product development feedback loops allow for a much more rapid discovery of the functionality and qualities that lead to significantly increased alignment between the needs of customers and the product. This in turn improves the competitive position of a company as the product better meets the market demands.

The short feedback loops in product development and evolution allow for a different approach to requirement engineering: the deployed system can now be used for experimenting with customers and with system behavior. Different deployed systems can get different versions of the software or of feature implementations. By studying the behavior of users and systems while using the different versions, one can empirically and based on statistically relevant data determine which version of a feature implementation or system software is preferred. As many studies have shown the major gap between espoused preferences and actual behavior, the ability to collect data on actual behavior is incredibly valuable.

The way companies evolve through their ability to use data proves to follow a predictable pattern. As shown in figure 1.3, companies start with a very ad hoc and manual approach to data driven by passionate and committed individuals. Then, the collection of data is automated, followed by the introduction of dashboards for relevant teams that get automatically updated with data from the field. The challenge with these dashboards is that they easily become outdated, which leads to the data innovation stage where there is a constant flow of new insights that results in evolving dashboards and focus areas. Finally, the entire company adopts data-driven decision making in everything it does including sales, performance reviews, hiring and other processes.

1.3 ECOSYSTEMS

The transition from internally focused to ecosystem-centric ways of working brings with it many advantages. It allows for companies to focus on their core competencies, to outsource all activities that are not strategic for the company and to employ ecosystems of third party developers to complement the

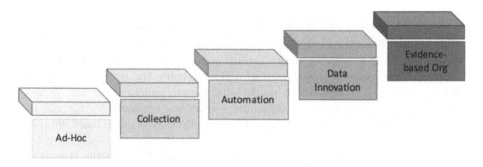

Figure 1.3 Data dimension of the Stairway to Heaven

core functionality provided by the company itself with extensions for specific customers and customer segments.

For the industry at large, our research shows that although the principles of core competencies, outsourcing and crowdsourced ecosystems are well understood, many companies are still quite poor at fully embracing these concepts. Many of the companies studied still have a preference to continue to do many things internally that should be outsourced and tend to manage their ecosystem partners during the selection, the execution and the conflict resolution stages, in a largely ad hoc and locally optimized fashion.

One of the reasons for the aforementioned challenge is that there are few really actionable models and frameworks for companies to use in determining the best course of action. Thus, every company has to build, over time, its own set of experiences and learn and structure its interactions with its ecosystem. There is little knowledge exchange beyond the vision level and, consequently, the operational level is ad hoc and executed based on the best efforts of the individuals responsible for the task.

Similar to the speed and data dimensions, we have defined, again based on our research, an evolution model for how companies work with software ecosystems. As shown in figure 1.4, starting from an internally focused company, the first interactions with the ecosystem tend to be ad hoc and locally initiated. Once the benefits are shown, the next step is to take a more centralized approach but to focus on short-term benefits and hence the company takes more of a tactical approach. Over time, one of the ecosystems that the company is part of will start to be managed in a more strategic fashion. Finally, the company adopts this strategic approach to all its ecosystems.

One of the models that we use to discuss the approach to software ecosystems is the three layer product model. This model distinguishes between the commodity layer of functionality, the layer of differentiating functionality and the layer of experimental and innovative functionality. The company has different ecosystems to deal with for each layer of the model as well as manage the transition of functionality between these layers. The three layer product model can be used as a conceptual model, but it can also be used as a physical

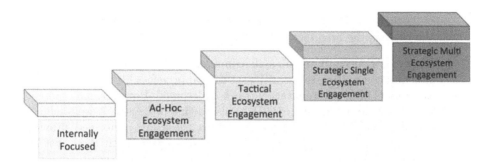

Figure 1.4 Ecosystem dimension of the Stairway to Heaven

software architecture with different teams, with different success metrics, associated with each layer. Although software ecosystems have associated technical challenges, in our experience, the technical challenges of realizing a software ecosystem are often quite manageable whenever the company is clear on the business strategy.

1.4 THE BAPO MODEL

As the topics in this book touch upon business and business strategy and technology as well as on process and ways of working as well as architecture, it is important to ensure that we establish the relationship and priority between these topics carefully. In earlier work [49], we presented the BAPO model. The BAPO model identifies four major areas of concern:

Business: The business and business strategy for a company is the starting point and everyone in the company (especially those in R&D) needs to have a deep and intimate understanding of the business the company is in, the vision, mission, goals and strategy for accomplishing those goals and the customers that are served by the company. Especially in engineering, there has traditionally been a culture where the business side is viewed as "not our concern" and engineers tended to ask for clearly specified requirements. In a fast moving world where technologies, customers needs and business models change rapidly, engineers can no longer afford to be ignorant of the business.

Architecture: Although the word *architecture* has become overloaded and in many contexts gets to mean whatever the user of the word wants it to, the fact remains that the top-level breakdown of a system, the design principles and patterns that form the fabric of a system as well as the design rules and constraints that result from the design decisions forming the basis of the architecture are of critical importance for the success of a system and its ability to realize and support the business strategy. Engineers and other technical staff, as well as product managers and others working with R&D, need to understand the architecture and the reasons the architecture is structured as it is.

Process: Especially in the agile community, process has a bad reputation and considering the straitjacket that approaches like CMMi [22] put developers into, this reputation is not undeserved. However, many forget that agile approaches like SCRUM also define processes. A well-defined set of process steps and order in which these are performed provide structure that allows individuals and teams to perform at their best by streamlining activities and minimizing coordination overhead.

Organization: People in any organization larger than a handful need to be organized in teams and departments. A company needs a work breakdown structure that ideally assigns most of the coordination to intra-team communication and minimizes inter-team communication. Also, individuals need to know who are in their team and who are not if only to know who to rely on and partner with. Consequently, the structure of the organization is important and requires attention.

In figure 1.5 we present the BAPO model graphically. It is important to note, however, that although all four areas of concern in the BAPO model are important, there is an order of priority. The starting point is the business and business strategy. The architecture is the next area as this is where the business strategy and its priorities need to be realized in the structure and architectural patterns through design decisions. The processes and ways of working are a consequence of the architecture as components of the architecture often can be released (internally or externally) separately and the process will be informed by the structure of the architecture. Finally, the other areas should result in an organizational structure that meets the needs of the business, architecture and process.

Although the BAPO model has a clear priority order for the different areas, in reality there are connections between all four areas and there is feedback from the lower priority areas that will influence the decisions around, for instance, business and architecture. For instance, an organization that has teams in different continents will influence the architecture to increase the amount of independence between the parts assigned to the different locations. However, to the largest extent possible, one should start from business and business strategy and adjust the other areas according to the discussed priorities.

In the remainder of the book, where we explore the speed, data and ecosystem dimensions of the Stairway to Heaven, the paradigm underlying the BAPO model should be considered as the basis even where we leave it implicit in the text.

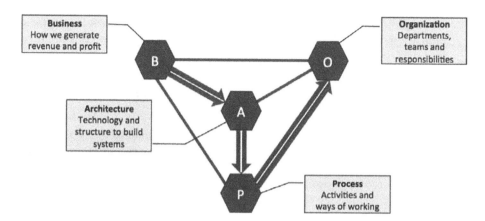

Figure 1.5 The BAPO model

1.5 WHERE ALL THIS COMES FROM

The content in this book is based on three sources. First is the industrial experience while working in industry and being actively involved in large-scale software development. The companies were concerned with mobile devices and with pure software and SaaS deployments as well as headquartered in Europe and in Silicon Valley.

The second source is the Software Center in Sweden. This is a collaboration between, at the time of writing, nine large companies and five universities. The companies involved are Ericsson, Volvo Car Corporation, AB Volvo, Saab AB, Jeppesen (part of Boeing), Axis Communications, Grundfos, Tetra Pak and Verisure. These companies are the employers of hundreds to tens of thousands of software engineers. In the research activities, we have been involved in a broad range of topics, ranging from agile development methods and continuous integration to continuous deployment, data-driven development and software ecosystems. The techniques, methods and tools presented in this book are in active use by some or all of the companies in the Software Center and consequently validated in industrial contexts.

The third source is the consulting engagements that I have been driving with a variety of companies over the last years. Having worked with well over a dozen companies on a range of topics including software architecture and platforms, development practices, continuous integration and deployment, innovation practices, the relationship between business and R&D, business and software ecosystems has resulted in a solid understanding of the practices and approaches that work and those that don't work in large-scale software-intensive systems.

Although I currently work in academia, I would like to ensure you as a reader that the content in this book is based on a solid empirical foundation with significant hands-on industrial experience underlying the concepts. Many of the topics that we discuss are hard to implement and realize in a typical organization, but the benefits exist and have been confirmed and documented in real, large-scale software-intensive companies.

1.6 FOR WHOM THIS BOOK WAS WRITTEN

The primary audience for which the book is intended are senior leaders in software-intensive companies, both from the general management as well as from product and R&D management. For the vast majority of organizations, technology has become too important to leave to the technologists. Interestingly, however, the opposite is true as well: the business of companies is so influenced by technology that it can no longer be left to the business leaders only. The technology leaders, both in product management and in R&D, need to be deeply involved in the business of the company as well in order to ensure optimal alignment between the business and the technology.

The main reason for this increased level of integration is that the traditional functional organization is unable to respond sufficiently quickly to changes in the market. Instead, organizations increasingly move to cross-functional teams holding the necessary skills in the team and jointly moving towards a goal. These teams have levels of autonomy that go significantly beyond the traditional approaches and are supported by levels of automation that allow these teams to respond rapidly. For these cross-functional teams to be effective, there is a need for a common terminology, perspective and paradigm. This book seeks to address that challenge by providing the common language and shared point of view that technical as well as business people can appreciate and use as a basis for their work.

Consequently, the third audience group is senior engineers and software architects. As technical staff need to understand the business, the business strategy as well as the trends and developments influencing the business and technology, it is no longer sufficient to focus just on the technological challenges. The alignment between business and technology needs to be driven by engineers and especially architects as much as by the folks in formal leadership roles.

The final audience group is researchers and students in software engineering, product management, technology management and innovation management. Although the book is predominantly written towards industry, the content is academically well founded and based on dozens of publications. Although not as extensive as in traditional academic literature, there are many references to the publications underlying the material in the book and this in itself may be relevant for researchers and academics in general.

Summarizing, the book has four audience groups for which it is intended:

General management and leaders outside of R&D

Leaders in R&D and product management

Technical staff such as senior engineers and architects

Researchers, students and academics in general

1.7 READING GUIDE

Although as an author one wants to have everyone read one's book cover to cover, the reality is that time is limited and that not all parts are equally interesting to all readers. There are two ways to limit the reading of this book to a subset of chapters. One is to read about the entire set of concepts in the book but at different levels of depth. The second is to focus on a topical slice of the book.

Covering all concepts in the book can be accomplished at three levels of coverage:

Elevator pitch: For you who just want to know the main concepts and ideas underlying the book, reading this chapter and the conclusion (chapter 14) will give you high-level understanding of the topics addressed. This will give you a first insight and help you decide if the content is relevant for your situation.

Just the basics: The second level of coverage is read this introduction chapter, chapter 2 to understand the trends that are driving the content in the book, chapters 4, 8 and 11 as the description for each of the dimensions of the Stairway to Heaven model and the conclusion (chapter 14).

The full monty: The final level is to read all chapters in the book and to understand not just the concepts, but also develop an insight into the methods, techniques and tools that we are introducing into the book.

If your interest is more focused on one of the Stairway to Heaven dimensions, you can read the content of each part independent of the other parts:

Speed: if your interest is predominantly concerning increasing speed and efficiency of software development, your reading should focus on part I (chapters 1, 2 and 3), part II (chapters 4, 5, 6 and 7) and part V (chapter 14).

Data: If the use of data to increase effectiveness of software development is your primary interest, please read part I (chapters 1, 2 and 3), part III (chapters 8, 9 and 10) and part V (chapter 14).

Ecosystem: Similarly, if software ecosystems and the strategic management of your partners, suppliers, customers and complementors are the key focus, you should read part I (chapters 1, 2 and 3), part IV (chapters 11, 12 and 13) and part V (chapter 14).

Finally, the book is intended for industrial professionals and aims to provide as much in terms of concrete, tangible solutions that can be directly applied in your organization as it is concerned with building an understanding between the strategic trends, developments and business implications and the role that R&D needs to play in response to these. As such, the book is not a cookbook with clear-cut recipes, but rather invites you as a reader to build a deeper understanding of the subject matter and to use this understanding to materially improve the competitive position of your organization.

CHAPTER 2

Trends in Society, Business and Technology

Whether one agrees with the development or not, the fact of the matter is that the world is moving faster. Customer adoption of new products and services has consistently been increasing in speed. It took the telephone around 75 years to reach 50 million users in the US, whereas the Internet reached 50 million users in 4 years. More recent, the game Angry Birds Space reached 50 million users in 35 days. In response to customer demand, industry has improved its ability to scale new technologies to keep up.

The technology providing the largest increase in speed, however, is software. Introducing software into a range of products allows for major improvements in the ability of companies to serve customers. Although traditionally treated similar to other technologies dealing with "atoms", increasingly companies are adopting continuous deployment in order to get new functionality in the hands of customers faster. To illustrate this, look at the automotive industry. A new car platform has a lifetime of 10 to 15 years before being replaced with a successor. Similarly, a new car model has a development cycle of around 4 years. This means it is only every 4, 10 or 15 years that a product designer can make decisions about the next generation of a product. At the same time, non-safety critical software in modern cars is (or can be) deployed every day or every couple of days. The short feedback cycle allows for a much faster rate of innovation, driving up customer satisfaction and, consequently, customer retention and adoption.

Anyone who has not heard the term "big data" must have been living under a pretty big rock during the last decade or so. With Moore's law continuing to deliver its fantastic progress, computing is increasingly powerful and can churn through vast amounts of data continuously as well as in response to queries. We read about amazing new insights that have been derived by sifting through vast amounts of data and correlating different variables.

Although this novel use of data originating from different sources was originally the purview of research groups at universities as well as dedicated data analytics companies, over time companies in different industries have started to adopt data-driven practices in parts of their business. For instance, in the Web 2.0 and Software-as-a-Service (SaaS) industry, companies adopted split testing (or A/B testing) as a way to experiment with different aspects of their products.

The use of data is far from novel and companies have used data in accounting, marketing and sales for calculating various KPIs such as return on investment for accounting, brand awareness changes in marketing and cost of customer acquisition in sales. Also, errors found in the field in deployed products are collected at most companies and used to direct quality assurance efforts as well as defect management.

The main transition that the industry is currently experiencing is driven by two factors. First, the cost of collecting, storing and analyzing data has, over the last decade, reached an inflection point allowing companies to collect and store data in areas where it was originally impossible to do so. Second, because of the increased availability of data, companies have shifted decision making for many issues from the traditional opinion- and experienced-based reasoning to decision making based on data.

No company, organization or even an individual is an island. Both as people and as organizations, we live in networks where we are connected to others. Through these connections, we interact and exchange, we collaborate and compete, we share and we learn. In fact, it is these networks that define any human endeavor, rather than the isolated actions of an individual or organization.

Even though we intuitively understand the importance of the networks that we operate in, many organizations have traditionally had a preference for operating independently, conducting all justifiable activities internally in the organization and keeping anyone who they are dependent on at arm's length through a strict, contractual interface. During the 1980s, the era of outsourcing started which focused on the notion of core competence. The basic premise is that any company that is successful has one or more core competencies where it is better than any other company and these core competencies are the reason for its success. In order to be more successful, the organization should focus its internal energy on the things that differentiate it and stop doing all the other things.

The structural changes in the industry that followed from the focus on core competencies and outsourcing were dramatic and caused a major upheaval in the social contract between companies and workers. At the same time, however, it led to major improvements in the efficiency of the restructured companies, at the expense of increased dependency on other companies in their network that now conduct the non-core activities earlier conducted by the organization itself.

Although outsourcing has proven its value, during the last two decades companies in, especially, the software-intensive systems industry have found ways to become increasingly ecosystem focused through, for instance, crowd-sourced software ecosystems. Pioneered to a significant extent by companies like Apple and Google in the iOS and Android mobile phone ecosystems, approaches were found for small development shops and individual developers to offer solutions to often relatively small customer segments. Here, Apple and Google provided the marketplace for customers and developers to find each other and, in the process, to vastly enrich the range of functionality provided to their customers through the use of external players.

Successful software ecosystems provide an economic and technical environment that provides competitive advantages to all parties active in the ecosystem in their competition with others in other ecosystems or those that operate more independently.

In this chapter, we dive deeper into the reasons behind the increasing need for speed, the use of data as a source for decision making and operations as well as the increasing ecosystem focus on organizations. With a major focus on efficiency and effectiveness, companies improve their competitiveness by shortening feedback cycles. It is challenging to change slow feedback cycles with faster ones, obviously, as it requires the entire company to change its ways. It needs data and a culture of evidence decision making. Finally, companies need to become much more intentional about deciding what to do internally and what to rely on the ecosystem for. Consequently, we need a model to guide the transformation from traditional "waterfall" style, internally focused ways of working to shorter, faster cycles affecting the entire company and not just R&D. Our goal is an agile business that can respond to changes and opportunities in the market instantaneously.

2.1 TRENDS AND DRIVERS

There are several developments in society, business and technology that drive the increasing "need for speed" that many companies are experiencing. In the following sections, we discuss some of the trends that are driving. These range from the transition from products to services to increased awareness of the financial benefits of moving faster.

2.2 PRODUCTS TO SERVICES

Sociology researchers often refer to the Gen-Y and Millennial generations when discussing the sharing economy. Whereas for baby boomers and Gen Xers, owning products is important; for the later generations, the priority is to have access to the services provided by those products, but without the need to own these. One explanation is that especially the baby boomers grew up in a world of scarcity and owning a product provides a sense of security for this generation that is not achieved in the same way by having access to the same product as a service. The later generations are increasingly experiencing that ownership brings with it many disadvantages as well. As an example, when living in a large city and owning a car, finding parking, paying congestion fees, arranging for maintenance, changing between summer and winter tires, etc., are chores, distractions and annoyances that are removed when opting for signing up for a service where one has access to a car as a service. Even though it may seem more expensive on a per use basis, the average car is used less than 1 hour per day and hence is a huge waste of capital for any owner.

Interestingly, in business a similar transformation from ownership to access is occurring. Most companies are looking to reduce capital expenditure (CAPEX) or long-term investments with operational expenditures (OPEX) or continuous cost associated with use. One example of transferring CAPEX to OPEX is to sell your office building and then to rent it back from the company that you sold it to. This increases your operational expense as you're now paying rent, but frees up the capital locked up on the building. Other companies have outsourced manufacturing in order to decrease their investment in factories and the associated equipment. Similar to the consumer space, also industry is shifting its focus from ownership to access to services.

Next to the transition from ownership to access, there is a second aspect: both private persons and companies are increasingly focusing their energy on the things that make them unique; where they add the unique value that only they can provide or that gives genuine pleasure and quality of life. By focusing on that which differentiates, the consequence is that we seek to eliminate everything else because it becomes a distraction from what we want to focus our time on. Cleaning services, for instance, are widely adopted in industry and in households. Pet services allow busy people to enjoy pets without many of the side effects. Security services are another widespread example. Although the transition to services is in part driven by financial incentives, there is a second driver which is concerned with time and attention. Both companies and households have limited time and attention and being able to free up those by acquiring services from other parties is a powerful value proposition.

The discussion up to now has addressed the general trend of the transition from products to services, but has largely ignored the role of software. However, software plays a central role in this transition in several ways.

The first factor is the role of software in the products used to provide the service. As an example, take cars. The goal of car companies is to sell as many cars as possible. Limiting the lifetime of cars and ability to upgrade are important drivers to get car owners to trade in their car for the next model. However, when the company transitions to becoming a mobility services company, the financial incentives suddenly change quite significantly. The goal becomes to sell as many mobility services against the lowest cost. As the cost is directly driven by the number of cars required to deliver the required mobility services, the driver now is to maximize usage of the available cars (remember that currently most cars are used for less than one hour a day) and to maximize the economic life of each car. One of the best ways to increase the economic life is to upgrade the car after it has left the factory and, in fact, throughout its economic life. And the lowest-cost technology that allows for post-factory and continuous upgrading is software. Already today, modern, high-end cars get new software during each service or, more recently, even through over-the-air updates. This allows us to incorporate new functionality into cars, extend their economic life and, consequently, lower the cost of mobility services.

Although we used cars and mobility services as an example in the above, the pattern applies to numerous industries and software-intensive systems companies need to accelerate their ability to deliver to the new economic drivers. The organizational change required to change a company from a products focus to a services focus is enormous as it requires companies to change fundamental beliefs in the organization that are becoming obsolete but that traditionally have defined the success of the company.

The second role for software is concerned with everything surrounding the service, ranging from ordering, planning and delivery. Earlier, many of the processes surrounding services were manual and required significant human effort to be performed. Now, increasingly these processes are fully automated and can be provided at much lower cost than earlier. Not only are software-based solutions significantly cheaper than human-based solutions, often they do a much better job as well. Software allows for order processing at unprecedented rates and scale at, for instance, Amazon. The ability of software to find optimal solutions for large problems, such as flight and crew planning for airlines, far exceeds the ability of human planners. Even if there are small parts of a service that require human intervention, some companies use crowdsourcing, such as Amazon's mechanical turk, as a mechanism to deliver the service.

An illustrative example of a software-enabled service is crowd-funding services such as Lending Club for loans to private persons and FundedByMe for start-ups. These services allow for disintermediation of traditional banks and venture capital firms and offer similar products at a significant cost advantage and at unprecedented speeds. Similar to earlier examples described in this section, it again is the software that drives the transformation from traditional products to services.

The final point related to the transition from products to services is concerned with customer expectations. For the longest time, acquiring a product meant buying it in its current state and experiencing slow degradation over time until the product lost its potential to serve the need and then it was replaced with the next instance of the same or a similar product. For several product categories, the expectations of customers have evolved to expect a continuous improvement of the functionality of the product through releases of new software that improve the user experience. This started with computer operating systems releasing "slip streams" to fix bugs and, later on, provide new functionality. However, now many products, including mobile phones, consumer electronics, cars and wearable electronics, are connected and update their functionality on a regular basis. This means that updating a product containing software after it has left the factory is no longer a choice, but rather a necessity for sustained success in the market.

2.3   TOWARDS CUSTOMER-DRIVEN INNOVATION

For a long time innovation was synonymous with new technologies that could address problems that were unsolved earlier. New technologies are still the foundation of major societal changes ranging from the introduction of the automobile to the role that the Internet plays in modern life. At the same time, it is important to realize that each of these and other technologies achieved such broad adoption because these addressed human needs that were in existence long before the introduction of the technology. For instance, the automobile addresses a mobility need that virtually every human has and it solved it so much better than earlier mobility solutions that it allowed for the creation of the suburb and changed the lives of millions of people. One of the uses of the internet is to solve the need of humans to connect over distance and with intensity not feasible with earlier approaches. The point we are looking to make is that no technology will be successful unless it solves a fundamental human or business need in a better way than contemporary solutions.

Although technology-driven innovation has powerful protection mechanisms available, such as patents, the interesting observation is that most companies are gaining access to new technologies at roughly the same point in time. There are several factors driving this. First, so many companies are concerned with technology innovation and the creation of patent applications that no company will be able to dominate a technology completely. Consequently, there are often multiple ways to gain access to new technologies. Second, in most industries, the incumbents have cross-licensing agreements to basically neutralize the role of intellectual property (IP). Of course, these patents are often used to keep new entrants away and to maximize the barriers to entry. Finally, for broad adoption of new technologies very often standardization is required to create a sufficiently large market. In these standardization efforts, however, the participating parties are required to give up their patent rights in order to allow all players to use the standard without having to worry about license fees. As the business benefits of a new technology platform often outweigh the IP license income, organizations most often do sacrifice their IP. There are, of course, pockets where the above does not hold, but as a general pattern it is important to understand that differentiating from competitors through technology is an increasingly difficult strategy.

If not technology, what is then the best way to drive growth through innovation? The answer to this was already hinted upon: all successful innovations solve latent needs of customers or solve known needs in ways that are better than the current solution. Through deep understanding of customer needs and creative, breakthrough insights into novel ways of addressing these needs, intrapreneurs and entrepreneurs find new ways of serving customers in new ways allowing them to achieve adoption and ways to monetize these new solutions in novel ways.

The growing importance of customer-driven innovation does not remove the need for technology-driven innovation. The company still needs to have access to good enough or even world-class new technologies. However, technology by itself is no longer sufficient to drive significant growth and customer adoption. One risk that technology-driven companies are prone to is to be so focused on improving the technology in their products that the performance of the technology exceeds the needs to customers. For instance, for years during the 1970s and 1980s, television manufacturers were struggling with improving the longevity of TVs. Their efforts paid off to the point that TVs lasted 15 years or more. This was hampering innovation in TVs as the replacement rate simply was too low. In addition, customers often found it difficult to buy a new TV with exciting new functionality if their old TV was still working perfectly well. This led to the adoption of planned obsolescence: TVs were explicitly designed to break after on average eight years. The danger is of course to pursue the path of technology performance improvement after the value for customers has seized to exist.

A second challenge is that most incumbents work closely with customers and evolve their solutions in response to customer requests. As the R&D investments by incumbents are increasingly meeting customer demands, fewer and fewer R&D resources are spent on exploratory innovations. This has as a consequence that, with the growing importance of customer-driven innovation, it opens up for disruption of the market by new entrants. From the point that the customer base has a latent need to the point that individual users are able to express their demand or desire, there is a period where new entrants can meet the need that users didn't even realize they had and establish a beachhead that makes it really difficult for incumbents to unseat them. Although sustaining innovations are often predicted in time by incumbents, there are times when a market goes through a fundamental course correction where new entrants actually have a significant advantage over incumbents due to their lack of historical baggage.

2.4   CHANGING NATURE OF INNOVATION

Especially in embedded systems, where mechanics, electronics and software play a role, there is a quite fundamental shift in the nature of innovation taking place. Over the last decade, the focus has shifted from mechanics and electronics to software and from being centered around intellectual property to focusing on the customer.

Since the industrial revolution, the innovation model was dictated by an approach that focused on intellectual property (IP), such as patents, creating a competitive advantage for the innovating company. Over time, the focus on IP has caused a situation where large companies own thousands of patents. These patents are used predominantly to keep new players out of the markets of these companies and as a bargaining chip between the incumbents. Unfortunately, in many industries, the resulting situation is one where IP is used to restrain innovation and maintain status quo.

The culture at many companies has traditionally focused on the mechanical parts that make up the products, systems and solutions. Over time, electronics was added to the focus as it obeys the same physical constraints as mechanics and it requires the same design, verification and manufacturing processes. With the advent of Six Sigma, financial discipline and other approaches to standardize and harmonize processes, the focus turned towards cost and cost reduction as a mechanism to maintain margins as the products were commoditizing and competition was increasingly focused on cost advantages.

Summarizing, both the focus on intellectual property and the focus on the mechanical and to some extent electronic parts of products, systems and solutions resulted in a slowdown of innovation and a focus on maintaining status quo. A contributing factor is, of course, that especially in mechanics there are few breakthrough innovations that allow for fundamentally new ways to meet customer needs. In addition, new IP is increasingly becoming available to all players in an industry at roughly the same time. The result is that the ability to differentiate is highly limited for any player and the focus shifts to cost and efficiency.

Of course, for new entrants to a market, there is nothing better than a set of incumbents that innovate slowly and treat their products as commodities. This sets up the market for disruption by offering solutions that address customer needs in fundamentally new ways. As we discussed in the section concerning the transition to services, the key innovation can be concerned with a different business and customer engagement model. However, it can also focus on automating use cases that were earlier conducted manually by staff at the customer or by offering a solution with very different properties as compared to the existing solutions.

One of the key technologies for driving the types of innovation discussed above is software. By focusing on software as the key delivery function of new innovations, new entrants have been able to disrupt incumbents and to meet latent customer demands not identified by existing players. As an example, in the spring of 2015, Tesla announced that it would release new functionality that would allow their cars to drive autonomously on highways. As part of the same announcement, it shared that all Teslas would get this functionality, including the cars sold during the last years. The incumbents in the automotive industry have always focused on selling as many new cars as possible and releasing new functionality only in new car models has always been a critical factor to drive customers to upgrade their car to the latest model. Tesla fundamentally shifted the customer expectations in the automotive industry by promising to car owners that their cars would continue to improve also after the cars had left the factory. Of course, the specific innovation of autonomous highway driving as well as many other features in a Tesla are driven by software and delivered over-the-air as the cars are connected to the internet.

In the previous section, we already stressed the increasing importance of the customer. The ability of software to rapidly deploy subsequent versions of functionality and to measure usage provides for a fundamentally different

Object Code in 1000 Instructions

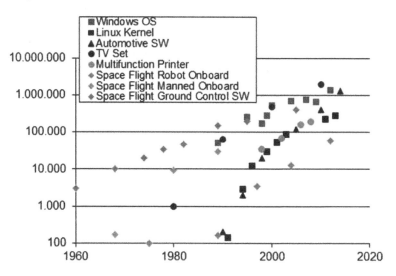

Figure 2.1 The growing size of software

innovation cycle. Although innovation in mechanics and electronics remains important and several industries are still very much driven by intellectual property, as an overall trend we see that innovation is moving towards meeting customer needs in novel ways through the use of software.

2.5 SOFTWARE SIZE

The first systems using software, going back to the 1950s and 1960s, were quite small and could often be built and maintained by an individual software engineer. Over the decades, however, an interesting development started to surface: the amount of software in systems grew and continued to grow year after year. In figure 2.1[1], the size of the software in typical systems in four different industries is shown over time. Especially for automotive software and the Linux kernel, the size of the software increases with an order of magnitude every five years. This means that a 1 million lines of code (LOC) system in 2005 will be a 10 million LOC system in 2010 and a 100 million LOC system in 2015. As Marc Andreessen famously said, software is eating the world.

Although not all industries grow as fast as automotive software, even slower

---

[1]Figure graciously provided by Christof Ebert. Used with permission.

moving industries such as telecommunications increase the size of their software with an order of magnitude every 10 years [26, 25].

The implications of this constantly increasing size are various, but there are a few that we want to highlight in this section. First, the continuously growing size of software requires the R&D organizations to constantly reinvent new approaches to designing and maintaining software architecture, invent new ways of working, develop and adopt new development, build, testing and deployment tools and experiment with new organizational structures. This means that experience, while still relevant, needs to be constantly reevaluated to confirm its continued relevance. It also means that, especially in the embedded systems industry, the more proactive management of commercial off-the-shelf software components as well as open-source components that provide required but commoditized functionality is increasingly important. As the size of software grows, pushing out internally developed and maintained software allows the R&D organization to focus on new, differentiating functionality.

As the company increasingly needs to focus on its differentiating functionality, it needs to be more intentional about the way it partners with its ecosystem. This ecosystem, of course, includes customers and suppliers, but also competitors and peers in adjacent industries as well as app developers and open-source communities. As we will discuss later, the continuously growing size of software demands from companies that they make very deliberate and intentional decisions about the functionality to innovate, develop and maintain internally versus the areas where the company will partner or even leave to ecosystem parties.

2.6 NEED FOR SPEED

The final trend that we discuss in this chapter is the central theme for this part of the book: the need for speed. Customer adoption of new products and new functionality in existing products is increasingly rapid. Research by [30] as well as [7] show the speed at which different major technologies have been adopted during the 20th century. Figure 2.2 below shows that the telephone took 50 years to reach 50 million users in the early 1900s. Radio and TV were adopted more rapidly, but still took 38 and 22 years, respectively, to reach 50 million customers. More modern examples such as Facebook only took 44 months to reach 50 million users and some new, mobile apps are rumored to acquire millions of users in a matter of days.

The key takeaway for most companies is not that they should prepare for customer adoption of new products in a matter of days, but rather that the societal acceptance and adoption of new functionality and products is occurring at much faster rates than earlier. For companies that traditionally adopted a fast-follower strategy, it is important to realize that the accelerating willingness of customers to adopt new products, technologies and solutions requires significantly faster response times than earlier. For companies that traditionally were the innovators in their industries, the danger may be even

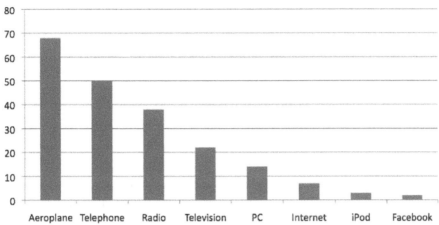

Figure 2.2 Years to reach mass adoption of innovations [30]

greater as the "next big thing" is likely to come from left field, rather than from one of the incumbents. As for companies that view themselves as industry leaders, it is even harder to accept that the desires and wishes from their customer base have shifted away from what traditionally made the company special.

2.7 FROM "NO DATA" TO "BIG DATA" TO "SMART DATA"

With the rapidly dropping cost of memory and storage technologies, companies have been dramatically increasing the amount of data that they collect from their systems deployed in the field as well as from their customers. The ability to measure the behavior of customers and of deployed systems gives a fundamentally better insight into the value delivered to customers.

In our research, and also recognized in the technology community at large, we have seen that companies move through three phases. The first phase is the "no data" phase where the amount of data collected is small and mostly focused on troubleshooting and bug fixing. Companies tend to collect trouble report data and may receive log and trace data from customers as part of their effort to resolve faults that have slipped through to the field.

The next phase is when companies have identified the opportunity for much more extensive data collection. Often without solid understanding of what it seeks to learn from the data, the company starts to collect everything that may be considered useful at some point in the future. The amount of data collected grows rapidly and the data analysts already at the company often are joined with new colleagues that are supposed to help generate value from the data. At this point, the company often works with retrospective questions, studying historical data to establish baselines and distill patterns.

The third stage is where the company realizes that the vast majority (upwards of 99%) that it collects is never used and consequently waste. At this point, the company moves towards a more intentional approach to collecting data and the analysis evolves into more of a forward-oriented and real-time approach. Analysts and R&D teams move towards formulating hypotheses and testing these with data from the field. In addition, streaming analytics allows for dynamic adjustment of behavior for the entire family of deployed systems and customers or personalized for individual systems and users.

2.8 FROM PRODUCTS TO PLATFORMS AND ECOSYS-TEMS

The final trend that we discuss here is a transition that many companies are attempting: to move to being a product company to a platform company connecting an ecosystem of customers with an ecosystem of complementors or service providers.

In a pure platform setup, companies offer the platform for free or at cost and charge third parties for access to the platform. In practice, however, companies take a hybrid approach where the platformized product is extended with third party solutions and the company monetizes both the product and the platform.

The fact is, however, that many companies, for a variety of reasons, seek to transition to being platform companies. Especially for successful products, the number of specific extensions requested by customers is unfeasible for the company to provide by itself and, hence, it requires a solution that allows others to contribute value to the ecosystem. In other cases, the company identifies that customers and others are extending the product using different forms of hacking, using unintended interfaces and access points. This is a clear indication that there is a need among customers and an opportunity for the company to transition to a platform business.

2.9 CONCLUSION

In this chapter, we discussed the key trends that drive modern software-intensive systems companies. One of the primary drivers, outlined in the previous section, is the speed of adoption of new technologies, products and solutions across society. This causes a situation where organizations need to be faster than their customers to adopt, introduce and scale new features and products. Although especially incumbents in many industries have traditionally adopted a fast follower role and done so with success, the increasing adoption speed makes this a far more dangerous strategy as the time to respond to market developments becomes so short that it is almost impossible to respond in time. Also, as the number of new entrants in any market is staggering, ranging from tiny start-ups to large business conglomerates entering new markets, the risk of missing a latent customer need, having a new entrant identify and capitalize on it and risking disruption by these new entrants is no longer a remote possibility. Consequently, organizations need to become better at identifying the needs of their customers before their customers even realize that they have the need. This requires the adoption of customer-driven innovation, as we discussed in this chapter.

The second primary driver is data and all the functionality and behaviour that it enables. In a fast paced world, bad decisions can easily unseat the company from its market position and consequently taking data-driven instead of opinion-based decisions is an important antidote to missing important shifts in the market.

Finally, the third primary driver is the transition towards ecosystems. As companies seek to become platform instead of product companies, there are significant opportunities both for the platform provider and for the complementors. This allows each partner to focus on the topics that it is uniquely good at and positioned to take on. Successful ecosystems provide benefits to all parties in it by reducing coordination cost and increasing efficiency and effectiveness. The transition itself, however, is difficult and several companies have failed to make the transition successfully.

There are several developments that make it even hard for companies to realize the above. First, the transition from products to services, i.e., customers having access to products as a service rather than owning the products outright, allows customers to switch to competing solutions even faster than earlier. This only adds to the challenge outlined above. At the same time, the value for embedded systems has, depending on the industry for a decade or more, shifted from mechanics and electronics to software. This has, in turn, led to a situation where the size of software in products has been growing with an order of magnitude every five to ten years. The increasing size of software, and the resulting complexity, has a tendency to slow down R&D in many companies, instead of speeding things up.

The need to become more innovative and responsive to customers while at the same time experiencing several drivers that make the company more inwardly focused, more reactive and slower is a key challenge for many organizations. In the remainder of this book, we present several techniques and approaches that allow product teams and the organizations they work for to address these challenges and maintain or even improve their competitiveness in increasingly challenging markets.

CHAPTER 3

Illustrating Our Story: VIGANBE

Over the last close to 25 years, we have worked with dozens upon dozens of companies around challenges associated with large scale R&D of software-intensive systems. These companies have experienced real challenges that, at times, risked the very existence of the organization. Some of these companies indeed are no longer around. Others have been acquired and integrated in other organizations. Yet others are shadows of their former selves. Finally, there fortunately is a sizable group of companies that met their challenges, overcame them and grew to be even more successful after battling with these challenges.

One of the patterns that we have experienced is that many companies talk about their success in public and about their problems, challenges and failures in private. However, it is so much more interesting to read about the specifics of the hard things rather than read the celebratory story afterwards. For a book, in its nature a public artifact, it becomes difficult to share the difficulties experienced by companies without anonymizing the cases.

As a solution to this challenge, we're introducing Viganbe, a virtual company that merges many of the characteristics of companies that we have worked on during the last years and decades. The Software Center (http://www.software-center.se), which has provided the research context for several of the theories, models and frameworks in this book, has nine companies involved, including Ericsson, Volvo Cars, Volvo Trucks, Saab AB, Tetra Pak, Axis Communications, Verisure, Jeppesen (a Boeing company) and Grundfos. In addition, outside of Software Center, we have worked with other companies. So, although the examples in the paper originate from real cases at companies that we've worked with, these will be presented at situations at Viganbe.

In the remainder of this chapter, we provide an introduction to Viganbe using the ESAO model (introduced in chapter 13). First we present an overall introduction to the company, then we present the business strategy of Viganbe and the way it fits in the overall business ecosystem. Then we present its technical architecture and technology choices and the dependencies and interactions the architecture has with outside parties. Finally, we discuss the processes, ways of working and organization of Viganbe and the way it interacts with its partners, customers, complementors and other parties.

3.1   VIGANBE: AN INTRODUCTION

Viganbe is a 50-year-old company that has its roots in mechanical engineering and has for many years served both businesses and consumers with its mechanical products. From humble beginnings, the company has grown to ten thousand employees divided over sites in more than a dozen countries. The company is publicly traded on an European stock exchange and files quarterly reports on its business.

The company provides products to five main markets, two consumer and three business markets. It still conducts some of its own manufacturing but for a growing segment of products, manufacturing has been outsourced to suppliers in low-wage countries. The company has a significant investment in R&D (around 12% of revenue) and has sizeable R&D groups at sites in four countries.

There are three main developments that affect the organization. The first is that the company is experiencing significant price erosion and competition in its traditional mechanics-heavy product ranges. In response, though focusing on cost-reduction activities, the company is seeking growth by forward integration in its value chain. This means that it starts to compete with organizations that are or, up to recently, were its customers. This leads to a significant shift in the business and the company is carefully maneuvering this transition in order to replace more revenue from its new customers, buying systems and solutions including the company's original products, while losing as little revenue from its existing customers as feasible.

The second main development, to some extent driving the aforementioned forward integration, is that product software is increasingly important for the company. This is a natural development in that the company started to include electronics in its products many years ago and started to add software more than a decade ago. However, up to recently, hardware and software were in support of the mechanical parts of the system. Over the last years, however, the relationship has been inverted and the most differentiating aspects of products these days are driven by software. The mechanical parts are increasingly commoditizing and the company is experiencing difficulty finding differentiating features that are mechanics driven. A novel development is that the company has started to develop and market pure software products that interface with its embedded products. The software products provide new levels of customer experience, allow remote operational management and other use cases. With the increasing importance of software, of course the organization is responding in terms of work processes, organizational setup and hiring.

A newer development is that the company is developing a new commercially driven services organization. Initially, this organization was intended to provide more support for the high-end product range and was mostly supporting sales. However, over time the company found new ways to monetize its product portfolio and set of competences. This led to alternative business models where the company sells services that might require deployment of its products at customers but as part of a service contract rather than an outright sale. In addition, as its products are becoming connected to the internet, through starting from high-end products, monetizing software upgrades that provide additional value for customers that have the company's products already deployed in the field. Finally, though surprising for old-timers at Viganbe, the company uses the cloud to collect data from its products in the fields. It uses this data to understand product use, provide preventive maintenance services as well as providing consolidated, aggregated data from its entire installed base back to its original customers as well as to a new group of customers that use this data for their own purposes.

The developments discussed above have major impact on Viganbe and the organization feels the pressure of having to change at a rate that it has never accomplished before. These changes are not constrained to one aspect of the organization or a single function, but, as we will see in the subsequent sections, touch the entire organization.

3.2 STRATEGY

The strategy of Viganbe is a case study in conflicted emotions. On the one hand, everyone in the organization knows what is needed to succeed in the future. The long-term vision of the organization as a software- and data-driven service provider, supported by its products, is accepted in the organization. The question is more concretely concerned with what is needed now to make this a realistic transition. Getting concrete on the short-term actions for the next quarter and year is a difficult balance between letting go of areas where existing revenue has been generated for decades, even though the margins have been under pressure, and jumping to areas where the revenue potential has not been fully confirmed. Especially with a senior management team that has responsibility to report to the stock market every quarter, it is extremely tempting to pay lip service to the vision. This often happens by stating that the company will do both, i.e., support the old business and create the new one, but without freeing up resources to actually invest in the new business opportunities. With shrinking margins, the amount of resources available to invest in new opportunities inspired by the vision is reducing constantly and the choices that need to be made are increasingly difficult. This, in turn, easily leads to a situation that Viganbe has experienced in recent years: a Hail Mary effort into a new business with the hope that it would result in rapid revenue growth. Of course, the revenue was smaller and growing slower than expected, resulting in a cancellation of the initiative. Currently, a competitor of Viganbe has established itself as market leader in the same area and garnered rapid revenue growth. Several innovators in the company lament the lack of patience in the company and stress the importance of having several innovation initiatives funded as the revenue growth of new businesses is a slow and time-consuming process.

The strategy of Viganbe, consequently, is threefold. First, it drives cost reduction initiatives in its core product businesses in order to maintain or at least keep down erosion of margins while maintaining or growing market share. Second, it executes a forward integration strategy where it provides systems and solutions that include its traditional products but with Viganbe providing the entire system or solution. Third, the company increasingly seeks to complement its product offering with value adding services with the intent of generating recurring income after the initial revenue from product sales has been generated.

Over recent years, Viganbe has become increasingly aware of the ecosystems in which it operates. Especially as it executes on its forward integration strategy as well as it explores adjacencies, the company needs to build relationships with new partners, reform or end relationships with existing partners and manage the relationship with partners that are not affected (yet) but that are concerned with the strategic moves that the company is conducting.

Starting with the last group, Viganbe has been systematic in exploring its forward integration, starting in markets where it has low market share or it could find a solution with its primary downstream partners that would not alienate them. In these markets, the company started to provide systems and solutions that include its traditional products but also many other parts. The challenge is that these systems and solutions offer higher margins, but at the same time require a higher level customer intimacy as the systems and especially the solutions require more customization and adaptation to specific customer needs. This requires a different engagement model in sales, more access to engineering competence and a reversion of the scale-driven approach that the company has been successful with in the past. As the company is also still in its traditional product business, it needs to manage a situation where different sales cultures are used in the same company. Several of its existing customers, however, are aware of the company's actions in these markets, even if they are not active in the same geographies. Their concern, however, is that this might be a sign of things to come in their own markets as well, meaning that one of their key suppliers might turn into a competitor. The knee-jerk reaction often is to select another supplier that is more likely to "stay in its box". The sales and customer relation teams at Viganbe actively work with their customers to limit the reaction and to stress that it's business as usual.

At the same time, the forward integration by the company does require it to redefine the relationship with several of its existing partners and customers. For instance, with some customers, Viganbe starts to compete at the low end of their product portfolio but has no intention to compete at the high end. Discussions and negotiations with the customers are then concerned with maintaining the relationship while reshaping parts of it. This requires finding win-win solutions that grow the cake for both parties. In some cases, either for entirely rational reasons or because of emotional reactions by the senior leadership of some partners, it is not feasible to maintain the relationship, requiring the company to shut down ongoing activities with that partner.

Finally, both for forward integration and concerning the development of supporting services, the company is required to select new partners providing capabilities that Viganbe does not have available internally and may not be interested in developing in-house in the short term. The selection of new partners, building trust as well as business models that fit both sides and finding effective ways of monetizing the fruits of the partnership require significant effort from R&D leadership as well as general management. However, as the company realizes that it is increasingly (inter-)dependent on its evolving ecosystem, it views the time and resources spent as an investment into its future.

As Viganbe seeks to become increasingly data-driven in its business, it needs to get access to the data generated by the products, systems and solutions it provides to its customers. However, its offerings are typically integrated in the solutions its customers offer to end-customers. As such, there is a natural tension as Viganbe's customers claim the data are theirs and not accessible to Viganbe. This has led to several discussions and the company has tested several strategies to get access to the data, typically concerned with offering something of value to its customers in response to the data. Examples include providing additional insights by aggregating data from multiple customers and insisting that data sharing is a prerequisite for any warranty on its systems.

3.3 ARCHITECTURE AND TECHNOLOGY

Viganbe has always viewed itself as a technology company and it has introduced new technologies before its competitors most of the time. It has a brand of providing reliable, high-quality products to its customers and that has helped it command premium pricing for its products. The challenge that the company is experiencing is that for its core products, competitors from Asia have been successfully increasing the quality levels of their products without increasing pricing. This has been eroding the price premium that Viganbe has been able to charge.

The realisation that it is increasingly difficult to differentiate in the core product has led to reexamination of what the company offers in terms of value to its customers. That has, in turn, resulted in a redefinition of the notion of a Viganbe offering. Rather than just thinking in terms of a physical product, Viganbe defines the offering as consisting of several parts:

The physical product as it has offered for decades.

The software that is embedded in the physical product. Although the software originally was treated much like the physical parts, the increasing connectivity of its products allows for treating software separately as it can be upgraded after the physical product has left the factory.

The data that Viganbe is collecting from its products in the field are growing in size and relevance and the company is increasingly able to provide data and information services to its customers.

The company increasingly offers operational services for its deployed products where it provides preventive and traditional maintenance, monitoring of system functions as well as optimization of product settings. Viganbe allows the customer to select between a traditional product sale and operational services as a separate service or to select the entire package as a service offering, avoiding the upfront product cost.

Finally, the company has been focusing on providing integration services during the construction and deployment of systems and solutions at customer sites.

All of the above elements make up Viganbe's new offering. In addition, it is in the process of defining a set of APIs that would allow for extending the product with additional software-driven functionality. This is loosely modeled after the IOS and Android mobile app ecosystems, but provides more domain-specific functionality and strict controls on resource usage and access to the underlying product functionality. As one of the strategies is forward integration, the company needs these APIs for its own integration services but the intent is to open the platform up for external developers as well.

Viganbe serves multiple market segments, ranging from heavy industrial to SME and consumers, but it has long strived to accomplish economies of scale in its mechanical, hardware and software parts through the use of platforms. For its software, it has adopted a software product line approach where it has modeled the variations between the different market segments as well as products within each market segment. Although it earlier allowed product development teams to deviate as much from the platform as needed, with the adoption of an ecosystem interface (APIs for 3rd party developers), the company now seeks to standardize the interface to functionality built on top of the product as much as it seeks to maximize the reuse of common functionality.

The behavior of these APIs may differ somewhat between different products, especially in terms of response time and performance but also domain functionality, as the products in the product line serve very diverse market segments. However, each deviation that is brought up in the architect team needs to be approved before the product can be released. If this was just for the external developers, the company might not have found the discipline but as its own integration and operational services organisations are depending on it and tend to complain loudly when interfaces behave different from specifications, the adherence to architecture guidelines has been broadly adopted.

The architect team has made a number of critical decisions that provide significant structure and context for the R&D teams. The first is that the architecture defines a component mechanism with clearly defined message-based interfaces that allow for significant modularity in the architecture. As the hardware architecture in which the software is deployed can vary widely between high-end industrial products and low-end consumer products, the software is architected to be independent of the specific deployment. This means that messages on the same core (in case of static allocation) are compiled to efficient procedure calls while the same code may use a message bus in case of a distributed allocation.

The second decision concerns data. The component mechanism supports a generic mechanism for data collection at each interface with a pattern for inserting probes, data aggregation and data analysis at the component level. Mechanisms are provided for combining data from different components in the architecture for more complicated data aggregation patterns.

The third decision concerns a fundamental decision about differentiating versus commodity functionality. The architect team has decided, following the three layer product model discussed in later chapters, to break the platform into two layers: a bottom layer containing functionality that is considered commodity by the architects and a top layer containing differentiating functionality. Periodically, the architect team, with support of product management, reviews the functionality in both layers with the intent of moving functionality from the differentiating layer to the commodity layer as well as to review functionality in the commodity layer that can be removed or replaced with external software, either commercial or open-source. In addition, variability still present in components in the commodity layer is reviewed and removed where possible. The goal is to drive down cost and resource requirements in the commodity layer to free up resources. These resources can then be applied to the differentiating functionality layer.

Finally, the organization has invested significantly in its build, test and deployment infrastructure. This was necessary for the platform approach that the company has adopted as derivation of products from the platform had to be automated. In addition, the company is exploring technologies for enabling its software upgrade business, including the ability for continuous deployment of new functionality in some of its products that are used in operational service deployments. This has required the company to build a continuous integration infrastructure that allows for continuous testing of all products as the platform evolves.

3.4 ORGANIZING

Viganbe is a typical software-intensive embedded systems company with the typical functions found in the industry. The functions include product management, R&D, verification, manufacturing, sales/marketing and support. In addition, it has started to build up its services organization providing both integration and operational services.

As we focus on software in this book, though in the context of mechanics and electronics, we take a closer look at that part of the organization. Though ambitious, the company has centralized its software development in a single platform organization that builds the features that may end up in a product. Originally, the central software R&D organization would assign teams to R&D projects intended to develop a specific product. The new way of working is concerned with teams taking responsibility for a feature and adding the feature to the platform as a configurable item. This means that products can decide to include or exclude the feature.

The teams follow typical agile development practices, including sprints, daily standup meetings, a backlog of work items and frequent check-ins of code as well as other practices. The company has tried to the largest extent possible to follow the "two pizza" rule and keep teams around six to eight members. Although the teams have a product owner role, this person is often one of the engineers or an architect, rather than a product manager. Although the ambition exists to move towards more cross-functional teams including product managers, this has not been realized yet. Teams can call on product managers to clarify features and to help the team prioritize the most important work items.

When the agile work practices were adopted, this initially led to a reduction of attention on architecture which led to accelerated erosion for a period of time. It soon became clear that there was a need for architects and architecture governance that was not easily met in the basic agile ways of working. In response, the organisation identified architects that have responsibility for the architecture integrity for a part of the overall platform architecture. These architects spend part of their time working as engineers in agile teams and another part of their time working as architects. These architects are coaches rather than police agents.

The architects operate in an architect team led by a chief architect. This architect team also identifies architecture refactorings that are required and maintains a prioritized list for resource allocation to teams when there is budget available for refactoring.

As mentioned in the previous section, the company has invested significantly in continuous integration infrastructure. The infrastructure, of course, needs to be complemented with ways of working that exploit the offered advantages. Consequently, the agile teams have adopted test driven development as part of their practices and check in code frequently, often multiple times per day. This has allowed R&D to catch errors early while the new code is still fresh in the minds of the engineers, leading to higher quality and less effort spent on bug fixing.

There is a separate team that maintains the build, test and deploy infrastructure. This team is also responsible for the final release of the code as this requires manual testing that has not yet been automated. The company does not yet support continuous deployment of software even though it has aspirations in that direction. As the continuous integration environment does not catch all defects, the team also maintains a prioritized list of known defects.

The product management team is responsible for the product portfolio and the characteristics and features that differentiate the products in the portfolio from each other as well as from competing products. For the software in these products, the team focuses on the identification of features that add value for multiple products in the portfolio. As products are largely automatically derived from the platform, new products are configured to include new features and differentiate in this fashion. To support this way of working, the product management team maintains a prioritized list of features that it requests R&D to build.

One of the important sources of new features is the integration service teams. As these teams are building integrations for specific systems and customers, the teams have a good understanding of value-adding features that might be relevant to more than a specific system or customer.

In some cases, functionality is requested that is so specific to a particular product that the architect team is reluctant to add it to the platform. In this case, the team responsible for the product builds, similar to the integration services teams, the product-specific functionality on top of the ecosystem APIs. In this way, the platform is not polluted with overly specific functionality and the products can still maintain differentiation through their features.

The final part of the organizational setup is the governance of the work in the organization. The three teams in R&D discussed above, i.e., the architect team, the infrastructure and release team and the product management team, each maintain a prioritized list of architecture refactorings, system defects and features, respectively. As the R&D organization insists on a single backlog of work items, representatives from the aforementioned groups meet on a regular basis to prioritize between features, refactoring and defects. The resulting backlog is used by the agile teams to select their next task after completing their current assignment. As different teams have different profiles, the items in the backlog have, if necessary, skill requirements associated with the item. This means that certain teams do not automatically pick the next item from the backlog, but rather search through the backlog until they find an item that matches their skills profile.

3.5 CONCLUSION

In this chapter, we have introduced Viganbe as the case company that we use throughout the rest of the book. Although it obviously is a fictitious company, it combines many elements of companies that we have worked with over the last decade or more. In that sense, it is representative of the reality at a wide variety of software-intensive systems companies. Of course, there are individual differences and companies are at different stages, but Viganbe provides a model that is quite common to many companies. In the remaining chapters of the book, we will use this case company to illustrate the models, theories and frameworks that we introduce to manage the ever-increasing complexity of software development.

II

Speed

CHAPTER 4

The Stairway to Heaven: Speed

The only constant is change. The adage is also true for companies and broadly accepted. Many companies have seen peers in their industry that looked to be bastions of stability being disrupted and falling from their pedestals. The result might be significant loss of market share, exiting the market in order to focus on other core businesses or even bankruptcy. Many examples exist, but companies like Nokia, Kodak and Hasselblad are shadows of their former selves (if the company indeed is still in existence). In most cases, the analysis is that the companies had become static, unable to change and only running forward along the trajectory that had made them successful in the past. Consequently, the consensus in industry is that change is needed to survive. However, to assume that these companies did not try to change is a simplification of the matter. Of course, these companies tried to change and tried to defend their markets and build new markets. Each of these companies took increasingly desperate measures to maintain solvency and develop new growth areas. The challenge, however, is that these companies tend to be out of touch with the market to begin with - they would not be in this situation if they were in touch with the market - so any radical initiatives often are too few and too late.

Industry as a whole understands that change is required to stay in business. The main challenge is to understand what needs to change and, as organizations have a limited capacity for change, what the ordering of changes should be: what should be changed first and what can be delayed until later. Both aspects, the overview of all changes required as well as their relative priority and inter-dependencies, are critically important to be clear on.

One of the fallacies of change is to underestimate the scope of the change required. For instance, introducing a new technology may seem like a local change relevant only for the R&D department. In many cases, however, the new technology requires changes in manufacturing and customer support.

Sales needs to be able to define the benefits of the new technology. Customers may realize that the new technology allows for new engagement models (and associated business models) with the company. General management suddenly realizes that what was initially perceived as "just" a technology swap is turning into a change that affects the entire organization.

A second fallacy frequently experienced by people responsible for a change program is that, when thinking through all the changes that are required, it easily becomes overwhelming. Everyone has to change everything right now! Of course that is impossible and we need a systematic approach to change that allows organizations to change fast, but not at breakneck speeds. This requires a framework for sequencing the changes required by the organization.

In this chapter, we introduce the Stairway to Heaven model as a mechanism to provide an overview of the changes required as well as the sequencing of these changes. Using this model, you can decide which changes need to be implemented now and which can, or even should, be delayed to a later stage. The Stairway to Heaven model consists of three dimensions, i.e., speed, data and ecosystems. This chapter is focused on the speed dimension, but will mention the others. In each dimension, the model presents several levels that can be achieved in a sequential fashion. In fact, each level represents a necessary precursor for the next. Each level not only has technical implications or implications just for the R&D department, instead, depending on the dimension and level transition, every part of the organization as well as its interfaces to the ecosystems it is part of can be affected. This potentially includes the business model, product and ecosystem architecture, the ways of working, processes and tools as well as the way the organization is structured.

Although the dimensions of speed, data and ecosystems are theoretically independent, in practice there are dependencies in that improvements in one dimension have significant benefits for other dimensions. For example, one of the steps in the speed dimension is continuous deployment, i.e. the frequent (at least once per agile sprint) delivery of software all the way to customers. Accomplishing this level significantly benefits the data dimension where A/B or split testing of functionality is one level. Fast deployment cycles allow for much more efficient A/B testing as we can run experiments with systems at customers more frequently. Similarly, when continuous deployment includes both the company itself as well as its ecosystem partners contributing to its systems, the business benefits of continuous deployment are significantly higher. These examples indicate that although the dimensions are largely independent from each other, there are synergistic effects between levels in the different dimensions.

For those familiar with the research presented here, a quick note on the Stairway to Heaven model. The model presented here is the second instantiation of the Stairway to Heaven. In earlier work, we presented the first version that only covered the speed dimension. As we have continued to work with a variety of companies, it has become increasingly clear that effective use of data and the ecosystem that the company operates in are equally important

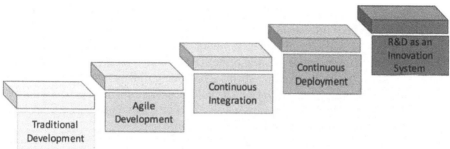

Figure 4.1 Speed dimension of the Stairway to Heaven

and that speed is more of an enabler for the other dimensions. In that sense, the model presented here should be referred to as Stairway to Heaven 2.0, but to keep things simple, we will not use the "2.0" in the remainder of this book.

In figure 4.1, we provide an overview of the Stairway to Heaven model, including the levels for each dimension. The remainder of the chapter introduces the model in more detail.

4.1 DIMENSION 1: SPEED

The first dimension of the Stairway to Heaven model is concerned with speed. As we will discuss, this speed is focused on shortening feedback loops in development. In general, faster feedback loops lead to faster adjustment to changes in the target environment. Consequently, it leads to more accurate investment of R&D resources.

The speed dimension distinguishes five levels that companies are moving through over time. These levels are:

Traditional: This starting point considers the traditional development approach before any modern development methods are adopted. In most companies the traditional exhibits many aspects of a waterfall style approach. These aspects include a relatively long time between the decision of what to build and the delivery of the associated functionality. Also, typically there is a sequential process where requirements, architecture design, detailed design, implementation, testing and release are performed sequentially. Finally, the R&D organisation is even organized in different functions related to the steps in the process.

Agile practices: As has been getting clear over the last decades, traditional development approaches have all kinds of inefficiencies baked into them. One of these inefficiencies is the number of internal handovers between different functions. This easily leads to a whispering game where the result as expressed in code is far from the functionality intended by the person describing the requirement. In order to avoid this, many organizations rely increasingly on formalized documentation, which in turn increases the overhead in development significantly. In response to these and other inefficiencies, many organizations have adopted a host of agile practices, including teams, sprints, backlogs, daily standups, clear definitions of done, etc. Adoption of agile practices focuses predominantly on the agile team itself and to a lesser extent on the interactions between the team and the rest of the organization.

Continuous integration: Once the agile teams have been established and are operating based on agile principles, the next challenge becomes to make sure that these teams are building code that actually works. This results in the introduction of continuous integration, typically a sequence of software systems that builds and tests software immediately after it is checked in. This gives teams and managers immediate feedback on the quality of the code delivered and it allows developers to fix errors that are found immediately while having the code fresh in their minds. The main advantage of continuous integration is that the organization has constant and accurate insight into the state of development. In traditional development, testing was performed at the end of the development cycle and many faults are found late, causing deadlines to be missed and the predictability of delivery dates to leave much to be desired.

Continuous deployment: When organizations have continuous integration established and institutionalized, in principle there always is a shippable version of the product software available. This version is constantly growing in feature content, but always at production level quality. Once customers realize this, there will be an increasing push for early access to the software as the new features provide benefit for them. If the new features are not providing value for customers, one should question whether these should be built in the first place. This pressure from the market often leads to continuous deployment, i.e. the frequent (at least once per agile sprint) release of new software to some or all customers. Initially, one or a few lead customers receive the software continuously, but as the benefits of the approach become apparent and concerns around quality have been allayed, the rest of the customer base will seek to adopt as well.

R&D as an experiment system: Once continuous deployment is established for some or all customers, organizations realize that the benefit is not just getting features out to customers faster. One can also test the implications of new features on customers and systems in the field by deploying partially implemented features to verify that the expected value of a new feature is indeed realized. This allows companies to redirect or stop development of features if the data from the field are not in line with expectations. The benefit of this is that the accuracy of R&D increases significantly in that we're only building features that deliver proven, rather than assumed, value to customers.

The levels for the speed dimension that we show above have been observed at dozens of companies through several empirical case studies. Although each studied company is at a specific level, we have been able to study the evolution as experienced by the company during recent years. In addition, we have studied some companies for years and have followed their evolution through these levels. As such, the levels describe a natural evolution that virtually all companies move through. As additional evidence, these levels are logical predecessors of each other. Thus, one can claim that each level needs to be accomplished before the next just because of the necessity of accomplishing one level before one can move on to the next. For instance, continuous deployment is impossible unless continuous integration is established as the quality of software deployed to the field otherwise is unacceptable. Similarly, continuous integration does not serve any purpose if there are no agile teams actually working with sprints and delivering software frequently.

Based on the previous paragraph and our experience in helping companies improve their software engineering practices, the Stairway to Heaven model provides a useful and practical approach for sequencing the change activities at a company. By first assessing current state, then deciding on the desired state and finally using the Stairway to Heaven to sequence the change management activities, companies can accomplish significant improvements in their practices at much faster rates than usual.

Although one may easily assume that the organization, as a whole, is at a certain level, in our experience, especially at larger organizations, there can be significant deviation between different products and different teams. In one of the organizations that we work with, at the time of writing, some product organizations have reached continuous deployment with lead customers. The majority of product organizations are working on getting continuous integration fully implemented. Finally, some product organizations are still working hard on getting agile development practices fully adopted across their teams.

In the following chapters, we describe each of the levels in more detail. For each level, we first provide a definition, followed by a discussion of the drivers that lead to the desire for adoption in the company. Subsequently, we identify the feedback loop that is improved by this level as well as the implications of adoption. Finally, we discuss the concerns and unsolved items that remain after the level has been fully adopted and a short example from Viganbe Inc.

4.2 TRADITIONAL DEVELOPMENT

4.2.1 Definition

Traditional development is concerned with three characteristics of software creation. First, there is an explicit definition of phases in software development and these phases are followed in a strict sequential order. In most cases, at least requirements engineering, high-level design, detailed design, development, testing and release are explicit phases. The process is concerned with completing each phase before as an R&D organization moving to the next one. Second, traditional development is concerned with stability. Once the requirements have been set, changes to these are resisted to the extent possible and, if the pressure is too high, grudgingly accepted and added against the smallest impact on the "stable" system. Finally, the system around traditional development is focused on making as accurate as possible long-term predictions, e.g., delivery dates that are a year or multiple years out, and rewarding people on their ability to deliver based on the long-term predictions.

4.2.2 Drivers for Adoption

Although it may be easy to scoff at these "old-fashioned" concepts, a waterfall-style development approach was developed in an attempt to handle the increase in systems size starting in the 1960s and 1970s. When the number of engineers working on the software of a system grew from less than a handful to dozens, hundreds and thousands [21], the software engineering community looked to other engineering fields to help bring the complexity under control. In any field concerned with "atoms", the ability to "undo" part of the system after it has been manufactured is non-existent. Consequently, traditional engineering approaches are concerned with designing a system very carefully and verifying at great length that the designed system indeed meets the requirements before the system is manufactured and produced.

Over the last two decades, we have learned better ways of building software, but also today there are companies that to a large extent still work according to the aforementioned principles. One example is the defense industry. Because of the nature of the customer interfaces, typically nation states and their military, and the long length of both the development phase (up to a decade) and the deployment phase (several decades), the development model is very close to the traditional one. During the contract negotiation phase, detailed requirement specifications are agreed upon between the customer and the defense contractor as well as a price. Once the customer has taken a formal decision, typically a highly politicized one, and the contract has been signed, things are largely cast in stone. Hence, defense contractors can assume the requirements to be stable over the entire development cycle. Second, since most defense contracts involve cutting edge mechanics and electronics, the software was traditionally only a small part of the system engineering effort. As changes to mechanics and electronics are expensive once the design is finalized, software development takes place in a very stable environment where the requirements and the system architecture are largely frozen. Consequently, the traditional development model works better in the defense industry than in many other industries.

A second industry where traditional development is still in widespread use is the high-security and high-safety embedded systems industry. Companies building systems where failure can lead to major loss of life and economic damage, such as nuclear power plants, aeronautics and medical devices, need excessive measures to ensure that the system performs according to specification. During the creation of these systems, the effort to maintain traceability between the artifacts and between identified risks and specific design solutions to address these risks takes priority over engineering efficiency. Hence, the overhead of traditional development experienced by most companies is not experienced by these companies as the artifacts need to be created and maintained anyway.

Concluding, although many industries have moved away from traditional development, it is important to recognize that the approach was developed based on the learnings of other engineering disciplines as a mechanism to handle the complexity of growing system and team size. Even today, and likely for a good long while to come, there will be industries where the traditional approach will be the central approach. It is important to realize, though, that the approach has significant inefficiencies as compared to more modern approaches. Unless there are very strong technical reasons to employ traditional development, any company that stays with this approach is setting itself up for disruption by competitors that can deliver systems at lower cost, faster speed and, surprisingly, better quality.

4.2.3   Feedback Loop

Whereas the next levels in the speed dimension of the Stairway to Heaven are concerned with shortening feedback loops at different levels, traditional development is concerned with minimizing or even removing the feedback loops throughout the entire development project. The approach aims to "feed forward" between the phases, while avoiding feedback from later phases back to earlier ones.

The only feedback loop that we can identify is between development projects where the learnings and experience accumulated in a previous project is employed in subsequent projects, assuming it doesn't violate the defined process.

4.2.4   Implications

One of the key implications is that, over time, different process models based on waterfall principles have been developed that have added more and more detailed steps, activities, milestones, artifacts and roles. Examples include the Capability Maturity Model (CMM and CMMi) [47] and [22] as well as SPICE (ISO/IEC 15504) [2]. These process models aim to deliver predictable and reliable output from development independent of the skills, experience and qualities of the individuals involved. In that sense, the approaches fall into the Tayloristic tradition in that engineers are treated as replaceable cogs in the machine. Career progress is concerned with learning the defined characteristics of acting as a bigger cog and then being selected for playing that role. Agile development practices, discussed in the next section, were developed as a reaction to the tendency of process models to standardize and harmonize professional engineers with the intent of making them interchangeable.

Of course, in this section, we provided a rather black-and-white picture of traditional development and several approaches have been developed that aim to combine traditional process models with more agile practices. For the industries that rely on and benefit from the stability provided by the model, this may be a viable way forward to increase engineering efficiency without losing the benefits provided by the traditional model. However, by and large, we have to realize that traditional development and the next levels in this dimension of the Stairway to Heaven originate from fundamentally different viewpoints about the role of engineers, the nature of development, the nature of a system, etc. To a large extent, these approaches are at odds with each other and trying to combine them is akin to mixing oil and water: it can be done, but it requires a lot of additional infrastructure.

4.2.5 Remaining Concerns

Although traditional development provides an answer to managing the complexity of large-scale software development, over the last decades the weaknesses of the approach have become more apparent as well. Fundamentally, this originates in the basic premise of the approach, i.e. strict sequential development, the focus on stability and rewarding the ability to make long-term predictions.

The insight that led to the development of agile development methods is that the basic aforementioned premises are flawed. Requirements are fundamentally unstable and change over time. Long-term predictions are very, very difficult and for many systems even attempting to do this is folly. This requires the activities of requirements engineering, architecture design, detailed design, development, verification and testing and, finally, release to occur in parallel rather than sequentially. The next levels on the speed dimension are all concerned with taking some of these activities and parallelizing them.

4.2.6 Example

One of the business domains in which Viganbe is active has very strong certification requirements due to the safety-critical nature of the solutions developed by the company. The certifying institute requires an evidence trail that clearly shows what risks have been identified and how each risk is mitigated in the design and realisation of the system. Although the business unit has explored more agile work practices, it has been unable to reconcile the strict waterfall nature of the certification process with agile work practices. In particular, maintaining a convincing evidence trail is difficult when employing sprints and iterative approaches. Consequently, the business has decided to stay with the traditional development process, despite the challenges associated with it, until there is more clarity on combining agile practices with the development of safety critical systems.

4.3   AGILE PRACTICES

4.3.1   Definition

As traditional development became more and more formalized, process-oriented and detailed, there was a reaction against the "straitjacket" that it provided. One of the most visible responses was by a group of programmers that met in Utah in 2001. One of the outcomes of the meeting was the agile manifesto. The authors of the manifesto stressed the importance of individuals, working software, collaboration with the customer and embracing change. The manifesto sparked a fire in the software engineering community that had long been frustrated with the constantly diminishing power of the folks that actually build software. Instead others, the staff functions, the process people, etc., had taken over and the amount of overhead created, the amount of rework and the overall productivity had been suffering for a long time.

The agile manifesto led to the definition of a set of agile practices. Some authors put all the activities in the levels of the Stairway to Heaven, including continuous integration and deployment, under agile practices. However, in reality the adoption of agile practices is almost exclusively focused on the agile team and the way it works with the software and itself. There are several agile practices that are at the core of agile software development. Below we discuss some of these practices.

One of the key factors is team size. In terms of Amazon's Jeff Bezos, two pizza teams work best. A two pizza team consists of six to eight people that work together. The team does not have to be entirely static, but it does require a level of stability in that the majority of the team members work together for several sprints in a row. The team works in sprints of one to four weeks, depending on the industry, the maturity of the software development environment, the interface to the rest of the organization and other factors. During a sprint, an agreed amount of requirements is implemented in the code, and working software is delivered at the end of it. The sprint is bookended with sprint planning at the beginning and a retrospective at the end. Each day, there is a meeting by the entire team where members report on progress, raise concerns, share their plans, etc.

In a small-scale environment where a team works with a customer, the team will, together with the customer, define user stories. These user stories are broken down into work items that are added to a backlog. The team uses a backlog of work items as the governance mechanism for work. Team members can take work items and move these through from "planned" to "in progress" to "done". A work item has a clear definition of done associated with it that helps the team determine if the work item really has been completed.

Several agile methods have been developed and Wikipedia provides a relevant overview [1]. However, few agile methods traditionally addressed the large scale of software development in many companies. When the number of teams grows to dozens or more for an individual product, not all practices can be implemented as described and additional governance mechanisms are required in order to facilitate the integration of all the software delivered by the different teams. There are some approaches, such as the scaled agile framework [3], that aim to address this, but by and large deploying agile development practices in a large organization remains a challenge where several organizations are struggling.

4.3.2 Drivers for Adoption

Although many developers may view their liberation as the key driver for adoption, the key driver for adoption of agile development practices was the constantly increasing overhead present in traditional software development. In a large organization, sales is the key function interacting with customers. Depending on the organization, product management talks to sales to learn about their experiences and formulates road maps, release content and feature specifications. These written artifacts are shared with the systems engineering department. Systems engineering converts these into higher level designs, including interfaces and protocols, and specifications for different subsystems and components. These artifacts, again written down and documented, are passed on to development who converts these into code. The code, once completed, is passed to the testing department, responsible for verification and validation. This department tests the software in response to its specifications and reports the results, often in written and documented form. We can describe traditional development in more detail, but the key realization is that development is organized as multiple stovepipe functions that communicate through documents. The amount of documents created for internal use only, the amount of incorrect interpretation of these documents as well as the resulting amount of rework results in major inefficiencies in software development. Even software engineers, the only ones building code, were reported to spend less than 10% of their time actually developing software. All other functions as well as 90% of the time of software engineers was spent on other activities that, by and large, could be construed as overhead.

In the early 2000s, most R&D managers with at least a basic understanding of software development had realized the inefficiencies associated with traditional large-scale software development and were quite open to trying out anything that offered the promise of improved efficiency. Hence, the seed of agile principles fell in very fertile ground and has been growing ferociously ever since its introduction.

4.3.3 Feedback Loop

Agile development shortens two feedback loops, i.e. the development loop and the requirements loop. In traditional development, individual engineers could work on a specific requirement for significant amounts of time. The time between check-ins could be weeks or even months at a time. In agile development, at least at the team level, the members check in their code frequently, i.e. daily or every couple of days, in order to share results and to allow the other members of the team to build on top of their code. Because of this the development loop is much shorter and the team can observe the realization of user stories in the software during and between sprints.

The requirements loop is at least as important. As part of sprint planning, the team seeks to clarify the user stories and work items. This requires close interaction with the customer or, as is the reality in large-scale software engineering, the product owner. The product owner ideally is a product manager close to the customer, but can also be a technical product owner. A technical product owner is part of the development organization, but acts as a bridge to product management. During sprint planning, the product owner works with the team to make sure that the requirements as well as the underlying drivers are solidly understood by the team. Instead of written documentation, this occurs through face to face interaction which leads to much higher degrees of understanding. In addition, the product owner is available to the team throughout the sprint for clarification. This allows engineers to confirm their interpretations of the requirements continuously, rather than guessing the correct interpretation, building the software and only later finding out that the interpretation was wrong.

These two feedback loops are shortened significantly with the adoption of agile development practices, resulting in a significant efficiency improvement once the adoption hurdle has been passed. The retrospective at the end of each sprint allows teams and product owners to frequently reflect on how to improve their work and over time additional efficiency improvements can be realized.

4.3.4 Implications

There are several implications of adopting agile development. The first is that it requires changes to the governance of software development. Rather than the traditional reporting on the stage that development is in, during agile software development, the focus tends to be much more on the system itself and the state of working software. This is, of course ,entirely in line with the agile manifesto which stresses the importance of working software. Rather than focusing on everything around the system, the focus is on the system itself.

The second, very positive, implication of the adoption of agile software development practices is that the relation between product management and R&D improves significantly due to the frequent interaction between the groups. In traditional development, the relationship between these groups can easily grow antagonistic. The typical complaint from product management is that development is always late and unpredictable. On the other hand, R&D teams complain about product managers who can describe what the customer want, provide vague and half-baked requirements and put unreasonable demands on the organization. The sprints provide the short cycles that allow for much more accurate planning and more reliable delivery. The frequent interaction clarifies the requirements and gives R&D teams an insight into the areas that are either not known by product management or a collaborative effort is required to understand what technology can be used to deliver solutions to customers.

One of the challenging implications is that some teams take an approach that is the other extreme of the process heavy traditional approach and refuse all structure, process and planning. This easily results in a cowboy culture and, over time, difficulty to deliver a system at quality. In this context it is important to remember that agile development is not about abandoning all process and structure, but rather to define just enough process and structure to maximize autonomy of teams without sacrificing the ability to deliver the system at quality.

In the same vein, during the adoption of agile development practices, the focus of architecture often diminishes as the R&D teams have a lot of freedom to implement features in the best way possible for them. As a consequence, decisions might be taken that are optimal from a local perspective, but that have negative implications at the overall architectural level. As a consequence, the risk is that the architecture of the overall system suffers a higher degree of design erosion as compared to traditional development.

Finally, there is some anecdotal evidence that the amount of bottom-up innovation by teams decreases in an agile context. As each team plans to 100% of its capacity and the sprints are relatively short, there is no time that is not filled with short-term work. In traditional development, because of the long cycles, it was easier for engineers to take time to work on an innovative idea or concept to add to the product next to their main area of focus. Consequently, organizations relying on their engineers generating a constant flow of smaller and bigger improvements may experiences a noticeable drop. As a counter to this, some organizations introduce the notion of unstructured or personal time. For example, Google's employees are allowed to use 20% of their time on projects based on their own interest, rather than aligned with the company strategy. Many employees use this time to build solutions or solve problems that they feel should have been prioritized by the company.

4.3.5 Remaining Concerns

One of the main concerns that agile teams experience as the organization transitions to this phase is the mismatch between their sprint model and the slow moving traditional cycle in the rest of the organization. This makes it difficult to achieve all of the benefits of agile software development and it tends to require a certain amount of overhead from the teams at different stages in the traditional development process to provide the process people in the rest of the organization with the information required in the traditional process.

A second concern not addressed at this level is that the verification and validation organization, at this stage, has not adopted the agile practices. Consequently, the teams build code, but then are unable to determine whether the software works at the system level. Unit and subsystem testing will provide some feedback, but the challenge is obviously that the more important and difficult to verify functionality can only be verified at the system level.

The key concern with late testing is not only that teams build software for a long time before they get feedback on quality issues; it also tends to disrupt the flow in agile sprints as certain sprints throughout the year will be disrupted as the trouble reports start to come in and need to be addressed.

The final concern is that the release of software to customers still is a "big thing" happening once or twice per year. This requires teams that otherwise work on their burndown charts and backlog to suddenly be available as the organization starts to release its software to customers and the issue from the field starts to be reported back.

Concluding, all the remaining concerns are related to the fact that even if the teams work in agile sprints, the rest of the organization is still working in the traditional development model. This leads to significant disruptions in the flow of agile development at different times and there will be a constant pressure to adjust to the rest of the organization.

4.3.6 Example

One of the consumer-facing business units of Viganbe adopted agile development practices in its R&D unit. Despite some wobbles during the transition, the engineers were pleased to get more autonomy and to work with modern, proven development practices. Also product managers quickly understood the benefits as it allowed them to perform re-prioritization of feature content every sprint, based on new findings from customers and feedback from systems in the field.

When the first release came around, however, the limitations of the approach became obvious as well. Even though software R&D teams were using the agile practices, the rest of the organization was still stuck in the waterfall ways of working. Consequently, when the testing of the software started, the agile teams rapidly got snowed under by a wave of error reports from the testing department and before long the agile teams were back in the crunch they had experienced in the old way of working before a release. Soon the teams joked that they could do agile nine months out of the year, only to fall back in the old ways of working for three months before release the remainder of the year. This caused a significant disruption in the agile ways of working, even though the teams sought to include defect management as part of the backlog and make it part of the normal work.

Product managers experienced their own challenges in that they enjoyed the frequent re-prioritization of feature content, but felt frustrated by the fact that whatever they prioritized would still take a year to reach customers. No matter how hard a product manager tried to counter moves by competitors, the fact remained that the software would not reach customers until long after the "sweet spot".

4.4 CONTINUOUS INTEGRATION

4.4.1 Definition

In traditional development the integration phase is handled as a separate phase towards the end of the development process. In the earlier phases, teams of engineers built software in their respective subsystems or components based on a break down of requirements and an agreement of interfaces between the subsystems and components. In practice, the integration phase, despite all good intentions, was the phase where all the misunderstandings of requirements, system level errors, mismatches in expectations between subsystems, etc., were identified. This led to an often major inflow of change requests and trouble reports and a lot of unscheduled work that resulted in unpredictable release schedules and high stress levels among those responsible.

Continuous integration provides a solution to these aforementioned challenges. A continuous integration system incorporates small chunks of new functionality as soon as these are developed, The integration has two parts to it. First, the new code is integrated into the code base and compiled and linked into a complete product. Second, through a sequence of test activities, the quality of the new product is established and any issues that are found are reported back to the R&D organization and specifically to the team that added the new functionality. In its final state, continuous integration ensures that the organization has a shippable product at any point in time, even if the feature content is growing continuously.

Similar to the previous level of agile development where different agile practices need to be adapted, continuous integration also is not binary, but rather a series of steps where the organization moves closer and closer to a state where any new functionality that is checked in is integrated and tested in minutes or hours. Later in the book, we present the CIVIT model as a visualization technique to support the transition towards continuous integration.

4.4.2 Drivers for Adoption

Continuous integration is the logical step after the adoption of agile development practices as it addresses one of the key challenges of agile teams: once the team has completed some functionality, it needs quick feedback on any concerns that the new functionality might have raised. If it needs to wait until the end of the development cycle, there tends to be significant impact on the development flow of the team as members need to go back to code developed sometimes months ago and try to figure out what is raising the problems. Especially in large systems operating in complicated contexts, finding faults is hard and time consuming.

A second driver for adoption comes from general and R&D management. The lack of predictability in the traditional integration phase is a source of major concern for any company as it is very difficult to make commitments to customers. As the customer perception of the company is a critical factor in a continued relation, making commitments and breaking these later is problematic if one wants to maintain a professional brand and image.

Third, as product management prioritizes feature content, the priority of a feature is a function of the predicted value for the customer and the cost and impact of implementing the feature in the system. Continuous integration provides insight into the impact of a feature on the rest of the system as it is being developed, providing mechanisms for developing only parts of the feature, implementing it differently or even removing it completely if it turns out that the cost outweighs the predicted value.

Finally, effective continuous integration allows for the correction of errors close to the time where the feature was developed. This helps development as the engineer has the code fresh in his or her mind. Second, error correction effort is spread out through the development cycle, rather than all piled up at the end of the cycle. This reduces disruption of the development flow of teams to a significant extent.

4.4.3 Feedback Loop

The adoption of continuous integration helps shorten at least three feedback loops. The first is the development loop of engineers and agile teams. Rather than having to wait until the end of the development cycle, feedback on quality issues is provided promptly, within minutes, hours or days. This has significant benefits for development.

The second feedback loop is between R&D management and the rest of the company; whereas earlier, the status of development was unclear until a shippable product was announced by R&D, i.e. at the end of the development cycle. After the deployment of continuous integration, there is always a shippable product and the entire company can follow the growth of feature content. This allows sales and general management to decide when sufficient new features are present in the system to justify a new release of the product to customers, or, alternatively, to adopt a periodic release schedule without having to bother about unpredictable delays in the end of the cycle.

Finally, the release process to customers is now more predictable. As the effort to release a new version is reduced with the adoption of continuous integration, many companies increase the frequency with which they release products to the market. There is an immediate business benefit as functionality, once it is developed, provides no value to customers or the company itself until it is deployed at customers. Hence, more frequent release of the product to customers, mutatis mutandis, improves the competitive position of the company.

4.4.4 Implications

Adopting continuous integration has a number of implications that the organization needs to address in order to achieve success. The first is cost and resources. In order to build up the capability to provide fast, qualified feedback once new code is checked in, some investment in the automation of testing is required. In traditional development, an amount of manual testing, ranging from moderate to extensive, is acceptable as the testing takes place only during the final stages of development. However, if the intent is to achieve continuous and fast feedback in response to new code, there can not be any manual testing in the process. Hence, all testing needs to be automated. For instance, in some of the companies that we work with, every agile team has a scaled down instance of the main product available.

Especially in the case of embedded systems, companies often have a very limited number of physical test beds available that are used by specialized manual testing teams for product-level testing. When adopting continuous integration, the testing on these test beds needs to be automated and all code needs to be tested at least nightly or every week (often during a weekend). Frequently, this requires investment in test beds that often are not available in the volumes that these are required in continuous integration. In addition, it may require investment in the automation of testing in these test beds to replace the teams that performed manual testing earlier.

Although agile development already assumes that engineers check in their code frequently in the team branch, in continuous integration, it becomes even more important for engineers to check in frequently in the main product branch. This requires a change in the behavior of engineers as many engineers have a preference to build large chunks of functionality in their own branch before sharing it with their colleagues. As the cost of integration as well as the cost of rework goes up non-linearly with the size of the check-in, it is crucial to change the behavior to frequent check-ins.

Finally, there is a level of trust in continuous integration that needs to be developed over time. Especially customer facing management has experienced many issues with the software at the customer site when the organization was using the traditional development process and will find it hard to believe that those problems are just gone. And, of course, these problems are not gone immediately, but rather continuous integration requires an associated improvement process where errors that slipped through are analyzed and test cases addressing the error are developed.

4.4.5 Remaining Concerns

The main concern that remains even after the organization has succeeded in a full roll-out of continuous integration is the diversity of environments in which the product is deployed at customers. Especially in B2B environments where customers have significant power, adjustments to the interfaces and behavior of the product are made to satisfy specific customer needs. As the configurability of the product increases, the ways in which the product is deployed at customers grows more diverse. When customers use the product in different ways, it becomes more difficult to test the product in the continuous integration environment for all the variations. This may lead to more issues to be found in the field than what one would expect considering the rigor and level of testing in continuous integration.

Addressing the aforementioned concern, however, should not just focus on expanding the continuous integration environment. Removing configurability that is no longer used and refactoring the architecture to increase modularity as well as other initiatives to reduce the amount of variation at customer deployment is very beneficial to address this. This is not just helpful for continuous integration, but also prepares customers for a potential transfer of the product from on-premise deployment to a cloud-based deployment of all or some of the functionality in the product.

4.4.6 Example

The R&D team of the consumer-facing business unit that had adopted agile practices and ran into the integration challenge of the traditional release process learned from its challenges during the first integration and release endeavor after it adopted agile ways of working. In response, it reached out to the testing department to improve the ability of agile teams to test their software frequently and to create system integrations that could be tested throughout the year. Initially, the testing department responded highly skeptical as many of their testing practices were manual and they could not see a way to conduct these continuously throughout the year as they needed to prepare for the next release. However, when the R&D teams offered help to increase the level of test automation, the discussion turned much more constructive. Using the CIVIT model, R&D and test jointly agreed on the most important initiatives to adopt and improve continuous integration and proceeded to partner on providing the resources to realise the initiatives. The next release still required crunch time from everyone in the company, but the consensus was that things were much better than in earlier years and that the overall direction for improvements was the right one.

Meanwhile, product management was still equally frustrated as earlier as despite all their efforts to speed up and continuously reprioritize release content, it still took a long time for the results of their efforts to release customers. However, as the quality of the software under development in between releases continued to improve due to the continuous integration efforts, some product managers started to wonder if this software was sufficiently mature to try out at some friendly customers in between releases.

4.5 CONTINUOUS DEPLOYMENT

4.5.1 Definition

As the quality of the software increases due to the adoption of continuous integration, the company will reach a point where it, for all practical purposes, has a production-quality version of the product at all times. When this point is reached, there will be a two-pronged push to increase the frequency of deployment. On the one hand, customers want to get early access to functionality as this gives a competitive advantage over others. On the other hand, development is eager to deploy the product in the field early in order to detect quality issues that the continuous integration environment might not catch.

Although many definitions of continuous deployment exist, we define continuous deployment to be reached when the results of every agile sprint are deployed at customers. As agile sprints are at most 4 weeks, this means that continuous deployment will deploy the product at customers at least that often. Of course, the frequency of deployment can be much higher, up to many times per day. The optimal deployment frequency is an optimization of multiple factors.

The term continuous delivery is also used in this context. We define continuous delivery as the process where the R&D organization delivers a shippable version of the product to internal or external customers, but the customer is still the one deciding whether to deploy the new release and, if so, when it deploys the latest version. Although providing several of the benefits of continuous deployment, it tends to create a complicated issue tracking situation as different customers use different versions and it may be difficult to determine if an identified issue is still present in the latest version or whether it was only a concern in an older version that is already obsolete. Customers, however, may demand support for the older version anyway, requiring valuable resources to be spent on resolving issues in old versions for just one customer.

The main difference between continuous delivery and continuous deployment is the party responsible for deciding when to deploy the version in a live system. In continuous delivery, it is still the customer who decides. Also, many companies use the term continuous delivery when the party delivered to is an internal customer, rather than a real, paying customer. In the case of continuous deployment, the producer of the software decides when it is deployed in real, live contexts at actual paying customers.

The transition to the producer deciding when to deploy software has major implications on the entire interface between the company and its customers. Depending on the number of issues found at the customer site, for instance in its test lab, there are significant trust and liability issues to be resolved during the transition period.

4.5.2 Drivers for Adoption

There are several drivers for the adoption of continuous deployment, both on the business side and on the technology side. From a business perspective, one of the "wasteful aspects" of traditional development is the fact that functionality that adds value for customers often sits on the shelf at the company for extended periods of time until it is taken in use by customers. Similar to manufacturing companies seeking to reduce inventory as it binds up working capital, significant amounts of finished but undeployed functionality is wasteful.

The second business aspect is concerned with the competitive position of the company. A competitor with a monthly release schedule can get an important feature out in one to three months, whereas a company with a yearly release schedule has, on average, to wait 18 months until functionality is available for customers. This leads to a significantly improved competitive position for the company releasing more frequently.

On the technology front, one of the key factors is quality. Frequently deploying the latest version of a product allows for identifying issues in the field early and with limited effect on the overall customer base, especially when using a staged roll-out and an effective roll-back mechanism. This means that errors that disable functionality in the product will be found earlier.

Another factor is that frequent deployment will not only identify clear errors, but it also allows for tracking quality attributes of the product, such as throughput and responsiveness as well as other attributes to be tracked over deployments. This allows the development team to see the impact of features on quality attributes as they are added. If, for instance, the throughput of the system falls in response to a new feature having been added to the system, the R&D team can immediately review the implementation of this feature and optimize the implementation. Thus, rather than having to reactively fix major changes in quality attributes between two infrequent releases, the team gets to respond in real time to smaller changes and avoid problems altogether.

One argument against the use of continuous deployment for quality concerns is that continuous integration should be able to identify any issues. In practice, however, products are often deployed in customer environments that have significant variation between them. Setting up a continuous integration environment with sufficient variation is particularly challenging and hence some testing at the customer site may be required to identify issues. Continuous deployment guarantees that the amount of new functionality and changes is limited and, consequently, the amount of variation in behavior between versions is manageable in most cases.

4.5.3   Feedback Loop

The primary feedback loop that is shortened by the adoption of continuous deployment is the quality monitoring loop. Although some companies have slip stream releases to fix errors, the ability to systematically and continuously release new versions after having identified issues in the field is very powerful once it becomes the norm, rather than the exception.

As we mentioned in the previous section, depending on the industry and relationship with customers, the variation in deployment environments can be significant. This makes it hard to use the continuous integration environment for all verification. Frequent deployment of small chunks of functionality at customers will surface issues due to variation in deployment environment much more rapidly.

Similar to functionality, the quality attribute feedback loop is shorter as well as customers often do not hesitate to share feedback on changes in performance, throughput, response times, robustness and other run-time observable quality attributes. As continuous deployment allows the R&D team to rapidly see changes, the team can adjust their efforts and direct more energy towards improving declining quality attributes. Especially in industries that are or have transitioned to a services business model, the use of service level agreements (SLAs) is prevalent. Having access to mechanisms that allows the company providing the service to optimize the quality attributes to ensure delivery according to the SLA is immensely valuable.

Once the trust in continuous integration and continuous deployment has grown to be sufficient, it will also provide additional support for product management in that customer feedback on the new functionality is received much faster as compared to the traditional model. This allows misinterpretations by product managers as to the needs of customers to be caught before they become large.

4.5.4   Implications

One of the most important implications in continuous deployment is the rather fundamental change in the relationship with the customer. As the frequency of releasing new functionality goes up, many processes and activities that originally were manual and relatively inefficient need to become automated. For example, especially in industries where the consequences of errors are significant, customers often built test labs to verify new software releases before deploying these. When the frequency of deployment increases to every couple of weeks or even faster, this manual, in-house testing becomes unfeasible and the customer needs to rely on the producing organization for ensuring quality and addressing concerns.

As the company takes more responsibility for the deployment process, it needs access to data concerning the software performance at the customer site to an extent it didn't have before. Due to competitive reasons, customers often were reluctant to share data as it gives significant insight into the business performance and, as the company frequently provides solutions to competitors as well, this is a sensitive subject. However, the company is unable to rapidly respond to operational issues concerning the product if it does not have access to operational data on a continuous basis.

If a service-oriented business model is employed in the industry, the above is often easier to accomplish as both the responsibility for quality as well as the data lie squarely with the company delivering the service. However, even if no services model is used, there are mechanisms to ensure confidentiality while getting access to data.

Another implication that requires a shift in mindset in the development organization is that certain types of functionality and especially quality attributes are difficult to fully test in the time frame between deployments. Especially for longitudinal tests, for instance to test for memory leakage or other issues that only surface after long operation, some of the testing may take place outside the deployment process. This also means that software is released and deployed even though not all testing has been completed. Releasing software before all testing has been completed goes against everything in the traditional development model, but is a relevant testing approach in a continuous deployment model.

4.5.5 Remaining Concerns

Continuous deployment addresses many of the concerns associated with traditional development. The different steps towards continuous deployment dramatically shorten the feedback loops, especially around quality assurance. The main concern is that even if the product is performing according to specifications, we do not have any data on whether it optimally meets the needs of customers. The data collected tend to focus on system performance and operational issues, but most companies that we work with have little to no insight into which parts of the system are used by customers and which functionality only looks good on paper but is not used by customers in reality.

To follow up on the above, in most organizations, even if they are using continuous deployment, the development of new features is driven by product management and "ordered" from the R&D organization. Once product management decides that a certain feature is required and prioritizes it in development, the feature will get built no matter what happens. This results in what we have called the "open loop" problem [40]: product managers prioritize new features based on their best understanding of customer needs. However, after the feature has been developed, they never verify if the expected business value of the feature is actually realized. Because there is no feedback loop to product management, there is also no learning or improvement in response to the feedback loop.

In short, the steps up to continuous deployment are concerned with building the product right. We now need to shift our focus to asking if we're building the right product.

4.5.6 Example

It started with a dinner with a major customer for the company. During the dinner, the heads of product management and of R&D had been expounding over the continuous integration efforts in the company, the great improvements of software quality because of it and the great feature content in the upcoming release of the product, still six months out, that was already implemented. Over dessert, the customer raised a seemingly innocent question: could they get early access to the release? The new features were very important to the customer's competitive position as some competitors were making its life difficult right now. The customer needed the new features now, not in six months. Aiming to keep the customer happy but at the same time unwilling to make promises they weren't sure they could keep, the PM and R&D heads agreed to investigate what they could do to help the customer.

The next morning, the R&D teams and testing organization learned about the customer request and, after the obligatory freaking out, started to lay out a plan that would help the customer while at the same time making the risks and limitations clear to everyone involved. The customer was brought in to discuss these in order to manage expectations and agreed to a limited trial in one of the factories both to work out any quality issues and to evaluate whether the new features indeed delivered on the value.

This simple request resulted in a significant improvement in the time to market of new features to (initially) this customer. Also, R&D teams approached their work with a reinvigorated focus on customer value and quality as the software they were building now would be running at the customer's factory days later. Finally, product management finally had an outlet for their fast, continuous reprioritization of feature content.

Obviously, continuous deployment was no silver bullet and the company struggled with all kinds of issues, ranging from quality issues in the field to overloaded individuals that had to perform tasks every three weeks that earlier took place only once per year. Also, convincing other customers to adopt continuous deployment proved to be an uphill battle in some markets. Overall, however, the customers and the teams in the company agreed that this was moving in the right direction.

4.6 R&D AS AN INNOVATION SYSTEM

4.6.1 Definition

Prioritizing the feature content of a software release often follows a process along the lines of the following: product managers are out meeting customers. During these interactions, both in response to requests from customers and based on observation, product managers have ideas about what could be added to the product to make it better. Some of these ideas can also come from the R&D staff in the company itself. In most organizations, the number of ideas far, far exceeds the ability of the organization to deliver on these. Hence, a prioritization of these ideas needs to take place in order to bring the feature content for a release down to a manageable set. This is where product managers meet, discuss, argue and finally prioritize a set of features. R&D managers and architects are often involved in some of these discussions to provide insight into the effort required to build certain features as well as the implications on the architecture, including the advantages and disadvantages of sequencing the implementation of features in certain ways. The output of this process is an agreement among the product managers and with the R&D organization on the new features that will be part of the next release of the product. Once this agreement is in place, the entire organization emits a sigh of relief and gets to work. Interestingly, however, in very few of the companies that we work with is there ever any attempt to afterwards establish that the features that were prioritized indeed were the most valuable. In fact, we have seen very little evidence that companies have any significant insight into the use of different features by customers at all. The prioritization of new features is very much driven by a set of organizational beliefs held by product managers and R&D staff about what adds value to customers. Also, at the other end of the lifecycle of a feature, the lack of understanding of feature usage also eliminates the ability of removing features that no longer are used by customers.

The final step on the speed dimension of the Stairway to Heaven is concerned with addressing the above concern. Rather than operating on beliefs and slow feedback loops about feature content, we employ continuous deployment to provide immediate and quantitative feedback on the use and, by extension, the value of new features as these are developed. By providing usage and other data concerning a feature when only 10-20% of it has been developed, product managers and the responsible R&D team can immediately respond if reality does not match expectations. The response can be to build more of the feature while monitoring the data coming back from the field, to change the implementation based on the data to see if a different implementation will improve things or, in its most extreme, drop the feature altogether if the assumptions underlying its prioritization proved to be incorrect.

The adoption of this level requires three activities that are not present in the previous levels. First, it requires that the responsible product manager and R&D team model the expected business value as well as the realization of this business value in the operations of the system. The team needs to identify what attributes of the system or customer behavior will change and to what extent when the feature is added to the system. Second, as part of the iterative feature implementation, the software is instrumented with probes that collect data concerning the aspects of the system or customer behavior that are expected to be affected by the feature. The collection and aggregation of this data needs to be implemented on the backend as well, as the systems deployed in the field need a destination to send their data. Finally, the team needs to analyze and interpret the results, reach actionable conclusions about the gap between the expected and measured results and then adjust the implementation of the feature accordingly.

The final level of this dimension of the Stairway to Heaven is related to the data dimension discussed in chapter 8. At this stage, the focus in development shifts from building the product right to building the right product. The data collected for each new and, over time, already deployed features provide new, quantitative insights and understanding of the use of the system in all its deployments that allows for an order-of-magnitude improvement in the accuracy of R&D investments. The amount of R&D effort that is invested before data are collected about the correctness of the investment is cut from months, or in some companies years, to days and weeks of person effort.

4.6.2   Drivers for Adoption

With the advent of Big Data, organizations everywhere are looking at better ways to use data collection, analysis and taking actions based on the data. Especially in the SaaS domain, companies have taken the opportunities to heart, and record literally every click and keystroke of users. Of course, many of these companies have freemium or advertisement-based business models and need to deeply understand customers in order to generate revenue.

Especially in the embedded systems B2B world, frequently the user and the customer are not the same person. This results in an engagement model where the customer is convinced with economic projections and the user is prioritized less as this is not the person paying in the end. The challenge, however, is that over time the brand of the company will be influenced by the opinions of users and it will start to affect sales. From a purely economic perspective, satisfied effective users are more productive so there is a benefit for customers as well.

Also, as mentioned earlier, with the adoption of a services business model where the product stays in the ownership of the producing company, the gap between the customer and the user is shrinking as the services business model often allows for easy change of provider. So, the company needs to earn its customers every day, rather than the "once every couple of years" sales model.

So, the drivers for adoption are a combination of a number of factors. First, there is an increased technical ability to collect data from products in the field as virtually any product is connected these days. Second, the overall trend toward "big data" is driving a general exploration of how data can benefit any part of the business. Third, the business models, especially the transition towards services, and the speed at which the market is moving benefit taking more data-driven approaches.

4.6.3 Feedback Loop

The primary area affected by this level is the prioritization of functionality built by the R&D team. The model allows product managers and R&D teams to learn about the benefits of functionality as it is being developed. This allows for immediate adjustment of the implementation of certain features or, in the worst case, even the removal of the feature if the benefits are not realized. This feedback loop is now measured in days and weeks, rather than in months and years as it is in the traditional model.

The second feedback loop is concerned with the optimization of features already implemented in the system. Using techniques such as split-testing (also known as A/B testing), we can experiment with alternative implementations of the same functionality in order to identify which works better for users or provides better operational quality attributes for the deployed systems.

Of course, the other feedback loops discussed in the previous levels stay valid as we go up the steps. However, these feedback loops are concerned with building the product right, whereas this level is more concerned with building the right product. This causes the close collaboration between the R&D team and product management.

4.6.4 Implications

Changing towards using R&D as a data-driven innovation system has implications on several aspects of the company. One thing important to realize is that instrumenting products in the field is not only driven by changes in the business model. The reverse is true as well: the fact that we can collect information about customer behavior and system performance allows for new business models that are much closer connected to the benefits for customers and users. In general, business models that align the value captured by the company more closely with the value generated for customers and users are often experienced as more fair and reasonable by customers.

One of the challenges is that, again, changes are required in the interface to the customer. Not only is the company becoming responsible for the deployment of new releases of software, it now also needs to collect all kinds of data from products in the field and at customers. This often requires a discussion and agreement with the customer as customers often are concerned with sharing information that is of confidential nature and may have strategic or tactical implications for the company. This means that proper safeguards need to be in place to remove those concerns, such as anonymizing data, aggregation of data that could, by itself, be used for identification, as well as other techniques to reduce the concerns that customers might have.

In some industries, the incumbents tend to flatly refuse to make their data available. In these cases, starting with new entrants with a higher willingness to take risk and innovate faster is a viable strategy to start building evidence that there is real value to be had in closely participating with their supplier.

In general, however, offering something of value in return for getting access to the data often is a viable strategy. For instance, one company that we have studied requires access to the data as a prerequisite for offering warranty.

A second implication is that the architecture of the product needs to evolve to better support instrumentation of code and collection of relevant data. Although it is, of course, always possible to "bolt on" some instrumentation, it is much better to have data integral to the architecture. This reduces the amount of architecture erosion as different aspects of the system are instrumented.

The development process needs to be changed in that up to this level, there is a predefined set of features that is built over the sprints. At this level, the work is more dynamic in that the feedback from the products in the field as well as qualitative feedback directly from customers should drive the development. This requires a much more close collaboration between product managers and R&D teams, to the point that in some companies product managers become a part of teams themselves.

Product managers joining R&D teams bring us to the organizational implications of this level. As with all the previous levels, there is a constant transition from a traditional, functional organizational structure to a team-based structure. There are several reasons why this leads to better outcomes for the organization, but the reduced communication overhead and the increased speed of decision making are two of the primary drivers.

4.6.5   Remaining Concerns

Even when reaching the highest level on the speed dimension of the Stairway to Heaven does not resolve everything, there are some concerns that need to be mentioned. One of the key learnings in our experience is that as soon as companies become more data driven in their decision making and start to do A/B testing, teams start to realize that they are often optimizing multiple parameters. And when an A/B test improves one of these parameters and is negative for one of the other parameters, there is little guidance on how to take the result forward. Product teams often need some sessions to get shared understanding on the key drivers and how to treat experiments with conflicting outcomes.

A second challenge is that, as the company becomes more data driven, it often becomes more difficult to take on large R&D tasks that will not provide feedback for several sprints. The culture of fast feedback loops collides with taking on large tasks that refactor parts of the architecture or that fundamentally change the way users interact with a part of the system. The organization needs to develop mechanisms to combine a data-driven, short cycle decision process with larger development efforts that require multiple sprints.

Finally some organizations have commented on the difficulty of driving more radical innovations that can not be tested quantitatively immediately, but instead require some time to grow and mature and initially will only get qualitative customer feedback. Similar to larger R&D tasks discussed in the previous section, it is, of course, important for the organization to have a pipeline of more radical innovations in addition to the smaller, evolutionary innovations that can be tested more easily using A/B testing and other quantitative techniques.

4.6.6   Example

As several business units at Viganbe worked on adopting continuous deployment of new functionality, there was an interesting development evolving between customers and product management. Product management would prioritize features based on their best understanding of the needs of customers, but customers would insist that they were misunderstood and that the promised value was not delivered by the features. This resulted in a shift towards instrumenting the systems deployed in the field with data collection "probes" with the intent of collecting data that could provide objective, unbiased insight into the value delivered by new features.

The discussion between product managers and customers shifted towards data and whenever there were questions, the first request was to collect data. The shift towards data-driven decision making was hard on some strong-minded and opinionated people, but generally resulted in much better alignment between the value delivered by the company and the value experienced by customers.

The value of data was now broadly understood in the company and improving its use of the data was the next order of action. For that, it turned to the data dimension of the Stairway to Heaven.

4.7   CONCLUSION

In this chapter, we have introduced the first dimension of the Stairway to Heaven that is concerned with speed in development. The speed dimension consists of five levels and each level is a necessary prerequisite for the next level. Starting with traditional development, the R&D organization first needs to adopt agile development practices. Once these are established, the next step is the adoption of continuous integration where every time an agile team checks in code, it is immediately compiled, linked and tested. This provides much faster feedback to the R&D organization that the new functionality works as intended and that it doesn't break anything that was working earlier. Once continuous integration is fully mature, the R&D organization has a shippable version of the software at any point in time. This gets us away from the situation where the company can not ship because the software is not done. The new motto is that we can always ship, but sometimes we wait to ship as we want certain features to be included in the release. The next step is continuous deployment. Once we have a production quality version of the software at any time, not deploying it at customers as new functionality becomes available is wasteful. Often customers are eager to get access to new features and if they are not interested in the features that the R&D organization is building, we're not building the right functionality to begin with. Finally, once continuous deployment is in place, we can shift from building the product right to building the right product. At the final level, we use data from systems in the field to build thin slices of new functionality, deploy these and measure the impact on customer behavior and system characteristics. Based on the data from the field, we can then dynamically adjust the way a feature is implemented, drop it altogether or double down on some aspect of the feature that resonates with customers.

For each of the aforementioned levels, we provided a definition, presented the drivers for adoption and discussed the implications. Also, we discussed which feedback loops get shortened by each level as it is adopted. As shorter feedback loops provide us with more accurate ways to allocate our R&D resources to the most valuable activities, it is very important to understand which loops are shortened at each level and what the business benefits are. Finally, for each level we also shared what the remaining concerns are that need to be addressed at subsequent levels or in other dimensions of the Stairway to Heaven.

In addition to the speed dimension, there are two additional dimensions to the Stairway to Heaven, i.e. data and ecosystems. The first is concerned with maturing the way the organization uses data in its decision making. This concerns the R&D organization, but also general management and complementing functions. The second, ecosystems, is concerned with how the organization effectively works with the other players in its ecosystem, ranging from suppliers to complementors and from customers to competitors. In many companies, decisions around partnerships and collaborations are taken in a bit of an ad hoc fashion by front line people. Our research shows that taking intentional and strategic decisions on how to engage with ecosystems partners leads to better outcomes.

CHAPTER 5

Throughput and Responsiveness

Companies serving a large group of customers seek to deliver as much value to as many customers of their products and services. The unit that this value is represented in is a feature, i.e. a unit of functionality that can be identified by a user as a logical entity. The role of product management is, basically, to identify features that add value to customers and then to prioritize those features that add the most value to the most customers. The R&D organization then is concerned with developing these features as rapidly as possible in order to get these deployed to customers. We refer to the constant stream of new features being developed as the throughput of the R&D organization.

Many R&D organizations work hard on maximizing their throughput as it directly supports the goal of delivering as many features to as many customers as possible. However, it tends to lead to a situation where customers of the company feel that the company is not very responsive to their needs and requests. This is not because of the ill will of product and R&D managers, but rather a consequence of the "filling the pipe" model that optimizes for throughput. Any new features requested by customers will be added to the list of already planned features and as the coming releases often are already planned in terms of feature content, the requested features often are delivered after a year or perhaps even longer since these were requested.

One of the key tenets of this book is the importance of getting closer to customers in order to build solutions that better address the needs of these customers. When adopting agile software development, companies often expect to become more nimble at the business level as well. The company is interested in responding more quickly to developments in the market as well as requests from customers. In the previous chapter, where we introduced the first dimension of the Stairway to Heaven, we stressed the importance of speed as well as the use of quantitative data and measuring the behavior of the system and of customers as a means to more intimately understand the needs of

71

customers. However, the latter becomes feasible only when the organization has reached higher levels on the stairway. Often organizations cannot wait that long in order to get closer and more responsive to customers.

One could, of course, suggest that the best way then is to work only with customers and build customer-specific versions of software as it allows the company to be the most responsive to individual customers. The challenge is, of course, that customers have similar needs and building bespoke solutions for every customer requires the R&D headcount to be linear with the number of customers. The beauty of the software business, of course, is that once a product is developed, there is little correlation with the number of customers as the reproduction cost is basically zero. So, in virtually any situation where functionality is requested by multiple customers, a solution where there is one configurable product is much more economical for R&D organizations as well as for their customers than any other approach.

In this chapter, we discuss techniques that can be employed in order to achieve a better balance of throughput and responsiveness and actually improve both. One of the techniques that we introduce is the notion of customer-specific teams, i.e. teams that work with one customer of the company to add functionality to the product that this customer requested. For those versed in agile development practices, this may seem like an obvious thing to do. Going back to the first agile development methods, involving the customer, almost having the customer part of the team is a central concept. However, in the context of large-scale software engineering where large, complex products serve a customer base consisting of hundreds, thousands or millions of customers, this becomes a much harder proposition. Most companies turn to the role of product management to represent the customer base towards the agile teams in product development. The challenge with this approach is that product management puts a level of indirection between actual customers and R&D teams. Also, product management focuses on building features that capture the needs from as many customers as possible and abstracts and generalizes the specific needs from individual customers to meet the needs of as large a segment of the customer base as possible. This is a natural development as the role of product management is to maximize the economic value generated from the R&D investment.

Customer-specific teams, as discussed below, provide a solution to the challenge of balancing throughput of features for the entire customer base and the responsiveness to individual customers. The technique is especially suited for companies where the number of customers ranges in the dozens or hundreds and where a smaller group of customers are critical to the company. Consequently, this scope is applied specifically to larger software-intensive systems companies serving B2B markets, although there are other application areas as well.

The remainder of the chapter is organized as follows. In the next section, we set the context that leads to the situation where better management of throughput and responsiveness makes sense. Then we describe the tension as it exists between throughput and responsiveness. Subsequently, we introduce the notion of customer-unique and customer-first features, followed by the description of customer-specific teams and the use of service teams complementing R&D teams. Finally, we present the experiences from one of the companies that applied this technique and discuss the implications of employing this approach, followed by the conclusion.

5.1 LARGE-SCALE SOFTWARE DEVELOPMENT FOR B2B MARKETS

Although many articles are written about companies serving consumers, a very large number of software engineers, if not the majority, builds software for B2B markets. These markets are characterized by large, complex systems that are deeply embedded in the IT or production infrastructure of customers. A company serving a B2B market typically has an addressable market that is counted in the hundreds or thousands and serves a segment ranging from dozens to hundreds of customers. This is very different from B2C markets where the addressable market is typically counted in millions or even billions of people.

A second major factor for B2B markets is the power of customers versus the company providing the system. As systems and solutions delivered to business customers often play a critical role in the infrastructure and main offerings of these customers, these customers are risk averse and often demand legal contracts and service level agreements to handle the times that the delivered system does not operate as specified. As the cost for these systems can easily range into the millions of euros, from a common sense perspective, it is also not unreasonable for business customers to demand terms that require the company to share part of the business risk. As the number of customers is smaller than in B2C markets, but their relative power is higher, companies serving these markets need to be more responsive to the needs, demands and requests from their customers.

At the same time, the number of customers is large enough that companies are unable to provide each customer with their own, bespoke solution. In fact, the best practice that most companies have landed on after trying out different solutions is to deliver a standard product to all customers and to provide configuration and extension capabilities that can be used by customers and third parties to ensure the proper integration of the system in the context of specific customers.

If the number of customers is relatively low, techniques such as software product lines [10] can be employed, but over time companies tend to move towards a configurable product base model [11] where the customer-specific solution is a configuration of a standard solution extended with customer-unique extensions.

As the diversity of contexts in which is system provided by the company is deployed is very high, quality assurance is particularly challenging for these companies. The system may behave very differently in different customer contexts and a continuous integration environment typically is unable to account for all the differences. In many organizations, this leads to a careful and elaborate product release process where the company seeks as much assurance as possible that the system can be deployed with minimal issues. As a consequence, the release frequency tends to go down which negatively affects the responsiveness of the organization towards its customers.

Finally, product management plays a very important role in the company as the representative of the customer base as well as contributing to maximizing revenue and margins for the company. In B2C companies, the number of customers is so large that listening to the customer is less feasible and these companies tend to focus on experimenting their way forward to new features. On the other hand, companies serving individual customers can focus on building bespoke systems. B2B companies tend to be in the middle in that they need to be responsive to requests from customers while being unable to respond to every customer request.

5.2   THROUGHPUT AND RESPONSIVENESS

Although Wiersema and Treacy, authors of *The Discipline of Market Leaders* [51], claimed that companies have to choose between product leadership, customer intimacy or cost leadership, in practice no company is able to focus on one of these dimensions. Every company has to combine the different dimensions in a model that allows them to compete in the market. This brings us to the concepts of throughput and responsiveness that we already raised in the introduction. Optimizing for throughput will result in better chances to achieve product leadership in the market. However, as a consequence customers will perceive company as being less responsive to their wishes and needs which will reduce the level of customer intimacy. Excessively focusing on customer intimacy, on the other hand, will cause the company to build too much customer-specific software which will drive up costs over time. In other words, the products will be too expensive for the customer base and customers will settle for more standardized but much cheaper solutions.

Especially in B2B markets, this is a particularly challenging problem for product managers. The company needs to balance product leadership and standardized solutions with the ability to respond to customers in a timely fashion. For a variety of reasons, it is often much more economical to focus on throughput. The organization is then able to plan the features for every release and develop a road map that contains the planned feature content for the releases after the current one.

From an organizational perspective, this means that the R&D organization is organized into road map teams that work their way through the features on the road map. Depending on the maturity of the organization, there may be other types of teams for quality assurance, release and deployment at customers, but the main role of R&D is to build features as they are specified from the . The approach has many advantages as it allows the organization to sequence development in such a way that there is little rework of existing features required as new features are added. Also, it allows sales and marketing to start their campaigns and other sales initiatives creating awareness of the new functionality before its development is finalized.

The major disadvantage of the approach, of course, is that requests from customers, even if these are prioritized by product management, end up at the end of the road map. This causes significant time to pass between the customer requesting a feature and the organization delivering the software realizing the feature.

5.3 CUSTOMER-UNIQUE VERSUS CUSTOMER-FIRST

Throughout this chapter, we have focused on the balancing between throughput and responsiveness. This balance assumes that an R&D team either builds a generic feature that will be available to all customers of the product or it will build something specific for a customer requesting specific functionality. In our research, however, we realized that this view is overly simple and does not really capture the reality of the situation.

When a customer requests certain functionality from the company, there are two categories of functionality that can be requested. The first category consists of features that are specific for the customer requesting the feature and there is very little likelihood that other customers will request the same feature. We refer to this category as customer-unique features. However, there is a second category of features. In this category, customers request features that have a high likelihood of becoming relevant to other customers as well. Although the feature is requested by a specific customer, it may be that the customer is particularly innovative or that the context in which the customer operates requires early demand of new functionality. We refer to this category as customer-first features.

The distinction between these two categories is important as a customer-unique feature is very expensive for the company to build. Just to illustrate this point: most companies express their R&D budget as a percentage of revenue. Depending on the company and the industry in which it operates, this may range from low single digits to 15-20% in mature software companies. Start-ups, of course, may even approach 100%. However, in software-intensive system companies the percentage tends to be around 10%. What many people do not realize is that an R&D percentage of 10% means that every euro spent in R&D has to result in 10 euros of revenue. Especially in discussions with customers where the customer is willing to pay for the R&D effort required to build the customer-unique feature, the company is basically choosing between a 1x return on the R&D effort and a 10x return on the R&D effort. At the same time, customers are, except for truly exceptional situations, unwilling to pay for 10x the required R&D effort. This basic fact is why many companies gravitate towards focusing on throughput rather than on customer responsiveness: it makes perfect sense from an economic perspective.

The above is exacerbated by the desire of companies building complex products to have one version of the software that goes out to all customers. This means that in the case that a company does agree to add a customer-unique feature to the product, it will be part of the product that goes out to all customers. Even if the feature is turned off, it will add complexity and code size to the product without any benefit for anyone except the customer that requested it. If the company agrees to add too many customer-unique features, the product will easily become bloated, complex and difficult to evolve, test and configure.

When it comes to the notion of customer-first features, however, the situation is fundamentally different. Even though there is a customer asking for the feature, over time it will become available to all customers and, more importantly, it will provide value for all customers. In addition, there is a significant benefit for many features to build it for one customer first. When product management defines features for the roadmap, there is an abstraction and generalization process where the responsible product manager combines all the input pertaining to the specific feature. Based on this process, he or she comes up with a description that captures all the different inputs that originate from different customer meetings, the company strategy, new technologies that may be coming available, etc. The resultant specification tends, as a consequence, to be relatively generic in description, cover many aspects and aim to solve more than one problem. When the R&D team receives the description, the challenge is to recreate a solid understanding of the purpose of the feature as the implementation will involve making dozens if not hundreds of larger and smaller design decisions for which the input can not be found in the specification. Instead, the engineers need to understand how the feature will be used. When there is no clear input on this, people will make decisions based on their best understanding which may not be in line with how customers would want to use the feature. This often leads to rework when a feature is released as customers provide feedback on changes needed to the feature implementation. Even if the company decides not to make changes, this will lead to lower customer satisfaction as the feature implementation only partially meets the need or requires inefficient routines to accomplish the goal. Returning to a topic discussed in the previous chapter, the focus on throughput will focus on building the product right, but there are risks that may result in the organization not building the right product.

5.4   CUSTOMER-SPECIFIC TEAMS

To address the challenge raised in the previous section, customer-first features provide the opportunity for an approach that allows the organization to improve throughput and responsiveness. The organization can appoint customer-specific R&D teams that work with the customer requesting a feature to build the feature according to the desires of this customer. This customer-specific team should have a product manager involved to make sure that the input from the customer indeed is generalizable to other customers and that the inclusion of customer-unique requirements is avoided to the extent possible.

At a high level of abstraction, the notion of an R&D team working closely with the customer is, of course, very close to the original notion of agile software development where the customer representative is expected to be available. Although this is certainly part of the model, there are several additional aspects that need to be considered and incorporated.

First of all, although there are constant interactions between customers and the organization, being available on a continuous basis to provide feedback to a customer-specific R&D team is typically not part of the role of those customer representatives normally interacting with the company. Thus, the first step needs to be to arrange for a customer representative team to be assembled that the R&D team can interact with. Although this seems obvious to the uninitiated reader, reality shows that in practice creating new roles and processes as well as allocating resources to these is far from trivial. Especially when initiating this, the customer must have a significant interest in gaining access to the feature early.

Second, there needs to be a way in which a version of the product can be deployed at the customer. Although we all have opinions about how software products and specific features should be built, being able to observe and measure the product as it is in operation has significant advantages over verbal feedback from the customer representative team in response to demos and screen-shots. The way to achieve this frequent deployment depends on the level of the company on the speed dimension of the Stairway to Heaven. If the company has reached continuous deployment, the customer-specific team can deploy the feature as part of the normal release process. The feature is just turned off and inaccessible for other customers and only activated for the customer working with the team. If the company has reached the continuous integration level, the team can at least use the quality assurance that continuous integration provides, but needs to develop an ad hoc mechanism for packaging and shipping the product. If continuous integration is not in place, the team will need to perform its own testing in addition to the aforementioned activities. The best approach in this case is the notion of a "feature alpha", i.e. deploying the last stable, verified version of the software with just the code for the feature added to the system. Although one might run into some unexpected problems, in most cases this allows the team to test just the functionality of the feature. If the organization still is working in a traditional fashion, it is unlikely that the discussion around customer-specific teams would ever come up. However, this can be an area where the organization starts to experiment with agile development. The challenge, of course, is that to make it work in that situation, significant amounts of scaffolding need to be put in place that will decrease the benefits of the approach significantly.

The process of developing a customer-first feature by a customer-specific team is very similar to traditional agile development. The team needs to first build an understanding of the feature, sketch out a solution and present it to the customer. Once there is a first level of agreement, development starts in normal agile sprints, but with the intent of creating a deployable version of the software as early as possible and, once accomplished, to continue to do so for every agile sprint in order to maximize the speed of the feedback loop with the customer. The number of sprints required to complete the feature depends on its size.

In this context, it is important to note that although many people consider a feature an atomic item that is either present or not, in practice a feature can be implemented to a greater or lesser extent. As the goal is to build customer-first functionality and build the part of the feature that provides maximal value for customers, it is important to keep the scope of the feature down to only the most important parts.

One of the topics that has not yet been discussed is the business model employed by customer-specific teams. Although the company most likely would have built the feature at some point anyway, there is sometimes significant business value for the customer who gets access to the feature first and gets it built largely to specification. Consequently, it is not unreasonable to agree on a model where the customer will pay a certain amount for these privileges. However, this requires a strategic discussion in the company in order to avoid local optimization of revenue while hurting the overall revenue generated by the customer.

5.5 FEATURE GENERALIZATION

The customer-specific teams discussed in the previous section work closely with a customer to develop a version of a requested feature that is an accurate realization of the needs of the customer, while ensuring that the implemented requirements are still considered to be customer-first, rather than customer-unique. However, once the feature is delivered to the first customer, it is not automatically also suitable for all other customers.

To make a customer-first feature developed for one customer generally available, product management needs to go through a feature generalization process. In certain cases, if the feature is quite generic in nature and the customer-specific team is experienced and has good understanding of the other customers, the feature generalization may be a matter of making it available to other customers through the configuration system. In many cases, however, there will be a need to extend the functionality associated with the feature to meet the needs of all customers concerning the feature.

There are, basically, three approaches to feature generalization:

Reactive generalization: In this case, the feature is made available to all customers without any further effort to generalize it. As customers start to use the feature, there will be feedback about functionality required by customers. The feedback from the customers is then used to drive the evolution of the feature. Depending on the amount of in-depth domain knowledge required to evolve the feature, these customer wishes can be implemented by road-map teams or by the customer-specific team that built the feature in the first place.

Customer-specific generalization: The second approach is to start working with a second customer that has shown interest in the feature as soon as the work with the first one is finalized. The second customer likely requests some extensions and the team works with this customer. The team can be the original customer-specific team rotating between customers or the customer-specific team that works with this customer permanently. Once the feature is sufficient for the second customer, the R&D organization takes it to the third customer and so forth. The experience is that after a handful of customers or even less, the amount of additional functionality requested by customers drops significantly and the feature can be made generally available.

Roadmap-driven generalization: The final approach is that product management specifies the characteristics of the feature that need to be added to the implementation of the version built for the first customer. These specifications are then implemented by a roadmap team and the software is subsequently made available for the entire customer base. This approach will likely be the fastest way to achieving a generalized version of the feature. It, however, suffers from the same challenge that caused us to introduce the notion of customer-specific teams to begin with: product management has a limited ability to understand the needs of customers and may make decisions that lead to a suboptimal implementation of the generalized feature.

One factor that complicates the generalization of a feature is that in some cases the first customer involved in developing a feature in a customer-specific model requests exclusivity for a period. Especially in situations where the company works with this customer and one or more of its direct competitors, this can be a way to accomplish a level of differentiation for a period of time. If the feature is visible to end-customers, the customer can then associate marketing campaigns and other initiatives to its exclusive access to certain functionality. Particularly when the customer has paid the company for getting early access to certain functionality, there are strong arguments to grant some form of exclusivity. In the end, however, this remains a business decision that should optimally support the strategy of the company.

5.6   PROFESSIONAL SERVICES

So far, we have mostly focused on customer-first features and the best ways to build these features in a way that supports throughput and responsiveness.

However, there are customer-unique features as well and customers will request the company to take care of these for them. The challenge is to keep these features out of the product as it will lead to a bloated product with even higher variability and configuration needs. This leads to higher testing cost, more issues detected post-deployment as well as other disadvantages. In addition, the product business model is at odds with the notion of customer-unique features. Consequently, we need to find a model that separates the product and product development from the customer-unique features and the development of these features.

One of the companies that we work with has adopted a model that addresses these conflicting requirements. They refer to this as the avocado model. The hard pit in the middle of the avocado is the product. The product has a clear, stable interface that can be used to integrate the product into the overall IT infrastructure of the customer as well as connect it to other, complementing solutions deployed by the customer. The soft part of the avocado is all the functionality that is developed to connect the product to the other IT systems at the customer site. Thanks to the product interface, customers are able to take in new versions of the product without or with minimal changes to the integration functionality as the product maintains backward compatibility to the extent possible.

From an organizational perspective, the company has two separate functions addressing the hard and the soft part of the avocado. The product R&D team works with product itself whereas the professional services organization works with the integration of the product at customers. The business models of these two organizations are fundamentally different. The product is sold using the typical license fee model whereas the professional services get reimbursed for the time required to integrate the product at the customer. The company does not insist on customers using the professional services organization and some customers use a third party for the integration. However, the professional services organization knows the product inside out and can often provide integrations more rapidly and at a higher quality level. Consequently, many of the customers use the professional services organization.

Whenever the organization receives requests from customers, product management assesses the request and categorizes it at a customer-first or a customer-unique request. Based on the assessment, the request is forwarded to the respective function inside the company. Although this is trivial in theory, in practice there are at least two factors complicating this model. First, even if a request is categorized as customer-first, the product R&D team may not be able to prioritize the development of the requested functionality and deliver it in accordance to the timeline requested from the customer. This may lead the professional services organization to implement the functionality outside the product but in the integration code. When product R&D gets around to building the requested functionality, the implementation performed by the professional services team may be used as input. But more importantly, the code that lived in the integration code needs to be removed and the integration needs to be adjusted once the functionality becomes available inside the product. In addition to the development overhead, there often are complicated discussions concerning the allocation of expenses, causing the professional services organization to occasionally perform work for free. The second factor is that product management is not perfect and may categorize the request wrongly. Either functionality is classified as customer-first and it turns out to be incorrect or vice versa. This may lead to situations where functionality needs to be shifted between the hard and the soft part of the avocado or the company and its customers agreeing to leave things in a sub optimal state.

One of the architectural challenges is the design of the product interface. On the one hand, product evolution will be simpler if the interface between the product and the code providing the integration is as narrow as possible. On the other hand, it should be possible to build customer-unique features outside the product and place the software associated with these features in the integration functionality. This requires careful decision making by the architects as it is very difficult to remove interfaces once these have been published and taken into use by customers.

The decision to handle customer-unique requests at all is a decision that the company needs to make strategically as the circumstances differ. For companies with few, but very powerful, customers, mixing customer-unique and customer-first development is unavoidable, but often the business model is typically closer to bespoke development. For companies that decide to focus on the product business, building partnerships with selected consulting companies and agreeing on a business model that works for all parties may be a more suitable approach. For instance, the company could get a share of the revenue generated by partner consulting companies whenever they perform a product integration.

Independent of the approach taken by the organization, the key challenge remains that any feature, originating from customers, the market or inside the company, needs to be carefully assessed to determine whether this is customer-unique or customer-first. Development of the feature for each category should then be handled accordingly. The main threat to the long-term viability of a product is to treat both types of functionality the same.

5.7   BRINGING IT ALL TOGETHER

So far, we have presented four types of teams performing development work. First, the default type of team is a roadmap team that takes features from the roadmap and builds each feature based on the specification provided. Second, we have discussed the notion of customer-specific teams that work directly with a selected customer on a customer-first feature. Third, we discussed feature generalization that may have its own type of team attached to it, although this is not necessary as the work can be performed by customer-specific teams or by roadmap teams. Finally, we introduced the notion of professional services teams that focus on building customer-unique features and typically work on the integration code between the product and the other solutions that a customer has deployed.

As customers in different industries have different expectations on throughput and responsiveness, each company needs to decide what types of teams it uses and what the right allocation of resources is for every type of team. For instance, one could consider using almost exclusively customer-specific teams that work very closely with customers. This is great for responsiveness and customer intimacy, but tends to lead to higher architecture erosion and higher levels of customer-unique functionality being part of the software. In the beginning of the chapter, we discussed the challenges with the other extreme, where the organization only uses road-map teams.

There are a number of factors to keep in mind when balancing these types of teams:

New entrants threatening incumbents: In situations where new entrants are entering the industry of the company, these new players tend to focus on customer intimacy and levels of responsiveness not delivered by the incumbents. In response, the company should respond by getting closer to its customers and customer-specific teams can provide an effective way to accomplish this.

Diverse deployment contexts between customers: The more diverse the deployment contexts for the product are between different customers, the more customer-specific teams should be stable and stay with the customer for an extended period of time. This allows the team to build up expertise and the customer feels less frustration about having to educate yet another R&D team about the intricacies of its specific setup.

Deep domain complexity: If it is rather the domain functionality that is very complicated, customer-specific teams should stay with the feature rather than with the customer. Employing a customer-specific generalization approach may be preferred in this case as the feature can then be evolved in a customer-by-customer fashion.

New technologies becoming available: At times when major new technologies become available to the industry, the company should focus on its roadmap teams in order to deploy the new technology as soon as possible to all customers. Assuming the new technology provides significant benefits, customers are willing to accept a less than optimal solution if they can get access fast rather than waiting for a perfect, personalized and configurable solution at a later point in time.

The factors discussed above provide some indications on how to balance customer-specific, feature generalization, roadmap and professional services teams. Effective balancing allows the company to improve throughput and responsiveness at the same time, rather than trading off between the two.

5.8 EXPERIENCES AND IMPLICATIONS

In our research, we have worked with a number of companies that employ a model where they employ the techniques discussed in this chapter. The companies have experienced the benefits that we outlined above, including the increased customer responsiveness, deeper understanding of the developed features and, consequently, a more accurate implementation of the feature that reduces rework and increases customer satisfaction. However, adopting these approaches does have several implications that one has to be aware of. Below we discuss some of the experiences of these companies.

The first reflection is concerned with the customers that get selected for customer-specific development. In general, the R&D organization has fewer R&D teams than customers. Consequently, the organization has to develop a mechanism for selecting customers. This can be done based on longer term strategic drivers or on short-term revenue. One of the companies assigns customer-specific teams to only the most important customers. These are the customers that have bought the most systems and are likely to be among the largest customers in the future as well. This company has a separate service department that provides, among others, professional services for implementation. Another company uses pricing as a mechanism to control which customers get access to a customer-specific team. The cost estimates for feature development are well above the professional services organization. This ensures that customers only request teams to work on features that can not be accomplished through software outside the product and that is so important for the customer that the business benefit outweighs the high cost.

Especially companies that have not reached higher levels on the Stairway to Heaven share that it is complicated to create fast, high-quality releases of the product software as part of customer-specific team development. Although some customers provide feedback by deploying the software in a test lab and use that as a basis for the iteration, in some industries and for certain customers this is not feasible. This means that the software will be deployed in live systems and quality concerns may quickly outweigh the business benefit of early access to features that are developed by the customer-specific team. Especially when customers pay for the development, balancing quality with fast deployment needs to be carefully managed. Also, the expectations of the customer representatives need to be set at reasonable levels.

Some of the companies experienced positive effects on innovation. As customer-specific teams work very closely with customers, they tend to identify new opportunities and valuable features that could be developed due to their exposure to the operational environment of the customer. Although this may be concerned with new product functionality, frequently this concerns aspects of the product that are not directly concerned with the main use case, but rather with less visible cost driving aspects of the product. For instance, installation or operation of the product may require more effort than what is strictly necessary as this aspect of the product was never optimized. In one company, a solution was developed to automate significant parts of the configuration of the product during installation in order to reduce the effort required by operators.

Finally, some companies have experienced more complicated situations where not only customers but also competitors start to play an important role. One company that we worked with provides mechanics, hardware and software to its customers. Traditionally, the company provided a turn key solution as a subsystem of the customer's product. The customers bought thousands of instances of the subsystem as part of their own product manufacturing. However, as customers wanted to bring in more of their own software into the product and to reduce the power of the company, the customers started to ask for widely different configurations. Sometimes the software of the company needed to be deployed on the hardware of a competitor. In other cases, it was the other way around. In many cases, software developed by the customer, software developed by competitors and software developed by the company itself needed to be merged into one product. Even though the company has dozens of customers, the change in customer behaviour and preferences causes a situation where it was very difficult to decide when to extend the product with customer-first functionality and when to put the solution in a separate customer-unique functionality component. The main point of this example is to stress that each industry and company is different and that the application of the principles in this chapter will require adaptation to the concrete circumstances. Doing so, however, will allow the company to improve both throughput and responsiveness, which, in the end, improves the competitive position of the organization.

5.9 CONCLUSION

Companies building software-intensive systems serving B2B industries are required to balance throughput, i.e. the development of features that serve all customers of their products, with responsiveness, i.e. the time it takes for a customer to receive a feature it requested from the company. Traditionally, these two factors are in conflict with each other and the company needs to balance. Due to economic realities, most companies tend to prioritize throughput, leading to unsatisfied customers who feel that the company is not focused on their business concerns.

In this chapter, we introduce the notion of customer-specific teams as a mechanism to improve responsiveness without sacrificing or perhaps even improving throughput. We do so by identifying two categories of requests from customers, i.e. customer-first and customer-unique features. By focusing on customer-first features, customer-specific teams can work directly with a customer to build a realization of a feature for that customer. As the feature is not just required by this customer, but also by other customers, the feature can, over time, be generalized by working with other customers. Working closely with the customer allows the team to build the feature based on a deep understanding of the real customer need and it leads to increased customer satisfaction because of the increased responsiveness.

The development of customer-unique features should be avoided by the product team as including functionality suitable only for one customer in the product leads to a bloated product with too many configuration parameters that is hard to test and configure and that often experiences an above average number of issues in the field. Instead, the company should direct customers to its own professional services organization or third parties that can integrate the product with the other systems at the customer.

The notion of customer-specific teams has been studied in research going back to the 1980s, e.g., Von Hippel [50]. Also in our own research, we have studied this concept from different perspectives, e.g. [17], [42] and [39].

One final note we want to close the chapter with is that this approach depends heavily on what customers say they want, rather than on measuring the actual use in the system. Consequently, the techniques are primarily intended for companies that have not yet reached the higher levels on the speed dimension of the Stairway to Heaven. Once continuous deployment and continuous data collection from systems in the field are in place, the need for these techniques is reduced and other mechanisms become available. This is discussed in part II of the book where we focus on the data dimension of the Stairway to Heaven.

CHAPTER 6

Managing Architecture

The challenge of scaling agile development practices to large systems, potentially including mechanical and hardware parts, serving B2B markets is a significant one. Traditionally, agile practices have focused predominantly on building functionality. Architecture, technical debt and refactoring have been aspects of software development that have received less attention. This has led to several cases where, over the sprints, the architecture of the system eroded to the point that adding new features became more and more complicated and effort consuming. The consequence tends to be a situation where assuring quality becomes increasingly difficult as changes in one part of the system lead to things breaking in other, seemingly unrelated, parts of the system.

The strong reaction of agile development advocates against architecture can be explained by at least two factors. First, when driving a rather fundamental change to development practices requires creating a mindset in the development community that is orthogonal to the prevalent one. If the change is presented as just a minor adjustment to what the organization has been doing in the past, people tend to fall back into their old behaviours and no change is accomplished. The second factor is that in many organizations, responsibility for the software architecture was centralized and a central team of architects sought to control the evolution of the architecture. This easily leads to a situation where architects act as police agents and developers feel constrained in their development without understanding why the constraints are required. Thus, architecture became lumped in with the traditional, heavy weight processes that constrained teams and that slowed down development. Hence, architecture was thrown out with all the other development practices that did not immediately fit an agile development mindset.

For many smaller and less critical systems that were based on industry-best-practice technology stacks, minimal attention to architecture works just fine. The technology stack, consisting of commercial and open-source components originating outside the company, provides a strict architecture framework already and teams naturally operate inside that framework. As the architecture decisions are taken elsewhere and architecture evolution is accomplished through new versions of components of the technology stack, the teams can, by and large, safely ignore the architecture and focus on building functionality.

When building large, complex systems that have complicated relationships to the environments they operate in, interact with mechanics and special purpose hardware and have strict quality attributes such as real-time constraints, security and safety, architecture becomes a challenge. In these contexts, architecture and architecture evolution need to be managed carefully in order to allow the system to continue to meet the needs of customers.

One important advance in the software process and agile communities over the last decade is the notion of "just enough". Whereas old process models were to a large extent "one size fits all" approaches, there is now an appreciation of the reality that different types of systems need different levels of process scaffolding, architecture management and quality assurance. To follow the principles of agile development, the idea is to provide just enough structure to maximize the empowerment of teams and individuals without the development of the system descending into chaos.

The topic of this chapter is to present ways in which the R&D organization can manage architecture and ensure the long-term viability of the system but without falling back into the traditional, centralized approaches. The traditional approach is disempowering for teams by putting up policing actions, approval processes and other hoops to jump through for teams that slow down development and that can easily create antagonistic tendencies in the organization.

The remainder of the chapter is organized as follows. In the next section, we discuss the notion of architecture technical debt followed by a section on architecture refactoring and a section discussing the role of the architect in this new context. Then we introduce the ART model, a way to organize development such that development of new features, maintaining quality and managing architecture technical debt are balanced. Finally, the chapter ends with a discussion of the experiences of companies applying these principles and versions of the ART model as well as a conclusion.

6.1 ARCHITECTURE TECHNICAL DEBT

Many pay lip service to the importance of software architecture, but when push comes to shove, the integrity of the architecture gets violated whenever there is an opportunity for short-term benefits. Typically this is driven by a request for some new functionality that is demanded from some customer or that a competitor has come out with and that needs to be matched by the company. Because of the time pressure, the implementation is performed in a "bolted on" way rather than in line with the architecture intent. Too many instances of this scenario and the architecture starts to erode and the debt levels go up.

Even if an organization is able to avoid the above scenario and instead builds all new functionality in line with the original architecture intent, the architecture will still accumulate technical debt. This is caused by the evolving purpose of the system for which the architecture was designed. When the system is first conceived and the architecture is designed, architects are typically quite able to design an architecture that optimally meets the functional and quality requirements of the system. However, the system as well as the purpose of the system evolves. The number of users of the system may go up significantly, the relative frequency of the different use cases may start to shift or new use cases are identified and added to the system, new security risks appear that the system has to handle, etc. As the saying goes, life happens, and as this happens, the architecture, through no fault of its own, accumulates technical debt simply because it was designed for a purpose that no longer fully represents the current purpose of the system.

To understand how this happens at the architecture level, we have to return to first principles. The first step is the definition of architecture. The IEEE/ANSI 1471-2000 standard defines *architecture* as the fundamental organization of a system, embodied in its components, their relationships to each other and the environment, and the principles governing its design and evolution [31]. Although most definitions identify components and their relationships to each other as part of architecture, this definition stresses the principles guiding the design and evolution of software architecture. This is important as many engineers working with architecture tend to focus on the observable aspects of architecture, i.e. the components and their relationships, without understanding how the explicit structure of the system ended up this way.

Understanding how an architecture ended up where it is brings us to the notion of architecture design decisions. In earlier work, we defined an *architectural design decision* as a description of the set of architectural additions, subtractions and modifications to the software architecture, the rationale, and the design rules, design constraints and additional requirements that (partially) realize one or more requirements on a given architecture [28]. The first part of this definition stresses the impact on the structure of the software architecture, but the second part is concerned with rationale, design rules and constraints as well as additional requirements on the system originating from the design decision. The second part of the architecture is as important as the first part, if not more so, but it typically is not explicitly modeled and primarily captured in the heads of the architects and, to some extent, in documentation.

If software architecture can reasonably be viewed as a set of architecture design decisions and if we view the resulting "boxes and lines" as a consequence or symptom of architecture work instead of the main result, it is easy to see why technical debt so easily surfaces: The decisions themselves as well as the part addressing design rule and constraints as well as the rationale are never made explicit and live only in the heads of software architects. During the lifetime of the system, architects make dozens, if not hundreds, of design decisions and each of these decisions bring additional design rules and

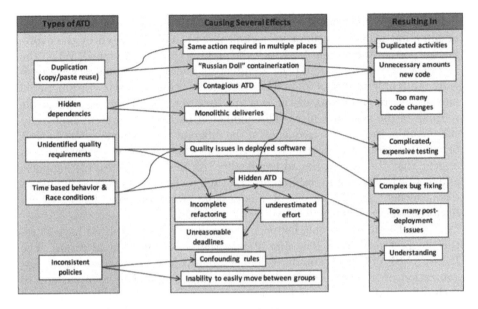

Figure 6.1 Architecture technical debt [33]

constraints. Thus in combination with software-intensive systems growing in size, it is harder and harder for anyone to maintain a solid overview of the overall system. For engineers developing within the architecture, it is very easy to start to violate the architecture, entirely unintentionally, as they add new functionality to the system.

The second challenge that causes architecture technical debt is that, as the system evolves, some design decisions no longer make sense and should really be removed from the system. However, as the architecture contains dozens or even hundreds of decisions that build on top of each other, removing the consequences of old design decisions is hard and effort consuming. As a consequence, architects and engineers tend to minimize the work needed and instead build on whatever is already there without cleaning things up completely or at all. Technically, it may even be impossible, or rather prohibitively expensive, to remove old architecture design decisions and instead we should focus on the key initiatives that improve the architecture against reasonable cost.

In our research, led by Antonio Martini (see [33], [32] and [34]), we studied architecture technical debt and its causes at seven companies in the Software Center. In figure 6.1, a summary of the findings is presented. The research identifies classes of architectural technical debt, the observable phenomena resulting from these types of debt and finally the extra activities that represent the extra effort or "interests" that the organization pays for the debt.

As figure 6.1 shows, there are several classes of architecture technical debt. The first class is debt originating from mismatches between the architecture of the system and the architecture of externally developed components that are included in the system. Although the reuse of these components obviously reduces the amount of development effort needed by the team itself, architecture mismatches result in additional effort due to the need to duplicate functionality in order to overcome the architecture mismatches as well as the need to wrap components that follow other architecture principles than the system itself.

A second source of debt is the implicit dependencies between components of the system. For instance, microservices architecture [36] is so popular in cloud systems precisely because it makes it impossible to introduce hidden or implicit dependencies in the system. When the number of implicit dependencies in the system goes up, it becomes more and more difficult to deploy individual components as the implicit dependencies will result in quality issues. As a consequence, the size of the deliveries tends to go up and as a consequence the frequency of deliveries goes down and the amount of testing effort increases as well. Implicit dependencies are an important source of contagious debt, discussed later in this section.

A third source of technical debt is non-functional requirements that are identified late in the development process or potentially only after deployment of the first or later releases of the system. Rearchitecting the system for non-functional requirements late in development or even after release of the first version is, for most quality attributes, far from trivial and often requires the introduction of "bolted on" solutions that could have been integrated in the architecture much more harmoniously if the need had been clear from the start. Of course, as the system evolves, it may be that new non-functional requirements surface that were not part of the original system design. For instance, in start-ups where the user adoption is very fast after the initial deployment, supporting the evolving performance requirements often leads to significant technical debt that is hard to pay off as the system grows. In more mature products, new security threats may result in increased debt as these threats often need to be addressed rapidly rather than properly architected.

New hardware architectures including multi-core processors and virtualization technologies may cause the system to incur technical debt due to temporal issues. For instance, when the deployment infrastructure becomes truly parallel and the sequence in which different threads finish becomes non-deterministic, the system might easily start to experience race conditions of different types. This could be viewed as a special case of the previous source of technical debt, but this is caused by evolution of the infrastructure in which the system is deployed, rather than the customer requirements.

These sources of technical debt often surface late in the development process and consequently need to be resolved under time pressure. In most cases, there is a choice between a short-term fix, just to get the system out, and a more proper rearchitecting effort, that will reduce the long term consequences. The danger in this situation is that architects and engineers easily underestimate the amount of effort required to realize the more proper approach. In this case, even later in development, under more severe time pressure, the rearchitecting needs to be halted before it is done and the short-term fix is applied after all. This results in a very messy situation where the amount of debt is much higher than in the case if the short-term fix was selected from the beginning.

Finally, especially as systems grow and development occurs over multiple locations and time zones, it becomes more and more difficult to maintain consistent policies across the entire system. As a consequence, in different parts of the architecture, security, persistence, robustness and other quality attributes may be solved using different architectural solutions. This leads to confusion and accelerated accumulation of debt as engineers work on different parts of the system and need to adjust to the architecture solutions selected in the specific part.

There are two key results of our research that need to be highlighted. The first is the notion of **contagious debt**. With contagious debt, the main insight is that not all architecture debt is created equal. Some types of debt are much more damaging to the system than others. We identified types of debt that have a tendency to spread through the system like a virus through a population or a human body, rather than stay in one place. An example of this type of debt is concerned with the design of interfaces. If an interface is designed as too narrow, it will easily cause a situation where engineers will bypass the interface and start to connect with interfaces inside components that were intended to be private. Even if the interface initially is not even accessible, it is often easy, in the spur of the moment, for one engineer to convince another to make the interface accessible as the information that is required from one component in another is not accessible in any other way. Once a private interface has been made implicitly public, the use of it tends to rapidly spread to other components. By the time the architects realize what is going on, understand why the need exists, agree to redesign the interface to the component and have freed up the budget to implement changes to the interface, the use of the illicit interface will have spread through the system like a contagious virus. Consequently, the cost of refactoring this violation of the architecture will be much higher than a localized suboptimal structure. In this context, please note that the interface may have been perfectly suitable when it was initially designed. However, during evolution, the need to get access to additional or different information hidden inside the component may be required, leading to this type of contagious technical debt.

There are other types of contagious debt as well, but the main point is that the interest that is paid over certain types of debt is higher than for other types of debt. As it is impossible to remove all debt from the system, we need mechanisms to prioritize different types of debt. As we prioritize, there are several factors to consider. One of these is the interest for the debt. If a debt item is of the contagious type, the cost for refactoring it will grow rapidly over time. Consequently, prioritizing resolving this type of debt will drive the cost of refactoring down.

The second key result from our research is the notion of **vicious cycles**.

In several of the companies where we conducted our research, we identified an unfortunate pattern that the organization did not realize until we made it explicit. The pattern starts with the architects identifying a critical debt item that they want to have resolved. After lobbying product management and others for the resources, the requested resources are allocated. Then the refactoring effort starts but during the work it becomes clear that the effort estimation was overly optimistic. Often, at the same time, some high-priority problem at some customer occurs, forcing resources to be redirected to addressing the customer concern. Once the resources and calendar time have been consumed, the result is that the refactoring effort is not finalized.

As an example of a vicious cycle, at one of the companies that we worked with, for historical reasons, there were three ways for components to communicate with each other. Obviously, this was far from optimal as it was unclear when to use which type of communication and it led to significant overhead in the organization, both in development as well as during quality assurance. The architects successfully lobbied for a refactoring effort to replace the three ways of component communication with one new way to communicate. The effort was started and soon experienced the situation discussed above: it proved to be more effort consuming than estimated and there were some issues with the system in the field that required resources to be reallocated. In the end, the refactoring was never completed and today the system has four ways for components to communicate with each other! The well-intended refactoring effort, because of the vicious cycle pattern, made the debt in the architecture worse rather than improved it.

To summarize, in the vicious cycle pattern, everyone makes the right decisions for the long-term viability of the system locally, but the overall, global outcome results in a situation that is worse than if no effort had been made to improve technical debt. Luckily not all refactoring efforts end like this, but the pattern was observed at multiple companies and needs to be safeguarded against. Unsuccessful refactoring efforts not only leave the system worse than initially intended, but also reduce the willingness of the rest of the organization to support refactoring efforts.

Concluding, in this section, we introduced the notion of technical debt and discussed its various sources and the consequences. We distinguished between the debt itself, i.e. the effort required to resolve the debt item at the time it is identified, and the interest, i.e. the effort required if the debt item is resolved at a later point in time as well as the additional effort that development requires due to the presence of the debt item. In the next section, we take a closer look at the refactoring process itself.

6.2 ARCHITECTURE REFACTORING

The accumulation of architecture technical debt is unavoidable. As we discussed in the previous section, even if the original architecture is perfectly aligned with the requirements on the system, as these requirements evolve, the architecture immediately is not perfectly aligned with the requirements anymore and debt has been accumulated. Thus, although architecture technical debt is often viewed as a problem, one has to realize that it is a normal consequence of evolving systems. The only systems that do not accumulate debt are those that are no longer in use.

A second source of unavoidable accumulation of debt is normal feature development. Feature development typically evolves through four stages. During the first stage, i.e. clarification, the team tends to have only a partial understanding of the requirements embodied by the feature and the precise definition tends to be in flux as product management or the customer is asked to make decisions. As development has already started at this moment, the design and code are altered in ways that may, in hindsight, not be optimal, hence debt is accumulated. In the second stage, lock-down, the requirements for the feature are clear, the team has agreed on the way to implement the feature and development is proceeding in line with the architecture. Often, some of the debt accumulated in the previous stage is recovered. The third stage, rushing, is entered when the deadline is coming closer and the team needs to meet it. At this point, teams tend to start to make shortcuts in the code in order to get the feature out. During this stage, more debt is accumulated as the team rushes to get the functionality out. After release, the fourth phase is entered, where the team, in an ideal world, recovers the technical debt that it has created and leaves the architecture in a place where it is as clean as before the start of feature development. In most situations, teams have very little time to actually recover any of the debt that they created. Instead the system accumulates debt for every feature added to the system. One of the agile practices is the notion of "clean as you go", which refers to engineers being expected to remove small debt items at the code level as they add new functionality to the system. Although this works for code-level debt, architecture technical debt tends to be too large and effort consuming for these purposes.

In our collaboration with companies in various industries, we have seen four approaches to managing architecture technical debt. These are (1) don't do anything; (2) hide it in feature development; (3) fixed allocation of resources and finally (4) dynamic governance. Below we describe each approach in more detail.

The first approach employed by companies is to ignore architecture technical debt. Although some engineer may occasionally do a little bit of local cleaning, by and large the organization tends to view the accumulation of debt as an unavoidable fact of life and focuses its attention on feature development while allowing for enough resources dedicated to testing to ensure quality. Over time, the cost of adding new features tends to go up as the architecture is less and less suited for the intended purpose. Also, the cost of ensuring quality goes up as more and more dependencies between different parts of the system exist, causing changes in one part to result in errors and quality issues in seemingly unrelated parts of the system. Finally, over time, the number of issues in the field increases as variation in the context at different customers also has unexpected consequences for the quality. The company marches on until it reaches a point where the cost of development and testing as well as the implications of quality issues in the field reach a crisis point and consensus is reached that "something needs to be done". At this point, the organization has two choices. The first is to retire the existing product and start to build a new product or platform from scratch, looking to avoid all the sins from the past. The second is to kick off a major reengineering effort to refactor the existing system architecture into an architecture that can serve the evolution of the system for another few years. Once the company decides and completes the development of the new platform or the reengineering effort, the accumulation of architecture technical debt starts again as it did in previous iterations.

There is a second pattern that often surfaces in the situation presented in the previous paragraph. The organization decides to build a new product platform and continues with the existing system to serve the market. The new product platform proves to be more effort consuming and complex than expected and even reaching feature parity proves to be a major engineering effort that takes much more resources and calendar time than initially estimated. Often, this process is exacerbated by the "borrowing" of resources from the team building the new platform by the team evolving the existing product as it continues to run into crisis after crisis. In the worst case, after the so many-est budget overrun and missed deadline, the company throws the towel in the ring and cancels the new product platform. In this case, the company is worse off from all perspectives as the old product has now eroded even further and is really hurting the competitive position of the company. And there is no new product platform to build upon. Although this seems like such an obvious thing to avoid, unfortunately, the history software industry is littered with examples of this process. My learning, after more than 25 years in the industry, is that new product platform development should be avoided unless all alternatives have been exhausted. Second, refactoring an existing product platform, though complicated, expensive and unsexy, is the low-risk, smart approach in the vast majority of cases.

The second approach taken at some companies is for the R&D organization to hide the cost of refactoring while still performing refactorings. Especially in organizations where the product management and R&D organizations have an antagonistic relationship, there is no basis for an open and transparent discussion of the need for refactoring efforts. In these companies, product management considers the R&D organization to be incompetent and lazy. Any discussion of architecture refactoring is viewed as yet another excuse to deliver too little functionality too late for what the company needs to be successful in the market.

In companies with the aforementioned relationship between product management and R&D, one strategy that is used is to hide the cost of refactorings in the feature development. So, when product management provides a list of features it would like to see added to the product, R&D performs effort estimation required to determine the priority of the features to be developed. As part of the estimated effort, the R&D leadership not only puts the cost required to specifically build the code for the feature, but also includes the effort required for performing refactoring in the part of the code affected by the new feature. In this way, the company manages at least part of the architecture technical debt accumulating in the system, but the antagonistic relationship, of course, complicates the alignment of architecture work with the current and future business strategy of the company.

The risk of hiding the cost of architecture refactoring in feature development is that it only reinforces the perception of the R&D organization as slow, inefficient and incompetent in the company. Product management often seeks to get independent and objective measures of reasonable development estimates and may reach out to outside consulting companies for estimates. Eager to make a sale and not encumbered by the need to maintain the long-term viability of the software architecture, these estimates often are significantly lower than those provided by the internal R&D organization. This potentially leads to efforts to outsource all of software development or to source the development of certain features from outside the organization. In the latter case, the internal R&D organization has no means available to protect the architecture integrity and may end up with an even faster eroding architecture.

The third approach is especially realized in companies with enlightened and strong senior leadership. In some of the companies that we have worked with, senior leaders, sometimes going back to technology-savvy founders, realized the importance of architecture refactoring. In order to safeguard the architecture, in these organizations a percentage of resources is mandated for refactoring. For instance, in one organization, the CTO has mandated that 25% of R&D resources for each iteration are allocated to architecture refactoring. A further 25% are allocated to quality assurance and the remaining 50% can be allocated to new feature development. In this case, product management can only allocate 50% of the resources and is free to prioritize feature development within these boundaries. Similarly, those responsible for quality can use their resources in the same way. And, finally, architects are free to identify, prioritize and implement architecture refactoring efforts within their 25%.

This third approach is infinitely much better than the first two approaches. However, it does bring with it a few challenges of its own. The first is concerned with the fact that each of the three activities, feature development, quality assurance and architecture refactoring, are performed largely independently of each other. The potential for synergy between the activities is, in this case, not realized. For instance, combining the development of a new feature and an architecture refactoring activity could result in lower overall resource usage and a faster realization of both. Similarly, an architecture refactoring effort to improve the modularity could be combined with a change in the continuous integration environment where one could shift some test activities from system level to subsystem level due to the increased independence of subsystems.

The second challenge of this third approach is that it is static and does not allow the organization to adjust to dynamic business realities. A major quality issue in deployed products needs to be addressed within the 25%, rather than allowing for temporarily increasing the resources for quality assurance. Similarly, temporarily increasing the resources for feature development to beat a competitor in bringing out an important new feature is not feasible as the model puts up rather solid boundaries between the different activities.

The final model, dynamic governance, addresses the aforementioned concerns. Rather than rigidly dividing resources between the three activities of feature development, quality assurance and architecture refactoring, the final model assumes a governance approach where product management, quality assurance and the architecture function jointly prioritize the work items in a single prioritized backlog. The governance team agrees on a target resource allocation, for example 60/20/20, but jointly agrees on deviations in response to market realities, quality issues or areas in the architecture that are in need of urgent refactoring. The model is discussed in more detail later in the chapter where we introduce the ART model.

6.3   THE ROLE OF THE ARCHITECT

At the start of the chapter, we discussed the adoption of agile development practices and the reasons that architecture was deprioritized during the transformation. Specifically concerning the role of the architect, the reasons were related to the role that software architects assumed or were assigned in the context of traditional development processes. In many organizations, the architect was part of a centralized team of architects and acted as an interface between product management and the R&D organization. In some companies, there still is a systems engineering department that acts in a similar way.

The architects also had the role of police agents with the ability to stop or reject development by R&D teams or enforce architecture design decisions. As architects were part of a different organization and not part of the daily development work, this easily resulted in an us-versus-them situation with the risk of the relationship turning antagonistic rather than synergistic.

The final challenge with the traditional role of the architect was that it was a full-time role. Even if the architect was a very talented engineer, which is how many got the promotion to architect in the first place, moving out from development causes a few interesting effects. First, the understanding of the realities of software development for the system at hand starts to fade in the months after an engineer transitions to a full-time architect. After a year or less, the architect tends to be so out of sync with the actual reality of software development of the system that the design decisions easily start to become questionable. Second, some architects develop some form of superiority complex where they pay little attention to the feedback of the engineers. Architecture design and evolution requires significant abstraction and it is easy to end up in a place where the design decisions make perfect sense in this clean, abstract model in the head of the software architect, but make no sense in the reality of the software development for the system. Having been promoted because of one's engineering chops, it is easy to assume that any feedback from the engineering team that is not positive is interpreted as lack of understanding or talent by the engineering team, rather than a reflection of the oversimplification performed by the architect. Finally, the danger of full-time architects is also that the role easily slides into the PowerPoint domain where discussions with product management, general management and R&D management increasingly occur in a parallel universe of PowerPoint slides that have no bearing on the reality of the system software. In short, the full-time architect is at risk of becoming a politician.

The above makes it clear that the traditional role of the architect does not deliver on its potential. Of course, in many organizations, common sense successfully avoided the negative consequences of the architect role discussed above. However, we have learned that there are two important aspects of the role of the architect that need to addressed.

First, the role of the architect should be a part-time one. This means that an architect should work as a member of an agile team for part of his or her time and spend the remainder in the role of architect. This ensures that the architect stays connected to the reality of software development and avoids the alienation of the architect from the team. As we will discuss in the next section, architects are best organized in a hierarchy where each front-line architect reports to a group architect. A group architect, if the system is large enough to warrant three levels of architects, may report to a chief architect. Each architect owns a part of the system from an architecture perspective and uses his or her time in the architect role to work with agile teams that are building software in the part of the system that the architect is responsible for. In addition to working with teams, architects are also responsible for identifying architecture technical debt items that should be refactored. These debt items can be sent up the chain to a single, prioritized backlog of architecture technical debt items.

The second learning about the role of the architect is that he or she should be a coach, rather than a police agent. The architect should coach agile teams to make the right decisions of their own volition because they understand the purpose of the design decisions that have resulted in the current architecture. By educating teams in this way, architects can also reduce the amount of technical debt accumulated as teams pay more attention to these aspects. Finally, if it becomes clear that the design decisions presented by the architect (no longer) make sense to the team, maybe the time has come to revisit these decisions and consider if these should be removed from the system.

Concluding, for any non-trivial system where the architecture is not completely dictated by the external open-source and commercial components, the role of the architect is of significant importance. We have, however, learned, over the years and with the adoption of agile development practices, that architects need to be engineers too and need to act as coaches instead of police agents. As keepers of the architecture integrity, they also identify debt items that can be added to the prioritized backlog of refactoring tasks.

6.4 ART: AN ORGANIZATIONAL MODEL

Earlier in the chapter, we discussed dynamic governance of architecture refactoring and the other development activities of quality assurance and the development of new features. Based on experiences from several companies, we have generalized a model from the best practices at these companies. Here we refer to the model as ART, which stands for Architecture; Requirements; Testing. In some publications, however, we refer to the CAFFEA model [34]. The model assumes that the organization is in the process of reaching the continuous integration level in speed dimension of the Stairway to Heaven.

The ART model defines three roles in agile teams, i.e. the architect role, the technical product owner role and the quality assurance role. These roles are ideally carried out by three different individuals within each agile team. Their responsibilities are to instill responsibility for their particular focus area, but in the end it is the team as a whole that owns the final decision and responsibility for its choices.

The architect role carries responsibility for the design and evolution of the software architecture of the system. The architect role does this by being knowledgeable about the design decisions that form the basis for the current architecture and the design rules, design constraints as well as the rationale that the team needs to be aware of and respect. Typically, the person in the architect role, in addition to being a regular member of the team, also owns a part of the software architecture and acts as a coach to teams that build software in his or her part of the software architecture. Finally, the architect role is also concerned with identifying architecture technical debt items and proposing architecture refactorings that would resolve the debt item.

The technical product owner is, again, a regular member of the agile team but the role assumes a specific focus on the requirements that the team needs to understand in order to successfully develop the feature that the team is concerned with. If the feature is part of a larger set of features, this role is responsible for making sure the team has a solid understanding of the feature itself as well as the interaction with other features.

The quality assurance role is concerned with ensuring that sufficient and sufficiently challenging test cases are developed by the team. These test cases need, of course, to be integrated in the overall continuous integration environment and added to the testing at the appropriate branches. Most R&D organizations have adopted single branch development, but still support a team branch for each agile team and individual sandboxes for members of the agile team. The test cases need to be placed in the correct branches to ensure quality without unnecessarily slowing the automated testing process down. In the next chapter, we discuss this topic in more detail. One responsibility of this role is to identify and raise awareness of system defects that for some reason are not caught at the time of introduction but are at some later point identified. At that point, it is no longer feasible to identify the team that introduced the defect or, if it is feasible, the team has already moved on to other tasks. In that case, the system defect needs to be resolved in another way.

Each of the discussed roles are part of a hierarchy. All the architect roles in the agile teams are part of a team that is led by a group architect. In large systems with many agile teams, there might be two hierarchies of architects where the group architects managing their own teams and are part of a team of group architects led by a chief architect. The number of architects is determined by the amount of work that is required. For a part of the system with little change, one architect can cover several components or subsystems and the scope is mostly limited by one person's ability to keep all the technical details in his or her head. For parts of the system where there is a lot of change, the scope of one architect may be only a single component. Here the limiting factor is the number of teams that require coaching. As architects are part-time in this model, it is important that each architect spends enough time integrated in the team and performing as a regular team member.

In addition to architects responsible for part of the overall software architecture, the organization can appoint architects responsible for specific quality attributes in case these attributes are central to system success. For instance, some companies appoint a security architect or a networking architect if these are aspects that are particularly challenging for the specific system. Again, these architects are part of agile teams for part of their time.

The technical product owner role is also part of a hierarchy. The technical product owner roles are led by a group product owner. Similar to the architects, for large systems with many agile teams, there might even be two levels of hierarchy. For this role, the interesting challenge is how to connect the technical product owners, who spent half or more of their time working as engineers in an agile team, with product managers who are more focused on the customer and the business. The better the relationship between these roles, the more accurate the feature implementation will meet the customer needs. As we discussed in the previous chapter, the actual intent of a feature is not always easy to communicate through written requirements and the communication with customers or their proxy is an important aspect of successfully building the system. In the case where the organization uses customer-specific teams, the technical product owner of the team plays an important role as well.

Finally, there is a hierarchy of quality assurance people with a group quality assurance leader who represents the group. The main role for the group is to share best practices, identify system defects that go beyond the responsibility of a single team and to prioritize the known system defects for their prioritized backlog. Of course, this team is also concerned with improving the continuous integration environment and, when the organization moves to continuous deployment, work with the release organization to minimize the number of post-deployment issues identified.

The ART model is concerned with optimally balancing the freedom and autonomy of agile teams with coordination among the teams. By ensuring that the A, R and T roles are deeply embedded in the agile teams, we avoid the challenges associated with the traditional functional organization.

The second point of balancing is the relative allocation of resources between features, architecture and quality. For this, the first step is that product management, together with the R role representatives, create and maintain a prioritized backlog of features to build. Similarly, the architect community maintains a prioritized backlog of architecture refactorings. Finally, the T role community maintains a prioritized backlog of system defects and improvements to the continuous integration environment as well as other parts of the overall software development infrastructure. Representatives for each of the groups form a governance team, potentially complemented with other roles in the company, to create and periodically update one prioritized backlog of work items that includes features, architecture refactoring tasks, system defects and improvements to the development infrastructure.

The agile teams use the prioritized backlog with all work items to pick the next item to work on when the previous task has been finalized. In systems where the skills required to perform the tasks in backlog are very homogeneous, all teams can take all tasks on the backlog. Especially in embedded systems, however, development tasks can range from building firmware software for FPGAs to improving the GUI using Java code. In this case, it is not reasonable to assume that any team can take any task and we need to introduce the notion of team skills. In the companies that we've worked with where the set of skills is too diverse for any team to take any task, teams tend to gravitate to certain parts of the architecture. This causes the team to reinforce their skills in that area of the architecture and to atrophy the skills in other parts of the architecture. In other words, each team builds a skills profile. By building a common skills vocabulary, the A, R and T roles that put work items on the single, prioritized backlog tag the work items with the skills required to successfully and efficiently complete the work item. Once this model is in place, whenever an agile team selects the next work item, it scans through the prioritized backlog until the first work item where the skill requirements match the skill profile of the team. This means that teams will, over time, conduct feature development, architecture refactoring and system defect tasks, ensuring that the team stays experienced in all aspects of software development.

It is important to note that although teams with skill profiles tend to gravitate to certain parts of the architecture, this does not result in a return to the component team model. In the ART model, any team can make changes to any component in the system as long as they take advice from the responsible architect. Also, when the work in the system shifts towards other areas in the systems, teams will shift towards these as there is too little work in their area of expertise and consequently the teams will take tasks that are on the boundary of their skills profile. This will result in new learnings for the team.

One area where different companies take different approaches is the development environment, including the work benches, the build system, the continuous integration environment and, over time, the continuous deployment infrastructure. Some organizations appoint separate teams to handle this as they feel that the type of work is very different from working on the product. Other organizations want the teams to own their own environment and ask the teams to build and evolve their own environment. One aspect that tends to affect this is the continuous integration environment. If the product that is tested contains significant mechanical and hardware parts that are specific for the product, it often is more effective to have a dedicated team build and maintain the development environment. In other cases, where the environment is general purpose and generic, sharing the responsibility for it between the teams provides a good understanding of the development environment across the development organization. Better understanding of the tools one uses for the job often leads to a better job overall.

In figure 6.2, we show a graphical representation of the discussion so far. The architecture of the system, shown as the boxes marked with "C", has several agile feature teams working on it. These teams check in code that is verified by the continuous integration environment. Any defects that slip through are added to a prioritized list of system defects. Each part of the architecture has a person associated with it. These architect roles are part of a group represented by a group architect. Together, they maintain a prioritized list of architecture refactoring tasks. Finally, there is a continuous analysis process, indicated by the CA block, that maintains a prioritized list of features that should be added to the system. These three groups are part of a governance team and meet periodically to create a single, prioritized backlog for the teams.

Concluding, in this section we presented the ART model that, based on our research with several companies, captures several best practices of large-scale software development. It provides an effective mechanism for balancing different types of work items in an objective, dynamic fashion and allows product management, architects and those responsible for system quality to jointly prioritize such that the organization reaches the best balance between the short-term demands and the long-term needs. As any model, the ART model should not be employed blindly in the organization, but rather provides a set of elements that organizations can decide to adopt in their own product development.

6.5 EXPERIENCES

Elements of the ART model have been deployed at several of the companies that we collaborate with and there are some experiences that are worth sharing. As this chapter is about managing architecture, we start there. One of the takeaways from some of the companies is that introducing a model akin to ART does not automatically resolve the difficulty in the organization to pri-

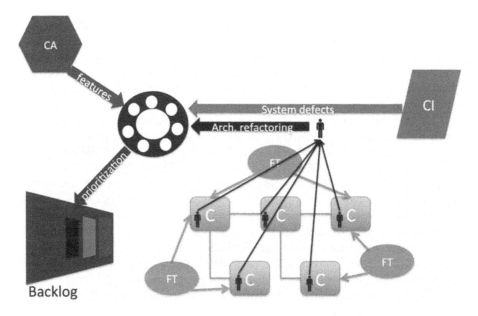

Figure 6.2 One view of the ART model

oritize architecture refactoring. One of the popular sayings in agile says that agile doesn't solve anything; it just makes problems so painfully obvious that the organization realises it needs to solve them. The same is true for organizations that have not found effective ways to prioritize architecture refactoring and put all their resources on feature development. This behaviour does not automatically change with the introduction of a new model, but rather the model creates a venue, the governance team, where the discussion can be had. However, especially in organizations where product management and R&D have an antagonistic relationship, the prerequisite for any progress in this area is a company-wide agreement that there is a need for allocating some resources to other tasks than feature development.

A related learned fact is concerned with the beliefs surrounding product evolution and new platform development. Especially less experienced and less technology-savvy people have a tendency to believe that building a new product platform will be far superior to evolving the current product platform. All the weaknesses of the current product platform are known and the organization easily develops a negative association towards it. The new product platform has no known deficiencies, as it hasn't been built yet, and every stakeholder can believe whatever he or she wants to believe about it. This leads to a significant underestimation of the risks of building a new platform and a lack of appreciation for the importance of refactoring the current platform to keep it fit for its purpose going forward.

When the organization becomes a bit more mature and starts to dedicate some resources to refactoring efforts, making sure that especially the first initiatives are successful is critically important. If one of the first initiatives fails and leaves the architecture worse off, as can easily happen due to the vicious cycles that we discussed earlier in the chapter, there tends to be a backlash in the organization and the progress made so far will be undone surprisingly rapidly.

Related to the ART model, one area where companies have experimented with different approaches is the stability of teams. Some companies initially formed teams for each feature taken from the backlog and disbanded the team after completion. This led to a situation that the bonds within the team never fully formed and each team was more of a loose group of individuals that just happened to sit together. The reaction was to create fixed, static teams and once you were part of the team, leaving it was akin to getting a divorce, slow, painful and expensive. The learning was that this created an overly static structure where team dynamics were negatively affected by the fact that people felt condemned to each other. The learning was to allow some level of rotation between teams where once every couple of sprints one or two members would move on to different teams, but where the core of the team was preserved and esprit de corps was maintained.

6.6 CONCLUSION

This chapter was concerned with architecture and its role in large-scale agile software development. We started the chapter with a discussion of the reasons for architecture to become deprioritized during the transition from traditional to agile development practices. We discussed the notion of "just enough" architecture which may range from hardly anything in systems where the externally sourced components enforce the architecture to quite a lot in typically embedded systems where the mechanics and hardware as well as strict quality requirements demand significant attention to architecture.

Subsequently, we introduced the notion of architecture technical debt and the sources that lead to the accumulation of this debt. The main takeaway is that there is no way to avoid the accumulation of technical debt and the removal of debt from the architecture needs to be explicitly managed. We discussed the importance of the less visible parts of architecture, including the architecture design decisions as well as the design rules and design constraints resulting from these decisions. Finally, we discussed the notions of contagious debt and vicious cycles.

Architecture refactoring is the process and activity of removing debt from the architecture. We discussed the four mechanisms that we have identified in the industry, including doing nothing and waiting for the crisis, hiding refactoring in feature development, static allocation of resources to refactoring and dynamic governance. We discussed the ART model as an instantiation of dynamic governance of architecture technical debt that balances refactoring, feature development and addressing quality issues.

The ART model is also an organizational model and we discussed the role of the architect. Rather than a full-time, powerpoint pushing police agent, we see the role of the architect as a part-time coaching role while continuing to work as an engineer in an agile team. This avoids many of the challenges with traditional, functional organization of software development and maximizes the freedom and autonomy of agile teams.

Software architecture is important in large-scale software development, whether we use agile development principles or not. But rather than designing the perfect architecture before the development of a product and then holding on to it for as long as feasible, it requires continuous evolution and refactoring to keep the architecture optimally suitable for its strategic purpose. It requires architecture and architects to transition from a "built to last" to "built to evolve" mindset.

CHAPTER 7

Continuous Integration

Continuous integration is a critical level on the speed dimension of the Stairway to Heaven as it provides the basis for the subsequent level of continuous deployment and is a major enabler for full adoption of agile work practices. Organizations have difficulty reaping the full benefits of adopting agile development practices without having access to continuous integration.

In traditional development, the verification of product functionality is performed at the end of development. With development cycles that often run for 12 months or longer, it is clear that real testing that allows for releasing the product to customers is conducted very infrequently. As it is performed so seldom, the organization sees little reason to invest in automation of the testing activities, resulting in a situation where manual testing is a major and important activity as part of the overall development process.

Some of the concerns that originate from this is that most errors are found late in the development cycle and often are unpredictable in terms of the effort required to resolve these. Consequently, the release of software becomes a highly unpredictable process which causes large amounts of stress and frustration both inside the organization and at customers.

Of course, more experienced companies do not leave all testing to the end of development, but rather perform some unit testing and subsystem testing throughout development. But everyone knows that many issues will be found late in the development when everything is brought together.

The goal of continuous integration when fully achieved in the organization is to ensure that there is a shippable version of the product at any point in time. Although the continuous integration level is an evolution of testing practices, when fully established, the organization will never have to worry about missing deadlines for delivery, but rather the decision becomes to either ship now without a certain feature present or to wait another sprint and to include the feature in the product that is released then.

The path to get to the state described above, however, is not entirely trivial. It requires mindset and behavioral changes in the R&D organization as well as in other functions in the company. There is often investment required to achieve the levels of automation and coverage needed. Finally, process and organizational changes are required. This chapter is concerned with providing insight and guidance on the transition towards continuous integration and on preparing the company for the next steps.

The remainder of this chapter is organized as follows. In the next section, we describe some of the benefits the organization can expect when adopting continuous integration. These are important as we need to be clear on what we are looking to accomplish. Then we discuss the challenges that many companies experience around testing. The subsequent section introduces the continuous integration improvement method (CITIM) as well as the continuous integration visualization technique (CIVIT). We use CIVIT as a basis for modeling current state as well as modeling desired state. Based on these two visualizations, the organization can prioritize the improvements it wants to engage in to bring the current state closer to the desired state. This section is followed by a discussion of the process and organizational changes required to realize continuous integration. The chapter is concluded with some of the experiences by companies that have used the CIVIT model to drive improvements in continuous integration and a conclusion section.

7.1   BENEFITS OF CONTINUOUS INTEGRATION

The speed dimension of the Stairway to Heaven is almost exclusively concerned with shortening the feedback loops that are central in large-scale software development. Continuous integration is concerned with shortening several of these feedback loops and the benefits of continuous integration are to the largest extent concerned with those.

The first benefit originates from the faster feedback that agile teams receive on the code that they have written. Traditional development performs testing at the end of the project, which means that engineers may have to wait for months before receiving feedback. At one of the Software Center companies, an engineer told the story of finishing up a feature before leaving for a nine-month parental leave and receiving the first test results in the first month after coming back to work. Especially in projects with yearly release cycles such long waits are not uncommon, but any errors that are found need to be fixed by engineers that have no idea of how they wrote the code and why they structured it in the way it now exists in the system. Continuous integration, on the other hand, gives feedback in hours or days, which significantly simplifies the fixing of errors as the code is still fresh in the minds of the people that built it.

Continuous integration results in a running version of the system for virtually any check-in of new code. As continuous integration typically assumes single branch development, there often is some testing performed on the code that is checked in by teams in order to minimize the risk of a check-in breaking the build. Teams, on their team branch, have scaled down test suites of the tests that are run on the integration branch and can test their code to a significant extent before checking it in on the main branch. This approach increases the quality of the code that is checked in and minimizes the number of broken builds. As a consequence, product management and others can use the new features that are under development as they are developed and provide feedback on the way the feature is implemented.

An additional benefit concerned with product management and others being able to try out new features during development is that it builds trust towards the R&D organization. Traditional development often experiences unpredictable delivery schedules, easily resulting in R&D being viewed as an organization that can not really be relied upon. With the ability to see new features in a system that is largely functioning at production quality, the rest of the organization will start to experience R&D as a reliable partner.

For product management, the ability to see features implemented in the product also makes it easier to determine if the feature delivers on the expected business outcomes. Seeing the feature in operation allows product managers to change their mind on how the feature should be implemented. It might even cause a situation where the responsible product manager decides to remove a feature altogether as the side effects of the feature are much worse than the value delivered by the feature itself.

Finally, obviously customers of the company building the system acquire the system for a reason and over time the system tends to become part of the network of critical IT systems that drive the business of the customer. Because of these reasons, customers tend to be very conservative in upgrading to the latest version of the software. Typically, customers are caught between fear and greed: greed as the latest version of the software contains features that are valuable to the customer; fear as the consequences of errors in the new version of the software can be quite devastating. Because of these risks, customers may develop testing labs or other ways of verifying the software in their environment. Due to this intermediate step, customers often deploy new software versions months or in some cases even years after it has been made available by the company. Implemented right, continuous integration will reduce the number of issues customers find in the field or in their testing labs. Consequently, customers will increase their trust in the software and reduce their own verification efforts. Simplifying the upgrading software versions will cause more customers to upgrade more quickly to the latest version, causing the company to support fewer versions in the field. Finally, this is an important enabler for the next level, continuous deployment.

7.2 TESTING CHALLENGES

We have established the importance of continuous integration and none of the companies that we have collaborated with in our research disagree on its relevance. It is, however, interesting to note that within the case study companies there was little understanding of all the testing activities that were performed. In our workshops, it was clear that everyone had a solid understanding of their own test activities, but very little understanding of all the other test activities in the organization.

The lack of end-to-end understanding of testing activities, of course, leads to several inefficiencies. First of all, when a version of the software is handed over from one function to the next, the new function has little understanding of the testing that has taken place during previous stages. In order to be safe, the default behavior is to test everything again. This results in significant inefficiencies during testing where the same test cases are executed over and over again, potentially crowding out more important, but more esoteric, testing activities.

A third challenge is that in many companies the feedback loop during testing is rather slow with multiple handovers and significant manual testing activities. Even if the slow feedback loop is viewed as problematic, which it is viewed as across the board, the lack of end-to-end understanding of test activities makes it virtually impossible to determine where improvements should be focused on to shorten the length of the feedback loop.

A fourth challenge is that, for a variety of reasons, quality attributes are often tested late in the development cycle. Perhaps special hardware is required or there is a manual process and test set-up specifically for testing quality attributes, but quality attributes receive little attention until late in the cycle. Between unit tests and subsystem tests, functionality often is tested early in the cycle, though it tends to focus on locally verifiable functionality.

Finally, the fifth challenge is that, due to the aforementioned factors, improvement efforts tend to be ad hoc, localized and tactical in nature. Some team may decide to improve the way they perform testing, but this often occurs without a clear relation to what others in the company are doing. Although improvements, of course, are welcome, a concerted, strategic effort optimizing the end-to-end testing activities would create a significantly greater impact for the same expenditure of resources.

7.3 CITIM

So far in the chapter, we have concluded that continuous integration is considered important by the companies, but at the same time these companies are experiencing challenges in their testing practices. To address these challenges and help companies achieve continuous integration, we developed the continuous integration improvement method (CITIM).

As shown in figure 7.1, CITIM at the highest level is a basic improvement loop consisting of four steps. The first step is to establish current state through visualization of all the testing activities currently occurring in the company. To aid the visualization, we have developed the continuous integration visualization technique (CIVIT) that will be presented in the next section. CIVIT provides a high-level but sufficiently detailed insight into the testing activities, the type of testing, the frequency of execution and the system scope that the testing entails. Based on establishment of the current state,

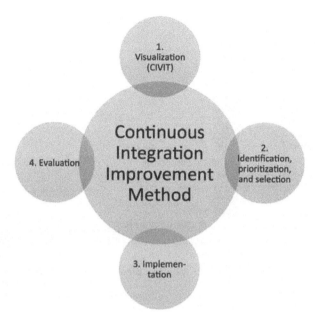

Figure 7.1 Continuous integration improvement method (CITIM)

the next step is concerned with the identification, prioritization and selection of possible improvements. We accomplish this by first using CIVIT to create a visualization of the desired state of continuous integration. Based on this, we can then put current state and desired state in the same visualization and identify the biggest gaps between the two. The gaps are then used to identify potential improvement activities. Once identified, the potential improvement activities are then prioritized based on their cost/benefit ratio. Finally, the highest priority activity or activities are selected for implementation. Step 3 is concerned with performing the improvement activity so that it is actually implemented in the continuous integration infrastructure. Upon completion, step 4 is concerned with evaluating the outcome of the improvement activity and is intended to determine the accuracy of the cost/benefit assessment. Any learnings from this step are used to improve the estimates in the next round of improvement. Finally, we return to step 1 and update the current state visualization and repeat the steps discussed above.

In the next sections, we first introduce the CIVIT model, then describe how CIVIT can be used to capture current state. Next, we model desired state as well as the process for performing gap analysis. Then, we describe step 2 of CITIM and briefly discuss step 3, implementation, and step 4, evaluation.

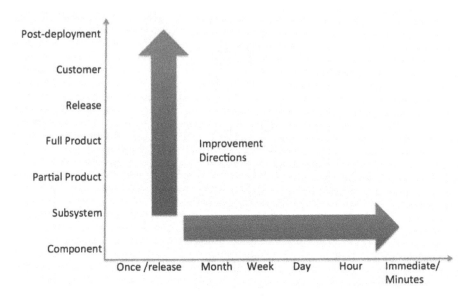

Figure 7.2 The two dimensions of a CIVIT grid

7.3.1 CIVIT

When we started our research on continuous integration, we performed a literature search to find earlier work that could help us provide an end-to-end understanding of all testing activities ongoing in a company. We were disappointed in our search in that it seemed that no techniques existed to visualize this. As the lack of an overall understanding of all testing activities in the company is a significant problem for the companies that we worked with, we decided to develop a visualization technique that evolved into the CIVIT model.

In figure 7.2 we show the grid on which we will lay out the testing activities conducted by the company. There are two dimensions: the x-axis focuses on the speed and frequency of the testing activity and the y-axis focuses on the scope and the development phase of the testing activity. The x-axis is relatively self-explanatory. A testing activity may execute and finalize immediately or in minutes, it may run every hour or every couple of hours, every day or couple of days, weeks or months. The final position is held by the testing activities that are conducted only once for every release. In traditional development, testing mostly takes place at the end of the development cycle, so many of the testing activities are performed once per release. With the adoption of continuous integration, the frequency of testing activities will increase, hence the arrow pointing to the left indicating the improvement direction.

The y-axis of the CIVIT grid is concerned with the scope of testing as well as the phase of development when it takes place. These include the following:

Component: The component refers to the smallest unit that is identified in the architecture. Depending on the system, this may be a file or a set of files with a single API towards the rest of the system. For other systems, a component is a unit that can be independently deployed. There is also an organizational dimension in that for the companies that use component teams rather than feature teams, a component is the scope of responsibility for a team. Testing at the component level is often concerned with unit tests that test for functionality, both new and legacy.

Subsystem: As the name implies, the subsystem is an architectural organizational mechanism that is in between components and the full system. As such, it contains multiple components and is responsible for a clear set of responsibilities. Testing at the subsystem level is wider in scope, but can only cover parts of the system use cases.

Partial product: The partial product level requires a bit of explanation as it is only used in embedded systems. Several of the companies that we work with build systems including mechanics, hardware and software. Examples include cars, trucks, base stations and radar systems. Performing system level testing in the final product, however, is cumbersome because of the overhead of conducting the tests. For instance, for a car, there are safety concerns, drivers need to be available, software downloading into the vehicle is cumbersome and it is hard to conduct the tests in an automated fashion and to remove humans from the loop. So, most companies build a test bed where part of the mechanics is simulated, rather than physically present. Even some of the hardware can be simulated. In the test bed, the software can be tested in realistic settings without the overhead of the actual system. Also, testing can be automated and humans removed from the loop.

Full product: Even though software is tested successfully at the partial product level, it is also necessary to test it in the actual system in which it will be deployed. Although often executed less frequently in embedded systems, it is a necessary step to ensure that the product performs according to specifications.

Release: Most companies have a separate testing activity at the end of a development cycle that is concerned with verifying, to the largest extent possible, that the software is free of critical and major defects. Release-level testing is concerned with this.

Customer: Especially in B2B markets where the number of customers is relatively low, i.e. dozens or hundreds, companies deploy the new release of the product first with one customer in order to verify in an actual customer context that the product works as intended.

Post-deployment: As organizations increase the frequency of deployment of their software, certain types of tests require more time than the period between deployments. Alternatively, companies decide that certain tests can be performed outside of the release process for other reasons. The types of testing often have a longitudinal nature, such as robustness testing, ensuring the system has no memory leaks, etc. The notion of first releasing the software and then continuing to conduct tests is an alien thought to many as our default way of thinking is that we first test the entire product to ensure it works and only then release it. In reality, however, any realistic system deployed at customers has several, if not many, known defects and issues. Fixing all these defects or deploying the system at customers so that they get access to the new features is a business decision and also customers are fine with the balance that their suppliers strike. As long as the basic value delivering use cases work and the system exhibits no safety or security concerns, there are several types of testing that can be conducted post-deployment.

Now that we have defined the two-dimensional grid, the next step is to introduce the blocks that we place in the grid to indicate testing activities. In figure 7.3[1], we present these blocks. Each block has four squares inside and a line around the block. The four squares are concerned with the following:

F: The "F" is concerned with the functional requirements that are being built as part of the ongoing sprint or release. In this square, we are concerned with the test cases that have been developed for testing this functionality.

L: Functionality that has been built in earlier sprints or during earlier releases should continue to work even as we are building and adding new functionality to the system. This legacy functionality needs to be tested.

Q: In addition to functional requirements, systems also have quality requirements such as performance, security and reliability. The quality attributes of the system need to be tested as well and the test cases in this square are concerned with that.

E: Finally, in our research we identified that most companies have, in the past, experienced weird, infrequent error conditions that were very resource intensive to resolve. In order to avoid ending up with one of these again, companies developed test cases to check for these. We refer to these tests as edge cases.

Each square in the block receives a color that indicates the level of coverage that the testing activity in this location in the grid. In figure 7.3, we use a five scale range from black to white indicating different levels of coverage. However,

---

[1]Originally in [38]. Used with permission.

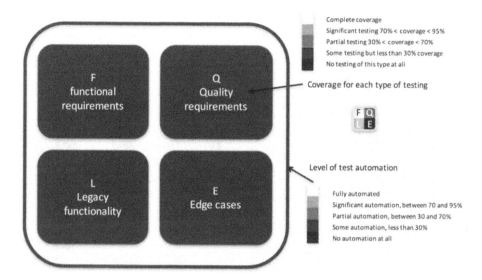

Figure 7.3 CIVIT block legend

companies have used three scale ranges, i.e. red, orange, green, or could use even different ways to indicate coverage, such as putting a coverage percentage in the box. Finally, the line around the four squares indicates the level of test automation for this testing activity. Again, the same five-scale range is used, but now to indicate the automation level rather than the coverage. Similarly, other ways to indicate the automation level can be used.

In figure 7.4[2], we present an example of a CIVIT model for one of the companies that we worked with. In this case, the company chose to use a three level scale. As the figure shows, there are nine positions on the grid that are in use for testing activities. We briefly discuss some of these. First, in the bottom right corner, the first block indicates the testing that takes place in the sandbox of an engineer. As the company uses test driven development, the engineer runs the test cases that he or she developed for the specific feature. No other testing is conducted. Upon success, the code is tested in the branch of the agile team. More functional tests are run, but also some legacy and quality tests. From there on, the code is offered to the main branch. It first needs to pass an acceptance test that focuses on functionality and legacy. Once accepted, the code is added to the main branch. Then the company has three levels of automated testing on the main branch. Every two hours, a test suite of prioritized test cases is run. Then, every night the system performs a 10-hour test with significant coverage. Every weekend, a 50-hour test suite is run. The latter test suite focuses mostly on quality attributes, but also tests some functionality and legacy. At the end of every sprint, a separate release team

---

[2]Originally in [38]. Used with permission.

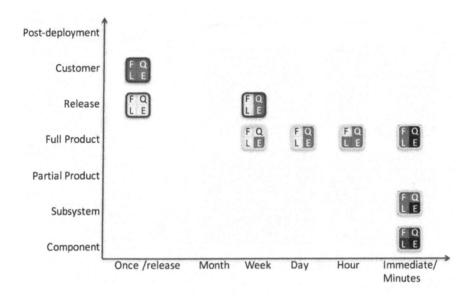

Figure 7.4 CIVIT example

receives the code and subjects it to more tests that, however, are conducted manually. For every release, the release team performs a very elaborate test at the company, then deploys it at a first customer and upon passing all that testing, the release is made available for all customers.

In the above example, it is clear that significant amounts of testing are ongoing by different groups and focusing on different parts of the system. This case is an example of a company that is quite advanced in continuous integration, but that due to its complicated hardware and the reliability requirements still uses a traditional release process towards customers.

The CIVIT model continues to evolve and the version presented here is again an evolution of versions that we published earlier ([38] and [37]). The main changes are in the representation of coverage in the testing activities and the introduction of a new testing scope, post-deployment testing, in response to companies adopting continuous deployment starting to transition certain testing activities until after deployment.

7.3.2 Capturing Current State

Although we already showed an example of a CIVIT model of a company, the first step in CITIM is to create a CIVIT model to capture the current state. To illustrate this and the next steps of CITIM, we'll be using an anonymized case of one of the companies that we worked with, shown in figure 7.5.

From the figure, it is clear that the company has very little automated testing ongoing. Only at the component level is there some automated unit

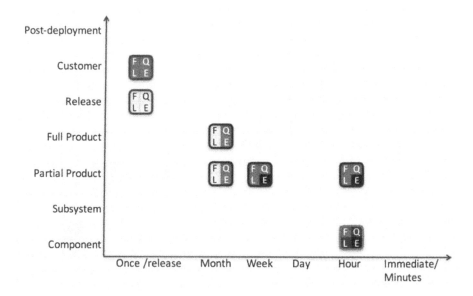

Figure 7.5 Current state CIVIT model for one case company

testing for new functionality. All other testing activities are manual. Every day, there is some manual testing on the partial product to test. Once per sprint, there is some additional manual testing. Then every quarter, both on the partial product level and at the full product level there is more elaborate testing. As the product gets ready for release, the full system is tested, deployed at the customer and then tested at the customer site before the product is transferred to the customer.

Although this case may seem exceptional in the low amount of automation and coverage, our experience is that many companies in the embedded systems domain, especially those serving smaller numbers of customers, have similar testing setups. Traditionally, test automation was not necessarily viewed as necessary and providing a sufficient return on investment.

7.3.3 Envisioning Desired State

Once the current state has been captured and agreed upon as being accurate by all the stakeholders involved in its creation, the next step is to envision the desired state, although one might assume that the ideal state is where all testing is done immediately, so an engineer knows immediately upon checking in that things work as planned. In practice, this is, of course, not realistic as testing takes time and many companies literally have thousands of test cases. In the case of embedded systems companies, speeding up testing requires parallelizing testing which, in term, requires more test beds. As these test beds

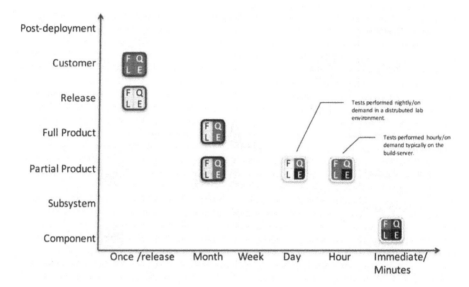

Figure 7.6 Desired state CIVIT model for the case company

cost tens of thousands up to millions of euros, the reality is that speeding up certain types of testing is simply prohibitively expensive.

Also, when envisioning the desired state, one does not have to model the absolutely ideal situation, but rather model a state that would provide a significant step forward with clear benefits for quality. In subsequent iterations, the goal posts can be moved and a more ambitious desired state can be modeled.

Our case company decided that as a desired state, it wanted to focus on automating the development close to the engineers, so its desired state has two main changes. First, its desire is to have automated testing at the point of check-in for a component. Second, its desire is to replace the manual testing at the end of each sprint with hourly and night automated testing. We illustrate this in figure 7.6.

7.3.4 Gap Analysis and Improvement Planning

Once current state and desired state have been modeled, identifying the gaps and prioritizing these is typically rather easy at the level of the CIVIT models. However, one now also needs to look into the actual changes that would be required for each of the identified gaps. Each identified gap should also have an estimated budget and resource requirement associated with it. That allows the team to prioritize the improvements based on the cost/benefit of each improvement.

For the case company, in the previous section, the main items desired by the organization were already identified, so the gaps can readily be derived from these. The company sought to do three improvements:

Automated unit level testing at the time a component is checked in. This required installation of a test program and the associated test cases on the machine of each engineer. As the software was open source and no additional hardware was required, the company decided to start with this task.

The second was to run **hourly tests** on the build server. As the build server already was getting slow, the company invested in faster hardware such that the build and the automated testing were performed significantly faster than the old build process by itself. There was some investment required, but the cost were manageable. This was the second task the company committed on after completing the first.

The third was to automate the **nightly testing** on the actual, distributed hardware of the system. This proved to be the most challenging task as this required the allocation of one instance of the distributed system that the company sold to be allocated for testing purposes. Although it could be used for other uses during the day, every night it needed to be put back in a shape so that the automated testing could be conducted. This also required the addition of special testing hardware to simulate system interaction that earlier was done by humans as well as simulate input from sensors and actuators that could not be activated without human presence. As the company sought to first build evidence on the value of test automation before asking for significant investments, this improvement was scheduled last.

7.3.5   Post-Deployment Testing

In this section, we introduced CITIM and CIVIT and illustrated their use. One of the cases we did not yet share is post-deployment testing and in figure 7.7 an example is shown. This case company is a Web 2.0 Software as a Service (SaaS) business that releases new software up to 25 times per day. Basically, every time an engineer finishes some functionality, it is checked in, tested at the component, subsystem and release level and within minutes the software goes live. As customers are using the product in their web browsers and the page automatically refreshes, customers constantly get access to new software.

Although the case company prides itself on its release process, it realized that it needed to complement the pre-release testing with separate testing or customer feedback activities that run outside of the release process. Specifically, it uses three techniques to ensure quality:

It uses an **automated, model-based testing system** that performs exploratory testing of the product and checks for some quality attributes, such as performance and memory usage.

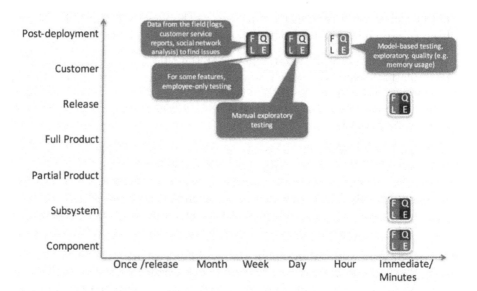

Figure 7.7 CIVIT model of a SaaS company

Second, the company employs some **manual testers** that just use the product as any customer would and raise concerns when they appear.

Finally, the company looks very carefully at any **feedback coming back from the field**. This can be more automated sources, such as logs, but also more qualitative sources such as customer service reports and complaints in social media. In some cases, the company turns on features only for its employees, who are fervent users of the product, and receives feedback from its own staff in case things are not working as they should.

As we discussed earlier in the chapter, the notion of testing after the product has been released may initially seem unnatural and beside the point. However, in situations where there is a lot of diversity in the environment in which the product is deployed and customers are using the product in very different ways, this can be a very effective technique to test significant parts of the functionality of the system.

In fact, most companies already today use different techniques to identify, track and resolve issues coming back from the field and their customers. This can be viewed as post-deployment testing, even if it tends to be more ad-hoc than what we discuss here and less appreciated by customers. In that sense, it is better to have one's own testing infrastructure identify post-deployment issues before too many customers are confronted with it.

7.4 PROCESS AND ORGANIZATION

Continuous integration requires significant changes to the build and test infrastructure of the R&D department. Up to now, we have focused on those changes through CITIM and CIVIT and we have shown how companies that we work with have used these techniques to drive the changes necessary to get to continuous integration.

In addition to the technical changes, however, there are also several changes that need to be driven in relation to process and organization. In this section, we discuss some of these that were experienced by the companies that we worked with in relation to continuous integration and related topics.

The first transition that companies seek to effect is the reduction of the number of versions of the code that are maintained and developed by the R&D organization. This is a significant change, especially if customers have received specific versions with their specific requirements added. Even if there is only one version at every point in time, customers may upgrade at different points in time and demand support for errors found in their specific version. Especially as the company is getting ready for a transition to continuous deployment, the behaviour by sales, product management and support needs to shift towards urging customers to upgrade to the latest version and to resolve issues only in that version.

Also inside R&D, continuous integration functions optimally when the company employs single branch/track development. Although engineers can have their sandbox and agile teams can have a team branch, all code needs to end up in a single branch and proper testing takes place for that branch. In cases where R&D has sought to manage certain types of complexity by creating separate branches for certain regions, customer segments or based on another segmentation, the handling of variability needs to shift from the different branches to configuration in the single branch.

One of the surprisingly frequent and non-trivial changes that need to be implemented is the habit of engineers and teams to check in their code early and often. Engineers, as a group, have perfectionism characteristics and if left unchecked may want to work on a problem or feature for a long time, create a complete and comprehensive solution, test it locally and only then offer it to the rest of the organization for integration. The challenge is that the amount of integration work that needs to take place can then be very large. However, in traditional development approaches, often the integration was not performed by the engineer him- or herself, but rather by a separate team.

The best practice that several companies employed is to let the team that runs into integration challenges deal with the integration problem. Thus even if the integration challenge was caused by another team, if the other team checked in first and passed all the test cases, it is this team that needs to deal with integration. This rule encourages teams to check in early and often in order to avoid having to spend significant time integrating their code into the code developed by other teams.

As a basic principle, the goal of the organization needs to be that of having a shippable version of the product at any point in time. We can always ship and feature content grows continuously.

7.5 EXPERIENCES

The CIVIT model and CITIM have been taken in use by several of the companies that we work with. Especially the CIVIT model is useful not only for documenting the testing activities, their frequency and their coverage, but also because it provides an artifact that all stakeholders in the company can gather around and discuss. This helps in establishing shared understanding of current state, but also to constructively discuss the desired state, the gaps, the improvements needed and their relative priority. The shared understanding also helps in implementing the changes required to realize the improvements. As this typically requires changes in several places in the organization, having established shared understanding of the rationale behind the changes results in better support across the organization and faster implementation of the changes.

Interestingly, some companies have started to use CIVIT models as a boundary object in discussions with other functions in the company. As a CIVIT model gives a clear overview of what testing takes place when in the development process, it can also be used to give testing activities to other functions in the organization. It also allows for discussions around which testing needs to be successfully performed pre-deployment and which testing activities can be conducted post-deployment.

7.6 CONCLUSIONS

This chapter is concerned with continuous integration. We started by defining and describing the concept and the benefits that continuous integration provides to the organization. Then we discussed the challenges surrounding testing that companies experience, ranging from the lack of end-to-end understanding of all the testing activities that take place in the company to the late testing of quality attributes, leading to unpredictable delivery schedules as changes are required late in the development process.

In response to the challenges, we introduced the continuous integration improvement method (CITIM) and the continuous integration visualization technique (CIVIT). These techniques have been successfully adopted by several of the companies that we work with to help in the transition towards continuous integration.

It is important to realize that continuous integration is not a binary step, but rather a gradual process of faster feedback loops between engineers building and checking in code and the results of the testing efforts being available to these engineers. The goal is to have a shippable version of the software available at any point in time. Once this goal has been achieved, one can consider moving towards continuous deployment, the next level on the speed dimension of the Stairway to Heaven.

Data

CHAPTER 8

The Stairway to Heaven: Data

Anyone who has not heard the term "big data" must have been living under a pretty big rock during the last decade or so. With Moore's law continuing to deliver its fantastic progress, computing is increasingly powerful and can churn through vast amounts of data, continuously as well as in response to queries. We read about amazing new insights that have been derived by sifting through vast amounts of data and correlating different variables.

Although this novel use of data originating from different sources was originally the purview of research groups at universities as well as dedicated data analytics companies, over time companies in different industries have started to adopt data-driven practices in parts of their business. For instance, in the Web 2.0 and Software-as-a-Service (SaaS) industry, companies adopted split testing (or A/B testing) as a way to experiment with different aspects of their products.

The use of data is far from novel and companies have used data in accounting, marketing and sales for calculating various KPIs such as return on investment for accounting and brand awareness changes in marketing as well as cost of customer acquisition in sales. Also, errors found in the field in deployed products are collected at most companies and used to direct quality assurance efforts as well as defect management.

The main transition that the industry is currently experiencing is driven by two factors. First, the cost of collecting, storing and analysing data has, over the last decade, reached an inflection point allowing companies to collect and store data in areas where it was originally impossible to do so. Second, because of the increased availability of data, companies have shifted decision making for many issues from the traditional opinion- and experienced-based reasoning to decision making based on data.

The transition towards data-driven decision making is an organizational change management activity as much as a technical problem or a skills development challenge. The employees at a company typically do not wake up one morning and all start working in a fundamentally new, data-driven fashion. Instead the process is a gradual one where the organization starts by trying out collection, analysis and decision making based on data in some small, relatively insignificant area in order to build experience. Based on these experiences, assuming these were successful, the company will take subsequent steps to build additional expertise and to expand the set of decisions made based on data.

One of the most promising areas for data-driven decision making is concerning the customer's use and appreciation of the product or system provided by the company. In the decision making about what to build for customers, there are significant amounts of opinion-based decision making by product management as well as assumptions-based guessing by R&D teams. Enriching these decision processes with relevant data would go a long way to improve the accuracy and relevance of R&D investments.

A second major area is the use of performance data generated by products in the field. When prioritizing feature development or other improvements on the system, product management and R&D teams have predictions about the implications of the effort on the system. However, in practice there is little effort allocated to actually measuring the impact of new features or refactorings on the system. Hence, actively instrumenting the code for tracking relevant metrics about the general performance of the system can provide much more insight into the effects of development of the system and provide quantification of the value provided by new functionality.

Summarizing, the transition from opinion-based decision making to data-driven decision making is critical for the success of companies. The power of big data is not just found in novel applications that were unfeasible until now, but as much if not more in better, more accurate and more real-time decision making in areas where organizations used the opinions of managers and leaders for decision making.

This chapter is concerned with introducing the second dimension of the Stairway to Heaven, i.e. the data dimension. After working with dozens of companies on data-related topics, we have found that, similar to the speed dimension, companies move through a predictable set of steps as they transition towards becoming data-driven organizations. The remainder of the chapter is concerned with introducing and discussing the levels that are part of this dimension. In the next section, we provide a high-level overview of the five steps in the data dimension. In the subsequent sections, we provide a more detailed description of each level. Finally, we end the chapter with a conclusion.

8.1 DIMENSION 2: DATA

Even among hard-core engineers, the use of data remains a challenging topic for many. As engineering education tends to focus on formulas, clear cause-effect relations and predictable behaviours of the systems built by engineers, the notion of statistical behaviour, analysis of large data sets and the use of averages and deviations feels less tangible, or, if nothing else, requires an alternative mindset from the people working with the data.

A second challenge is that everyone has opinions about the performance of the system as well as the preferences of customers. Especially when these beliefs are held by many in the organization, it starts to be treated like a truth. Of course, the problem with these "truths" is that, even if these were true at some point in time, system behaviour as well as customer preferences evolve. This may cause these truths to transform into shadow-beliefs, i.e. a belief that has no grounding in reality but is still widely held across the organization.

The main antidote to an organization riddled with shadow-beliefs is the use of data to confirm or disprove any beliefs and assumptions by constantly collecting data and demanding evidence as part of decision making. Evidence should be demanded for every decision, especially those where it is "obvious" what the right course of action is. The "obvious" decisions are those where the shadow-beliefs that exist in the organization are hardest at work and where providing evidence to the contrary provides the most powerful learning opportunities for the company.

The transition towards a data-driven or evidence-based company is an organizational change process that evolves through a number of stages and levels. The data dimension of the Stairway to Heaven is concerned with this transformation. Based on our experience with dozens of companies, there are five levels that organizations evolve through. Below, each level is presented and described at a high level.

> **Ad hoc:** At the lowest level, the organization has no systematic use of data concerning the performance of the system or the behavior of users. Not only are data not used, they are not even collected or analyzed. At certain occasions, based on the initiative by individuals in the organization, some data are used to learn more about a specific aspect of the customer or the system. In these cases, as the company is not geared for working in a data-driven fashion, each step, including instrumentation of the system, collection and aggregation of data, analysis of the collected data as well as decision making based on the analyzed data, require significant amounts of one-off work. This requires significant initiative from the individual or team that has expressed an interest in using data for learning or decision making. As the barriers to using data are so high, the times a team or individual decide to expend all this effort tend to be few and far between, even if many see the potential benefits. The interesting observation, however, is that when data are presented to inform decision making, they stir up attention and many get inspired and see the opportunities. Hence, in an organization that is at this level, creating these cases, despite the sometimes Herculean effort required, is necessary to create the awareness that will cause the organization to move to the next level. Of course, any software-intensive

systems organization does collect data about quality issues in the field, as well as quality issues identified pre-deployment, so there is some use of data in the organization. Also, any company will have to collect and use financial data and one could view sales data as a measure for the value that the products and systems sold by the company provide to its customers. So, it is not that the organization uses no data anywhere, but rather that in product development, little data are used to steer decision making but rather product managers and others rely on their experience and their opinions that are formed by their experience and other background.

Collection: Once a certain level of awareness of the relevance of data is established in the organization, the next step is to start to instrument the software in its products and systems with the intent of putting the data in a data warehouse. One of the drivers for this is that when collecting data in an ad hoc fashion, teams often fall into the challenge of not knowing what the normal state of the system in operation is. In order to be able to identify deviations from the normal state, we first need to establish what is the normal state. This provides a starting point for data collection, but it also initiates a discussion on what data are relevant to collect. The initial position typically is that as much data should be collected as possible as it is impossible to predict what types of analysis we might want to perform at later points in time. At the same time, just blindly recording anything that can be measured is not a suitable approach either. Hence, some balanced needs to be found between proactively collecting and storing data and accepting that certain data will not be collected, but that the data collection infrastructure can be extended to facilitate new needs as they surface. In this stage, often the data are stored in a data warehouse. In response to specific requests, a data analyst (or team) structures the request, finds the data in the warehouse, runs analysis on the data, creates a report and presents the results to the requesting party. These requests often come from different management levels in the organization, but can also originate from R&D teams that seek to better understand how to build a specific feature. The main characteristic at this stage, however, is that although data are collected proactively, the analysis and decision making based on the data is performed reactively in response to requests from different parts of the organization. In addition, access to the data is, either intentionally or unintentionally, reserved for the data analytics team. Others in the organizations either are barred from having access or, if they have access, the interface to and ability to engage with the data requires so much expert knowledge that non-experts are unable to engage with the data in the system.

Automation: As managers and others provide requests to the data analytics team, it will become clear that certain queries come back frequently. In addition, people start to ask for the multiple reports over time to be provided with the intent of observing the variation of certain data points over time. When this happens, often dashboards are defined and initiated. This allows the data analytics team to implement a specific type of analysis, make it repeatable and then automate it to the extent possible. Once certain types of analysis are automated, management teams as well as other groups can start to use these automatically generated data dashboards for information sharing and decision making. At this point, management and R&D teams have identified a set of key metrics to track that and, based on current understanding, provide the best insight into how the organization delivers value to its customers. The dashboard is updated either periodically or continuously and the new data can and often are used for decision making. At this point, one will start to observe an interesting behavior: whenever there is a change, large or small, in the data, different people will start to discuss the cause for the change. Especially in areas where there is contention within the team, there will be a tendency to use the data to explain the consequences of decisions taken earlier and to put these decisions in either a negative or positive light. However, as there are very little data to back up any of these interpretations, the discussion has moved squarely into the domain of (shadow-)beliefs. Of course, the data analytics team is still available and these kinds of discussions may easily lead to queries being fired off to the analytics team to try to answer. One of the important items to be aware of at this level is that the metrics that are considered to be important, and that consequently are on the dashboard, may not continue to be important over time. Hence, the dashboard should be viewed as a map of a constantly changing area, rather than as the truth itself. At this stage, not only data collection is automated, but also parts of data analysis and reporting are automated through the use of dashboards and other reporting mechanisms.

Data innovation: As dashboards and continuous reporting of data become the norm, the awareness of the limitations of static dashboards becomes apparent. As management and R&D teams learn about their deployed systems, customers and the market, the frequency of queries to the data analytics team will increase. In response, the data analytics team realizes that it requires more domain knowledge about the system, its customers and the market. This results in a closer collaboration and partnership between the management/R&D team and the data analytics team. This can take several forms, but a typical model is where one or a few data analysts are appointed to work with the management/R&D team on a continuous basis. This may then lead to the next level where, between the team and its analysts, a behavior develops that results in a constant flow of innovative ideas on new correlations to test in the data. Whenever a relevant new insight is found, it is presented to the management or R&D team and its meaning and importance are discussed. If the new metric is sufficiently relevant, the associated correlation is added to existing data dashboards, potentially replacing existing items, or new forms of reporting are created to provide insight to the right people in the organization. At this point, dashboards evolve into fluid, constantly evolving reporting mechanisms, driven by a continuous flow of new, innovative insights into the evolving system, customer base and market. Teams learn that even if certain correlations or experiments were unsuccessful in the past, changing conditions may cause a situation where the same correlations or experiments will result in statistically relevant insights. In this stage, the organization also starts with experimentation in deployed systems or in lab contexts. Until now, analysis, tracking and decision making were predominantly performed sequentially: as the system evolves, customer usage of the system evolves and the market evolves, management and R&D teams respond to these changes by taking actions that correct negative trend data or that support positive trend data. At this level, the organization realizes that data-driven decision making may require running experiments to evaluate the relative strengths and weaknesses of alternative ways of realizing certain types of functionality.

Evidence-based company: Once we reach the final stage, the entire organization has embraced the motto attributed to Deming: In God we trust; everyone else bring data. The entire organization employs data-driven decision making and experimentation considered to be the most powerful tool to accomplish this. Rather than tracking data from an evolving system, the organization proactively runs parallel experiments, also referred to as A/B testing or split testing, or at least sequential experiments where different alternatives are deployed sequentially to determine the superior alternative. An additional element to this phase is that once relevant metrics and correlations have been identified and used by management and R&D teams, the next step can be to embed the analytics and related data-driven decision making in products and systems in the field. This then allows these systems to dynamically adjust behavior based on customer and system context profiles. Fully automated, instance-specific selection of alternatives to system behavior is then accomplished within the organization. One can not stress enough the cultural change that organizations need to move through as we reach this level. Especially in hierarchical organizations, much positional and reputational power is derived from having collected years of experience and sharing, sometimes loudly, opinions about the system, the customers and the market. When moving to an evidence-based company, especially those that traditionally have embraced the traditional model have to fundamentally change their behavior and admit that they don't know the answer to many questions that surface in the organiza-

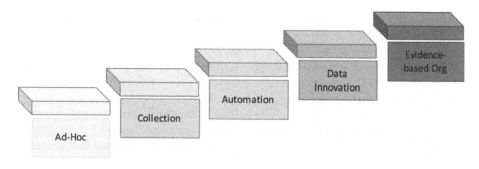

Figure 8.1 The data dimension of the Stairway to Heaven

Table 8.1 Stairway to Heaven - Data dimension

	Collection	Analysis	Reporting	Decision Making
Ad hoc	manual	manual	manual	manual
Collection	automated	manual	manual	manual
Automation	automated	automated	automated	supported
Data innovation	dynamic	dynamic	dynamic	supported
Evidence based company	dynamic	dynamic	dynamic	automated

tion, that the only way to find the answer to many of these questions is by trying it out, either in the lab or on systems deployed in the field, or by using both approaches. Building a culture where decisions are made based on data, rather than using the HIPPO model (highest paid person's opinion), requires the leadership of the organization to model and reward the right behavior.

Having introduced the five levels of the data dimension of the Stairway to Heaven, the next sections are concerned with defining and describing each level in more detail. In table 8.1, however, we first summarize the levels introduced above.

8.2 AD HOC USE OF DATA

8.2.1 Definition

All companies use data in different parts of their business. For instance, government regulations require companies to keep track of their financials. However, around product management and R&D, the main use of data in many companies is around troubleshooting and support only. As having good insight into the quality of the software deployed at customers is of critical importance to the company, this use of data is clearly helpful. Also, it helps to provide customers with insight into the performance of their instance of the system. In the first level, however, there is very little use of data beyond the legal requirements on the company.

The only exception are individuals that, often driven by personal curiosity, seek to collect data to answer specific questions or to test concrete hypotheses. In this case, often the individual is required to create the needed instrumentation in the product software, get the new version deployed in the field, collect the data and analyze it before any conclusions can be drawn. The amount of effort required for a single test is quite significant so the frequency of tests will be very low. Because of the amount of effort the organization views this as very inefficient.

8.2.2   Drivers for Adoption

As this is the lowest level of the data dimension of the Stairway to Heaven, there are no drivers required for adoption. The company is driven by the opinions of its leaders and ad hoc experiences with customers. As the company is not data-driven, but rather driven by individuals that make decisions based on their "gut" and convince others using rhetorics and other techniques to win over others, the organization may even develop a negative attitude towards using data for decision making. In some of the organizations that we worked with, leaders that suggested data-driven approaches were considered to be visionless bean counters that were shirking their responsibilities. Of course, this attitude would need to be overcome for the organization to move to the next level.

8.2.3   Data-Driven Principles

As the company at this stage does not employ data in decision making, there tends to be an "open loop" as it comes to decision making. The term "open loop" originates from control theory and indicates a situation where the controller does not receive any feedback from the controlled system. Organizations that do not use data tend to resemble this situation where the feedback loop between the market and the decision makers in the company is slow, contains lots of noise and focuses on high-level aspects, rather than tangible and actionable feedback.

Of course, all companies collect some forms of feedback from the market. The challenge is twofold. First, the feedback is primarily on the product and the portfolio level and much less on individual features. In short, the granularity of the feedback is coarse. Second, the feedback is often not representative as it is often collected from those customers that are the loudest in sharing their feedback. These customers may not represent the most important market needs and, especially in B2B contexts, the individuals representing the customer may not provide feedback on the most important aspects of the product, but instead focus on the topics that are currently top of mind. Thus, the feedback contains a lot of "noise" and requires significant interpretation.

8.2.4 Implications

The primary implication of operating at the ad-hoc level is that the accuracy of R&D investments is likely to be low. This is due to the coarse granularity of feedback and especially the amount of noise in the feedback. This opens up for interpretation by different players in the organization. A likely result is that the decision processes become politicized as people can take pieces of data and interpret these for their own purposes. Although office politics is often viewed as a necessary evil, one should not underestimate its destructive nature. The attention of the organization turns inwards, rather than being focused on the customer, which leads to a significantly increased risk of disruption by new or existing competitors.

8.2.5 Remaining Concerns

The concerns remaining at this level are many. The feedback collected from the field is minimal if existing at all. Decision making is opinion based and organized along the hierarchy of the organization, meaning that those higher in the organization have orders of magnitude higher impact on the key directions taken by the company. Even if anyone in the organization decides to collect data for more informed decision making, the amount of one-off effort required to model the desired data, instrument the code to collect it, overcome all the internal and external resistance, set up a back end of collecting the data, analyze it and draw conclusions that are trusted by the organizations is so high that the number of initiatives will be few and far between.

8.2.6 Example

In one of Viganbe's B2B business units that has traditionally been predominantly mechanical in nature, management has considered the use of data from products in the field as too intrusive for customers. In recent months, however, the customers have experienced unexpected breakdowns of products in the field. Analysis showed that the breakdowns are caused by normal wear and tear of a specific part. The company has decided to develop a preventive maintenance process that can be used by customers or that the company can offer as a service. In order to decide when to initiate the preventive maintenance, however, the company needs to analyse the data from product breakdowns, separate out the part failures for which it intends to initiate preventive maintenance and develop a statistical model for when to trigger maintenance. As the data have not been collected automatically, the responsible team experienced great difficulty in collecting, analyzing, presenting and decision making and the amount of manual effort was outsized when compared to the size of the task.

8.3 COLLECTION

8.3.1 Definition

Once the first successful cases of ad hoc data-driven decision making have run their course and the culture of the organization becomes more willing to recognize the relevance, the organization becomes ready to move to the next level: automated collection. The line of reasoning in the organization typically is that it does not know what it will do with the data, but that collecting and storing it may be a good idea that justifies the allocation of resources.

In this stage, the company will collect data from its products automatically and store it, but all subsequent steps still require manual work from individuals and most value derived from the data is created by reactive initiatives. In most cases that we have studied, there is a driver around quality. For instance, in order to support customers experiencing issues with deployed products, it is required for the company to collect data logs to understand where the system in operation starts to deviate from the expected behavior. This troubleshooting often requires that the company stores the data from different customers centrally. Over time, the company builds up an often significant database of operational data that can be used for quality issues, but obviously also for other types of analysis.

The challenge for companies often concerns deciding what data to collect. Initially, this is driven by the needs of troubleshooting and support, but it often becomes clear that the organization would benefit from other data to be collected as well. On the other hand, indiscriminately collecting everything that can be collected easily leads to unacceptable amounts of data. Hence, the collection process requires intentional decision making about the information to collect. This is not a one-off decision, but rather a continuous one where the data collected will change over time. There are challenges concerning baselining the behaviour of the system, which is difficult if a new data collection item has just been introduced when the analysis starts. However, dynamically adjusting (often expanding) the data collected is a natural process that needs to be supported.

The typical model that the organization employs in this stage is centered on the data analytics team. Different people, often management teams, have specific questions. These questions are given to the data analytics team that then reactively analyze the relevant parts of these data to answer the question. The analysis is presented in a report that is shared with the team asking the questions. The outcome is a model where the quality of data analysis is often quite high, but the amount of effort required is such that data-driven decision making remains the exception rather than the rule.

8.3.2 Drivers for Adoption

The key driver that starts the adoption of automated collection often is concerned with quality. As the complexity of the product or system grows, customers will start to experience issues in the field that have not surfaced in the lab environment of the company. In response, the company starts to collect data that, initially, are concerned with quality issues such as performance, system or feature failures. Once this is in place, the next step often will be to collect information about the specific configuration in which the system is used. This includes the internal settings in the product or system but also the systems that it interfaces with. As fault situations can not be easily reproduced in test labs, the company needs more information about the specific configuration in which the errors occur. The third step is concerned with determining whether changes made by the development team indeed resolve the problems reported by customers. It is important to note that the more complicated situations are not those where a fault is either present or not, but especially those where there are intermittent faults where the root cause is not well understood or situations where system properties, such as performance, number of concurrent users or other factors, suddenly change significantly. As, once again, these changes may only happen in specific contexts, the company now also starts to collect general operational data from its deployed systems.

An important factor holding the company back is the concern of its customers about sharing potentially business-sensitive data with one of their suppliers. Especially in this case, where the company is providing competing customers with its product or system, there is a concern that the data shared might leak to competitors and provide these competitors with an unintended advantage. Because of this, initially customers will only provide data as part of identified problem situations that require the help of the company. The next step is to transition customers from providing data occasionally to providing data continuously. This typically requires an incentive for customers to overcome the perceived risks. In some cases that we studied, product or system warranty was made contingent on data sharing whereas, in other cases, companies provided participating companies with aggregated and anonymized data that allowed them to assess their performance with these industries at large.

8.3.3 Data-Driven Principles

At this stage in the evolution of the company, the company realises that there are classes of questions that can not be answered based on opinion alone. One actually needs data of sufficient breadth and depth and systematic analysis of this data to provide answers to these questions. Although it already was mentioned several times before in this section, the starting point almost always is concerned with quality issues in the field. Until the company has reliable, quantitative data available to inform decision making around prioritization of quality issues, resolution of these and evidence that quality issues have been resolved, the discussion between the company and its customers will remain one riddled with opinions and accusations.

As the amount of available data increases, the tendency to involve a data analytics team for other purposes than purely resolving quality issues will increase. Management teams will start to request specific analyses to be conducted in order to inform their decision making. There will be cases where teams want certain types of analysis to be conducted periodically. At that point, the data analytics team will start to look into conducting these repetitive types of analysis in more efficient ways, often resulting in looking into automation of the report generation. That will then lead to the first steps towards the next step in the data dimension of the Stairway to Heaven, automation.

8.3.4   Implications

Although there are several implications from reaching the collection level, the primary one is that the first steps towards data-driven and evidence-based development have been made. This affects the company culture that, up to now, has been very opinion driven. Whenever an opinion meets data proving the opposite meet, obviously the opinion loses. In practice, things are often not that easy as there will be different interpretations as to what the data actually mean, how generic the data are as well as many other attempts at critically reviewing the data or, alternatively, attempts at discrediting the data-driven approach in general. However, with the automated collection of data in place and the benefits of meeting customers with analyzed data instead of opinions, the culture of the organization will start to change for the better.

A second implication is that the organization will start to experience the complexity of data and the importance of careful analysis to simplify and focus the data reporting in order to have clear, unambiguous answers. This often starts with those concerned with customer support for quality issues, where receiving log files from customers often initially creates more questions than answers. The data frequently needs to be complemented with configuration data and other contextual data before relevant analysis of the data can be performed. As H.L. Mencken quipped years ago: "For every complex problem there is an answer that is clear, simple, and wrong". Starting from resolving quality issues, the company starts on a learning curve where it understands that moving towards true evidence-based development requires appreciating and addressing the complexity of data.

8.3.5   Remaining Concerns

The primary remaining concern is that due to the need to manually analyze data by use of a data analytics team, the organization will still use data only in exceptional situations and the majority of decision making is still driven by opinions. As the company evolves to higher levels in the data dimension, this concern will resolve itself, but when the company is at this stage, it still is mostly opinion-based, except for areas related to quality issues.

A second concern is that the data analytics team has to perform its work in a relatively reactive and manual fashion, responding to the requests by different members of the organization. As these teams tend to be small and limited in capacity, we have seen several cases where senior management prioritized their own requests over others in the organization leaving little or no time for more operational teams to work with the data analytics team on their challenges. The next step on the data dimension, automation, however, goes a long way in addressing that concern.

8.3.6 Example

One of the consumer-oriented business units has automatically collected data on customer subscription and churn for years. However, these data have not been used by any teams. The new head of product management, however, decided to bring a team of data analysts together to study the data and to identify potential patterns in customer churn as well as early warning signs for customers that are likely to leave in the near future. The data showed that there are clear behavioral patterns by customers that are leading indicators for leaving. In response to the analysis, the company has put together a set of offers that are presented to customers when their behavioral patterns indicate that it would be wise to do so. These offers and the associated data analytics have reduced the churn by a significant amount and the management team is exceptionally pleased with the outcome.

8.4 AUTOMATION

8.4.1 Definition

When reaching the collection stage, the collection of data is automated but all subsequent steps are manual and reactive. However, once the organization gets a taste of the insights that can be derived from proper data analysis, the frequency of use will go up in two ways. First, there will be more requests around a wide variety of topics concerning the business the company is in and the behavior of customers as well the performance of its products and systems in the field. The second increase in frequency is concerned with repeated, periodic requests from management and R&D teams across the organization. Especially the periodic requests are suitable for automation. Automation, in this case, means that the collection, the analysis and the visualization of data is automated. The consequence, typically, is some form of dashboard where the analyzed data are presented in easily digestible form and can be used as the basis for decision making.

The advantage of dashboards of this kind is twofold. The first, obvious advantage is that the data analytics team is freed up and can focus its time and energy on more challenging tasks. The second advantage is that the frequency of reporting, as well as the data chain leading up to the dashboard, tends to go up significantly. For instance, rather than getting monthly reports on system performance or user behavior, the dashboard may present daily or even hourly data, allowing decision making to be conducted in real time to an extent that was impossible before automation.

8.4.2   Drivers for Adoption

The drivers for adoption of the automation stage are similar to all cases where automation is implemented: to reduce human effort and to increase the efficiency of work. The adoption of dashboards allows the data analytics team to focus on unique tasks that require human attention, rather than repetitive tasks, as well as the automation of tasks that used to be done manually. As the company climbs the data dimension of the Stairway to Heaven, it becomes more data driven, putting significant strain on the data analytics team. Hence, solutions for automating data analysis and reporting are of significant importance.

The second driver is the improvement in quality of decision making due to the faster feedback loop. In chapter 4, we discussed the speed dimension of the Stairway to Heaven and the importance of shortening the feedback loop. When automating collection, analysis and reporting, the length of the feedback loop can be shortened from the typical quarterly or monthly to daily or even hourly. There is no need to shorten the length of the feedback loop to infinitesimal. Instead, the feedback loop should have the same length as the real-world process that it probes. For system operations for products in the field, this may be near real-time, but for other metrics, e.g. robustness or B2B sales, a feedback loop length of weeks may be perfectly adequate. The important part, however, is that management and R&D teams have access to high quality and current data for decision making and this, in virtually all cases, results in better quality of decision making. The quality improvement is driven by the ability to more rapidly see the impact of decisions and to learn from the (often unintended) effects of decision making.

The final driver that we discuss in this section is the observation that when data collection, analysis and reporting become automated, it often creates a desire for more data, alternative perspectives and different types of analysis. Of course, it is quite easy to create an overload of data that will drown out any benefits and, at that point, focusing on the most important analyses is critical. However, initially, due to the initial lack of data, more is better as it provides insights into the behavior of deployed products and systems as well as that of their users.

8.4.3 Data-Driven Principles

The key principle at this stage in the data dimension is the automation of data analysis and reporting and, consequently, the order-of-magnitude increase in the frequency and availability of processed data and the insights and knowledge originating from this data. This increased availability allows for significantly increased quality of decision making, allowing management and R&D teams to reduce the frequency of opinion-based decision making as compared to earlier stages.

8.4.4 Implications

Access to data in a democratized fashion, i.e. without the help of the data analytics team, allows increasing the efficiency of R&D investments as we can start to build new functionality in an iterative fashion and to measure during development if the intended benefits indeed are realized. As there is quite a bit of evidence that a major part of R&D efforts does not result in value delivered to the customers, finding better techniques to focus R&D on those activities that add the most value is critical.

8.4.5 Remaining Concerns

The main concern that remains is that at this level, dashboards tend to be static and, once in place, change infrequently. As the old saying goes "you get what you measure ", there is a risk that as the market and the product evolve, other things than those that are measured become important. However, without a strong incentive to constantly improve and optimize the dashboard, teams may end up in a situation where they start to optimize for the dashboard rather than for the actual customer base and market. Similar to the drunk man searching under the street light for his car keys because it is so dark in the area where he actually lost them, teams can focus too much on the things that are easy to measure, but not necessarily important. Hence, we need an approach where we have a constant exploration and evaluation activity ongoing to ensure the evolution and continued relevance of dashboards. The next level is concerned with this.

8.4.6 Example

The professional services organization of Viganbe has developed a dashboard that tracks revenue, margins, customer satisfaction, project throughput and several other metrics. The organization has used project throughput as a key metric for productivity as earlier data showed that customers appreciate the company delivering value at a constant, high rate. More recently, however, there are signals that customer satisfaction is dropping despite the fact that the organization is delivering record level project throughput. One of the product managers decided that this was a sufficient reason to interview several customers to identify the cause of the decreasing customer satisfaction. The interviews provided qualitative input showing that customers have become more concerned with agility and reduced time from project start to finish than with the overall throughput. Currently, a customer request may take several quarters to be realized where customers want to have a solution in a month or something. In response, the organization developed a new metric that measures agility and uses that next to the throughput metric.

8.5 DATA INNOVATION

8.5.1 Definition

The key driver for the previous level, automation, is to remove the human from the loop in the reporting on key drivers in the business. However, this brings with it the risk of "getting stuck" in a particular worldview, through the data, that after a while may no longer be representative of the actual customer and market reality. This can easily result in management and R&D teams optimizing the business for a set of metrics that do not actually deliver optimal value for customers because the market has moved on. The data innovation level is concerned with institutionalizing a constant process of discovery of new market and customer insights that management and R&D teams can use to make decisions that are in line with the market.

At this level, there are activities at least at three levels. The starting point is a constant formulation of ideas, hypotheses and concepts to test on the available data. This backlog is added to by the R&D and management teams as well as the data analytics team, but the items on the backlog are evaluated by the data analytics team. If relevant insights are uncovered, these are presented to the relevant team and prioritized against the current set of metrics that are on the dashboard. Based on this analysis, the team can decide to add the new insights to the dashboard, replace an existing metric on the dashboard or decide that it should not be included because there is too little additional value offered in the new metric.

The third activity is concerned with seeking ways to automate the actions derived from the data analytics activities and from the dashboards in such a way that the deployed systems can start to make data-driven adjustments to their behavior automatically, without the involvement of the R&D teams. For instance, when it's clear that certain customer behavior is likely to lead to negative outcomes, e.g. decreased usage or abandonment of the system, the system can automatically trigger actions to drive customer engagement to an improved level. Similarly, system behavior or other metrics that have statistically been proven to indicate future problems with the system can be used to automatically initiate actions that will avoid the negative outcomes, ranging from automated defragmentation of disk memory or transferring the software to other servers to preventive maintenance of the hardware and mechanics of the system.

8.5.2 Drivers for Adoption

In an ever faster moving world, the preferences and needs of customers tend to evolve faster as well. Consequently, when R&D and management teams use static dashboards for their decision making, there is a significant risk that there will be shifts in the market that will cause the dashboard to be an inaccurate representation of customer and market preferences and needs. Consequently, there is a need to continuously validate, extend and replace dashboards and other mechanisms that are used for decision making.

In addition, in order to avoid overloading teams with too much information, we can off-load teams by moving the decisions that are becoming standardized to the software of the system itself. So, as the system operates, it can observe customer behavior as well as its own behavior and when certain patterns are detected in these behaviors, it can automatically initiate actions that would otherwise require human involvement.

These activities require a set of activities that we define as the data innovation level of the stairway to heaven model. The intent is that there is constant innovation in the data that are collected and the visualization of that data as well as the human and automated decision making based on the data.

8.5.3 Data-Driven Principles

The main principle driving this level on the data dimension of the stairway to heaven is the continuous evolution of the types of analytics that are done using a process of exploration and evaluation. Whereas at lower levels, just getting a single data analysis done or automating the creation of a dashboard is already considered an accomplishment, at this stage the research is concerned with continuous improvement of the analysis performed on the data.

The second aspect is a continuous questioning of beliefs about customers and the market in the organization. The company needs a culture where everyone can question existing beliefs and seek to reinterpret data in different ways in order to evolve the organizational understanding. This requires testing and retesting of hypotheses and not accepting earlier established outcomes of tests as a given.

8.5.4 Implications

The first implication of achieving this level is cultural. Traditionally, companies define their strategy by setting a certain strategy and agreeing that this is what the organization is about. This starts from a fundamental belief about the business that the company is in and this is the core and starting point for everything else. As the organization adopts constant evolution and testing of hypotheses about the market and its customers, the basic strategy of the company easily comes up for debate. As we want to establish a culture of curiosity and testing, this divergence needs to be allowed for as new insights can only be accomplished by breaking existing beliefs. At the same time, however, we also want the organization to experience a unity of purpose as well as a shared learning across the company where the organization as a whole learns about its purpose and direction. The challenge is to establish the mechanisms where everyone can test a wide variety of different ideas and feels unconstrained while at the same time ensuring that the organization as a whole learns about the outcomes of the experiments and jointly develops interpretation of these results.

A second implication is concerned with the scope and scale of experimentation. As the organization is now focusing on constant exploration and questioning, it also realizes that the number of things that can be tested and the number of experiments that can be conducted is, for all practical purposes, infinite. Thus, the organization needs to develop a model or framework for deciding what areas are relevant for testing and which ones are less relevant and lead to less progress. In this context, an important aspect is to focus on what constitutes success. Assuming that the organization is a for-profit enterprise, the experiments that lead to growth should be considered to be the most relevant. However, this can easily lead to smaller and smaller experiments focusing on narrow aspects of the existing business. Instead, experiments are required that are more broad and allow for reinterpretation of the business that the company is in.

8.5.5 Remaining Concerns

At this level of data innovation, the data-driven approach in the company is predominantly focused on what is relevant for R&D teams as well as product management teams. Many other aspects of the business are still operating under traditional opinion-based and hierarchy-driven principles. This will lead to a cultural divide in the organization where some aspects are considered clearly subject to data-driven decision making, other aspects of the business are clearly considered to be impossible to make data-driven decisions around and then there is a gray zone where we focus on a balance of where different parts of the organization take different approaches.

A second concern is that there is a human tendency to only focus on what is easy to measure. Once something is easy to measure, it tends to increase in prominence, largely independent on its inherent value. Similarly, things that are harder to measure tend to be removed or diminished in decision making because these require more interpretation and different people will easily reach different conclusions. The natural tendency to focus on what is easy to measure needs active countermeasures and the organization requires to be challenged on seeking solutions to measuring the hard to measure aspects of the business.

8.5.6 Example

One of the business units in Viganbe serves governments or semi-government institutions in different countries. The types of contracts are large and cover many years, both in terms of product delivery and product operations. As a consequence, the sales process is more driven by politics than the technical capabilities of the product. This has led to an interesting dichotomy in the organization where the R&D and product operations departments are data driven, but the sales and marketing organization is completely opinion and anecdote based. After losing a few bids that the sales organization felt very confident about, the management has decided to develop a more quantitative model for the sales funnel, using historical data, to better model the likely outcome of sales efforts. The company is starting to use the data to take proactive steps in its sales and pre-sales engineering to change course when data indicate that the current sales efforts may likely fail. Although the initial results show great progress, the organization has partnered with the data analytics team to constantly evolve the model, based on data, and to avoid falling in the "static dashboard" trap.

8.6 EVIDENCE-BASED COMPANY

8.6.1 Definition

The final level of the data dimension of the Stairway to Heaven model is the evidence-based company. At this level, not only decisions related to the products of the company are driven by data. Instead, all decision making in the company is driven by the available evidence and data and the culture in the organization resists opinion- or rhetoric-based decision making and instead demands data before any decision is taken. In addition, the organization tends to exhibit an experimentation mindset where any concept or idea is first tested in a small scale before iteratively applying it in larger and larger contexts when the data support the further roll-out of the ideas.

The evidence-based company often exhibits an interesting balance between the traditional hierarchical organization and an egalitarian, evidence-based organization. In principle everyone can initiate the collection of data to learn more about any aspect of the company, including its customers, employees, products, processes and related aspects. In addition, experiments to test the relationship between variables can typically be initiated very easily and with minimal management approval. Although the company, of course, has a history of data collection and experimentation around its products, now all functions tend to adopt the same mindset and technology. A good example is the human resources function which traditionally has been a function more driven by opinions and belief than by data. Driven by the need to convince managers that demand data, also the HR function will adopt quantitative approaches to address employee-related questions. These may range from peer-evaluation and ranking to ways of quantifying performance in general, which then allows for analysis beyond what is possible in traditional organization.

While the data collection and experimentation is very much driven by an egalitarian culture, decisions that affect the company at large are still taken by a hierarchy of management teams. Even in evidence-based companies, there seems to be need for hierarchy and managers to ensure effective decision making.

The second main aspect of this level is that decision making is automated. Whereas decision making earlier was predominantly driven by product management and R&D teams, during this phase decision making is automated and implemented in the systems themselves. Consequently, systems not only collect data, but also analyze the data and adjust their behavior based on the analyzed data. Initially, this is performed by automating decision making earlier performed by product management and R&D teams. Later on, systems can be extended with functionality that allows for automated experimentation by the system itself. Thus, within boundaries, the system will experiment with different responses to the same stimuli and measure the outcome. Based on the outcomes, it can learn which responses are more suitable and consequently improve its behaviour without human intervention.

8.6.2 Drivers for Adoption

The primary driver for adoption is the diffusion of data-driven or evidence-based practices from the R&D and product management teams to the rest of the organization. Once used to making decisions based on analysed data and using experiments to uncover relationships between variables, one will automatically resort to demanding similar things for functions outside R&D. Functions such as human resources, the legal department, hiring, finance, purchasing as well as any other function outside R&D are affected by the data-driven mindset. This then leads to a very different approach in these functions as compared to traditional organizations.

A second driver is the basic engineering mindset that tends to permeate software-intensive technology companies. As engineering in general is very much an evidence-driven discipline and engineers are specifically prone to asking why questions and insisting on understanding why things are done in certain ways, an evidence-based approach will demand much more respect from engineers than alternative approaches. As technology companies are exceptionally focused on hiring top talent, appealing to the preferences of engineers will improve the standing of the company with potential hires.

8.6.3 Data-Driven Principles

At this highest level of the data dimension, the basic principle is that everything can be measured and should be measured as well as that decision making should always be driven by data. The basic principle is that any decision that is made without proper evidence supporting the selected course of action should be considered as improper and perceived with a high degree of skepticism.

The organization, at all levels and in all functions, continuously searches for novel ways to measure aspects of the business, explores novel ways to collect data as well as reevaluates the existing data-driven decision mechanisms for effectiveness.

8.6.4 Implications

The primary implication is that although the organization is exceptionally data and evidence driven, it is also aware of the dangers of focusing on data. As the saying goes, when you have a hammer, the entire world looks like a nail. So, there is a risk to miss relevant new developments by focusing too much on what is being measured and is easy to measure. This is why a culture of openness towards experimentation and trying things out that go counter any accepted thought models is so important. Even if the vast majority of these ideas will fail, it keeps the organization aware of the limitations of the current view of the business.

8.6.5 Remaining Concerns

As indicated in the previous section, the evidence-based company is driven by data, experimentation and evidence to the largest extent possible. As such, the culture in the company is that of a left-brain individual: highly mathematical and focused on precise, quantitative answers. Although this is a major improvement over traditional opinion-based decision making that often is based on outdated experience, ad hoc encounters and personality traits, there is a risk that the company focuses too much on what can be easily measured rather than on the things that matter. As Albert Einstein allegedly said: *not everything that matters can be measured and not everything that can be measured matters.* The main concern in an organization that is extremely data driven is that it may gravitate to the measurable rather than to what matters for the prolonged success of the business.

8.6.6 Example

One of the consumer-oriented business units in Viganbe uses an online e-commerce site. The unit is extremely mature in using data and runs many A/B experiments continuously on its site. Over recent quarters, these experiments are no longer yielding significant improvements in the conversion rate of the site, the main metric that the unit tracks. However, competitor analysis and the qualified opinion of experts in the company give clear indications that it should be possible to reach significantly higher conversion. A team has been given the task to develop a fundamental redesign of site. After extensive customer research, lab testing and other smaller scale feedback, the team has finalized the redesign. Initial validation, however, shows that the redesign actually has lower conversion than the current site. This leads to extensive discussions in the organization. The main argument in favor of the redesign is that it needs significant A/B testing of all its elements and the expectation is that this will gradually improve conversion beyond the current "maxed out" site. The skeptics find it difficult to understand why the company would replace the current solution with a design that performs worse. After significant discussion, the company decides to move ahead with rolling out the redesign, against the data, and to drive up conversion through expanded experimentation in the new site.

8.7 CONCLUSION

Data in all its forms are playing an increasingly important role in technology companies in general and in the software-intensive industries in particular. The ability to rapidly and continuously make informed, evidence-based decisions is an immensely powerful tool that drives a major competitive advantage for organizations adopting this before their competitors.

The collection of data can concern the behavior of customers using the products, systems and services offered by the company as well as the performance of systems in the field as measured by the relevant quality attributes. The ability to measure data concerning customer behavior and system performance allows the organization to run experiments that measure the impact of changes on this data. These experiments in turn allow the company to uncover relationships between variables that otherwise may have stayed hidden and, alternatively, disprove relationships that many in the company assumed existed but that do not.

Organizations do not just jump towards an evidence-based approach of working, but instead evolve through a number of predictable stages that systematically transition the four main activities, i.e. collection, analysis, reporting and decision making, from manual tasks to automated tasks. These stages have been captured in the data dimension of the Stairway to Heaven model. The data dimension has five levels, ranging from ad-hoc to the evidence-based company and in this chapter we have described each level in more detail. The model provides a practical, operational improvement model for organizations that seek to build their capability to use data to their advantage.

Data-driven decision making is in many ways superior to traditional, opinion-based decision making. However, there are two inherent risks to the approach. The first is that the organization will have a tendency to focus on the things that can be measured and may easily move away from things that matter but that are hard to measure. The second is that with the investment in the collection, analysis, reporting and decision making based on data, the company may have an even harder time to move beyond the current conceptual model of what constitutes success in the market. The approach may lead to a situation where experimentation is used to squeeze the last fragments of improvement out of the existing model rather than jumping towards the next generation of innovation. In some ways, companies may become even more susceptible to Clayton Christensen's innovator's dilemma.

As we have described the basic model of using data to one's advantage, the next chapters are concerned with providing concrete techniques for using data in product R&D. The next chapter introduces the HYPEX model as a technique for feature level experimentation in deployed products. The subsequent chapter presents the QCD model that combines qualitative and quantitative data and presents a tangible approach to systematically transition from pre-development to development and, finally, to post-deployment collection and use of data.

CHAPTER 9

Feature
Experimentation

Millions of software engineers around the world build software according to the specifications provided to them by product management. For many years, this was an entirely fine way of building software. New product development could take years and new software releases for existing products would happen yearly or sometimes even less frequently. And even more important, the amount of competition was limited. Over the last decade, however, there has been a major shift in how software gets built. Very few companies can afford to invest R&D resources over calendar years before getting a return on the investment and consequently the time and resources available for new product development as well as product releases have been shortening and shrinking.

One of the key challenges that companies are becoming increasingly aware of is that the functionality that has been specified as part of the requirements elicitation process is not necessarily the functionality that is of most value to customers. In fact, there is evidence that many features do not provide any value to customers and only clutter the system. One of the well-known studies going back to the early 2000s was performed by the Standish group. As shown in figure 9.1, more than half of the features of a typical software system are hardly ever or never used.

Now, although this may seem like an easy observation to accept and move on, realize what this means: half or more of all software development in the world is wasted effort! Or even worse, it may be negative to the system and its users in that it makes the system more complex to use and hides useful features and makes these harder to use. If it is really true that only 20% of features are actually used and consequently add value, then this means that during a year, a software engineer will develop valuable software during January, February and a bit of March. The rest of the year whatever that person is doing is just plain waste and it would be better that engineering was not doing anything

Usage of Features and Functions in Typical System

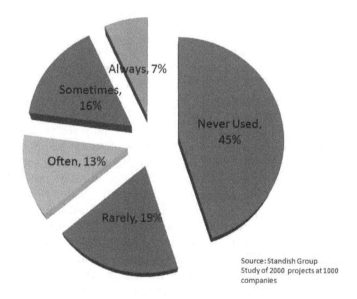

Figure 9.1 Feature usage in a typical IT system

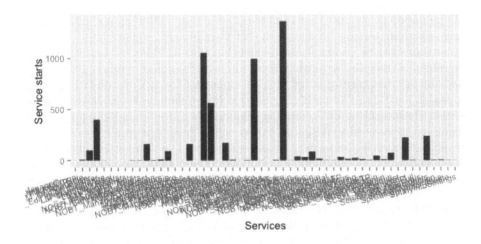

Figure 9.2 Feature usage for an IT system of a large Swedish company

at all. This is an outrageous statement and quite a tragedy for all of software engineering.

In fact, we felt obliged to conduct research of our own to gather more evidence that this is indeed an accurate representation of reality. At a large company in Sweden, we instrumented one of the large IT systems with the number of "service starts". This indicates, for each of the features in the system, the number of times it was started over the period that we studied the system. As we published in [8] and shown in figure 9.2, we see a pattern that is very similar to the findings by the Standish group a decade earlier. A very small number of the features sees frequent or constant use whereas the majority of features is hardly ever, if ever, used by users.

The above findings do not categorically say that any feature that is used infrequently should be removed from the system. For instance, one of the features in the above case study is to add and remove users from the system. Clearly, this is a necessary feature even if it is not used very frequently. However, at the same time, there are many features that are hardly ever used and that are not equally instrumental to the system and that could be removed and simplify the system.

In addition to the presence or absence of a feature, the relative importance of a feature can also be used to decide the amount of investment into the development of a feature. A frequently used feature can be developed more extensively, allowing for more exceptional situations. Also, the usability of important features can be improved by additional development and experimentation. Alternatively, features that can not be removed but are not used frequently can be developed in a rudimentary form and with only the bare bone functionality implemented.

The discussion on feature usage and our difficulty to predict what features will be important to customers and what are not is indicative of a much larger issue: planning feature content of the software in new products or subsequent releases of existing products is notoriously difficult. However, software engineering as a discipline is entirely focused on the notion of requirements being available as the starting point for development efforts. Consequently, a new approach is needed. We need to transition from planning to experimentation. Rather than focusing on improving planning practices such as requirements engineering, we need to adopt an experimental development approach where, using continuous deployment, we can deploy slices of new functionality that be put in the hands of customers. Once in use by customers, we can measure the way customers use the new functionality. Based on the data from customers and the system, we can decide on the next steps in development.

In this chapter, we focus on the more narrow problem of quantitative experimentation with new features during feature development for systems already deployed in the field. The next chapter focuses on the broader problem of collecting customer feedback throughout the end-to-end development process, including pre-development, development and post-deployment stages. However, we start by developing the more narrow concept and use that as a basis for the broader approach in the next chapter.

9.1   THE HYPEX MODEL

The main topic of this chapter is to adopt an experimental, rather than a planned, approach to the development of software features. The context that we assume is that there is a system already deployed in the field or on the web servers of the company developing the software. Also, we assume that continuous deployment has been implemented. This means that the company has reached the highest level on the speed dimension of the stairway to heaven and that it has reached at least the second level on the data dimension, but preferably the third or higher. In this context, the model presented in this chapter can be used.

The name of the HYPEX model ([41] and [40]) is a concatenation of the words "hypothesis" and "experiment". It is specifically intended for feature development using experimentation rather than a planned based approach. The HYPEX model is shown in figure 9.3 and has a number of elements. The first is that we assume that there is a backlog of features available. This backlog is based on the business strategy and goals of the company that has developed the product and deployed it at customers. This business strategy is translated into a strategic goal for the product. This strategic product goal is, finally, translated into a feature backlog. The feature backlog consists of a set of feature descriptions that are prioritized. Hence, it is known which features are more or less important than other features.

The HYPEX process starts with the selection of the highest priority feature in the backlog. Once the feature is selected, the first action is to define

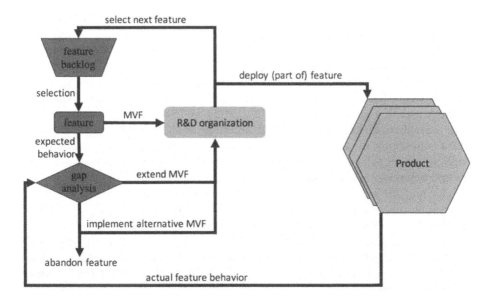

Figure 9.3 The HYPEX model

the expected behavior. This behavior is not concerned with the behavior of the feature itself, but rather with the way in which either the behavior of the system will change when this feature is added or the way in which the customer will behave differently. Of course, it can also be a combination of both. However, the very first step is to explicitly define what the implications of developing the feature will be on the system and its customers. This is so important as the change in system and customer behavior also defines the value of the feature. If the feature, once developed and deployed, would not have any impact on either the system behavior or the customer behaviour, it is clearly a waste of time and effort to develop it in the first place. Also, if the change in behavior is negative or positive, but very small, the feature will not give enough of a return on investment and should not be developed. By explicitly stating what the expected changes in behavior are that will justify the effort for developing the feature, the R&D team has an anchor point for the next steps.

The next step in the HYPEX process is to develop the minimal viable feature (MVF). The MVF is, in the assessment of the R&D team, the 10% to 20% of the feature functionality that will provide the most value to the customer or the company and consequently will affect the actual system and customer behavior the most. The team not only builds the slice of the feature but it also adds, where necessary, instrumentation to the code to allow for the collection of the "telemetry" or data concerning the aspects of the system and customer behavior that were identified as important when defining the expected behavior.

As we assume continuous deployment, after developing the first slice of functionality, the software will be deployed in some or all systems in the field and there will be a stream of data coming from these systems that will allow the R&D team to capture the actual behavior of the system and customers. Of course, both for defining the expected behavior and for the assessment of the impact of the feature under development, it is important to have collected reference data that indicate how the system and its customers operate under normal conditions before the introduction of the feature. Once sufficient data concerning the actual behavior have been collected to draw statistically relevant conclusions, the team can assess the gap between expected and the actual behavior. In addition, it can assess the delta between the reference behavior and the actual behavior and determine if there actually was a change in system and customer behavior that can be attributed to the slice of the feature that was added to the system.

Once the team has analyzed the (inevitable) gap between the expected and the actual behavior, the next step is to develop hypotheses concerning the nature of the gap. Typically, these hypotheses fall into two major categories. The first category is concerned with the amount of functionality associated with the feature that has been built so far. This group of hypotheses assumes that too little of the feature has been built to obtain all the expected behavior and that to close the gap more functionality associated with the feature has to be built. In practice, this means that the team decides on building an additional slice of the feature with the expectation that this will materially reduce the gap. The second category is of the "back to the drawing board" kind. This is where the team, after analyzing the data, concludes that they misinterpreted the way customers would use the feature. In response, the current feature implementation is removed from the system and the team builds an alternative slice with the expectation that this will reduce the gap. Although teams typically iterate through multiple rounds, it may be that already after the first deployment that the effect on the system and customer behavior is non-existent or, in fact, negative. In such a case, the R&D team may decide to abandon the feature and remove it from the system and the backlog.

Once the team has decided on the hypothesis to explore, the iterative process means that some more R&D is performed (feature extension or alternative implementation) and the resulting code is, once again, deployed as part of the continuous deployment cycle. The team can now collect data and once sufficient data have been collected determine if the hypothesis that they selected can be confirmed or is disproven. The intent is that with multiple iterations, the team learns about the system and customer behavior and manages to close the gap between expected and actual behavior to the point that it is sufficiently small to finalize the iterations and declare the feature done. It may, however, also be the case that the gap does not close despite the best efforts of the team. If this is the case after some or several iterations, the team needs to decide on a course of action. The decision basically boils down to shutting down the R&D iterations for the feature, but the key decision is whether to leave the code associated with the feature in the system or to remove it.

Whether to remove a feature or not should in principle be an assessment of the limited value provided to the customers, the system and the company developing the feature versus the cost of having the feature present in the system. For users, for instance, the presence of an unused feature will increase the complexity of using the system so it is important to consider such factors. Furthermore, leaving the feature in the system may affect future feature development in that the limited value of the feature may turn negative because of features added later. In the same vein, leaving the feature will likely complicate the development of other features in the future. Consequently, when in doubt about the removal of a feature, the right answer almost always is to remove it despite the R&D effort expended on the feature.

One of the concerns that is occasionally raised is that the HYPEX development process may seem inefficient in that there is lots of iteration and a significant risk that features are removed after (potentially significant) development effort has been expended on them. It is important to remember in this context that the goal of HYPEX is to maximize the effectiveness of R&D in terms of the value created for a measured unit of R&D effort. Building features that add no value is the worst waste of effort and it is better to build 30% of a feature and then remove it than to build 100% of a useless feature and then leave it in the system. In the former case, I at least have the 70% R&D effort left that I can now dedicate to another feature that hopefully will add value.

The remainder of this section is concerned with providing more detailed descriptions of each of the steps in the HYPEX process. In the next section, we start with the generation and governance of the feature backlog, followed by a discussion of the selection and specification of the feature as well as a section on the definition of the expected behaviour. The subsequent sections discuss the other steps and activities in the HYPEX process.

9.2 GENERATE FEATURE BACKLOG

Most companies have an existing process for defining the content for a release of an existing product or a new product. The traditional process, however, has a notion of "scarceness" associated with it. Everyone knows that there will be limited space in the product or release and, consequently, everyone focuses on the "obvious" features that customers "obviously" want. The challenge with this approach is many creative, innovative ideas never make it to the list of potential features as those involved already self-select away from suggesting them. The second challenge that we observe at companies is that because people inside the company think they already know what customers want and the feature content is already achieved with the things that are made up internally in the company, company staff easily starts to base themselves on outdated customer needs. Over time, a wedge starts to appear between what customers really need and want and the model of customer needs and wants as held within the company. This leads to the formation of shadow-beliefs, i.e. beliefs that virtually everyone in the company holds and beliefs to be true but that in fact are not true in reality. According to research, as facts and beliefs are the same in the human mind, it is incredibly difficult for anyone in the organization to constantly reflect over the beliefs held in the organization and frequently re-validate these.

The most effective way to avoid the aforementioned challenges is to ensure that the selection of release content is driven by data rather than by opinion. The mechanism that we propose in this chapter is to adopt an inclusive, rather than an exclusive, approach to identifying and considering features. Rather than treating the feature backlog as highly selective and only allowing features on it that have been approved by everyone, the approach should be to allow many and varied features to be added to the backlog and to use the HYPEX process as a way to either invest in or abandon features as the data concerning the first slices of feature functionality come back from the systems in the field. This allows for the company to constantly test its beliefs about the customer and the system and to learn whenever a gap between the expected outcomes and the actual outcomes is identified. The important distinction of this approach as compared to more traditional approaches is that the feature backlog contains a list of potential features that are included in the system rather than the definite list of features that will make up the functionality of a new product or the new functionality in the next release of the software for an existing product.

Even though we focus extensively on using data for decision making concerning feature content, the actual identification and generation of new potential features that might add value to customers requires human intellect and creativity. In general, one can identify three main categories of sources for new customer requirements, i.e., customers, business strategy and bottom-up innovation. Below, we discuss each category in more detail.

9.2.1 Customers

Every company needs to focus on the needs of its customers in order to have a viable business. Hence, when customers go through the effort of talking to their supplier to share their needs, wants and ideas for improvement, the company better pay attention. Although not the main topic of this chapter, it is important to realize three main aspects of using customers to identify potential features of new products. First, many companies have difficulty optimally balancing the (sometimes conflicting) requests from different customers. Even if the requests from customers are not conflicting, there still is the fact that it will be impossible to satisfy all the requests from all customers with a R&D organization that has limited resources. Hence, customer requests are always at conflict, either because of functional incompatibility or because of the resource conflict. Thus, there will always be a need to prioritize and sequence requests from customers. The process for accomplishing the relative priority of customer requests is inherently political in most companies, with different product managers eager to please different customers and with some customers having the ear of individuals in the higher level management. Consequently, without a mature process and organizational culture, this easily results in a situation where the customer shouting the loudest and calling the CEO the most often is the one that gets an unreasonable amount of requests implemented in the system. Thus, the company needs to build an approach where it makes sure that customers understand that their requests were heard, that there is a process in place to optimize the overall value of the product for the entire customer base and that their most important requests are handled to the best of the company's ability.

The second aspect that is important to realize as requests originate from customers is that many customers have a tendency to specify a solution, rather than a requirement. As the solution proposed by customers often fails to take into account the overall architecture and need to satisfy multiple customers, these types of solutions should be rejected. Instead, the discussion with the customer should focus on the underlying need that the customer has, rather than the customer perceived solution to that need. This discussion is often complicated by the fact that the system deployed by the company often operates in a much broader context of several other systems. These systems are integrated with the system developed by the company and this integration is often done by the customer's R&D team or by third parties hired by the customer. So, although the company knows its own system and the requirements, it is no expert on the other systems deployed at the customer. Hence, maintaining a clear focus on the need rather the solution is often rather challenging.

Finally, the third aspect that every company needs to be aware of is that new customer needs appear well before customers can express these needs. Although the time gap depends on the domain, it can be substantial and measure in years. During the time period that a customer need exists in a market, but customers are unable to express this need, there is an opportunity for new entrants to disrupt the market. This is especially the case in markets where the main players are customer focused to the extent that the vast majority of new functionality in their products is built in direct response to customer requests. This type of behavior also tends to shift the attention to the most demanding customers in the market, which then easily results in an innovator dilemma à la Clayton Christensen's book, meaning that new entrants serving the least demanding customers at the bottom of the market can gain a foothold from which they can disrupt the main players.

9.2.2 Business Strategy

The second main category of new features originates in the business strategy of the company. Assuming the business strategy can be operationalized (unfortunately not the case at all companies that we work with), the business strategy can and should be translated in a strategy for the product or system as well. The product strategy, being actionable, of course should result in several features that can or should be added to the system. One challenge, similar to customer requested features but even harder to counteract, is that the strategic features are easily expressed in terms of solutions rather than intended outcome or effect. That leads to a situation where the feature just has to be built rather than allowing for experimentation, adjustment and potential abandonment.

The aforementioned challenge is exacerbated by the fact that in many companies the term "strategic investment" is used to justify action that can not be justified by normal means of customer feedback, measurable impact on system performance or other factors. Thus, these strategic investments are treated as leaps of faith that can not be justified by any means until some point in the future, typically undefined. Although we recognize that there are cases where these leaps of faith are unavoidable, the fact remains that treating strategic investments this way remains the worst example of opinion-based decision making. In our experience, in the majority of cases there are ways to collect evidence about the correctness of the assumptions underlying strategic features. These ways, however, are different from the typical data collection in several ways. One of the ways is that one has to focus the data collection on a subset of the customers or system deployments that exhibit some of the characteristics that underlie the strategic feature. For instance, by focusing on young, urbanized, highly educated users, one can often gain insights into behaviors that over time will spread across the rest of the population.

Finally, once a reasonable set of strategic features has been identified and clearly described in terms of intended outcome rather than in terms of solutions, this feature set still needs to be prioritized and sequenced. Different from features requested by customers, strategic features often have inherent dependencies that require the realization of these features to occur in a predefined order as these build on each other. Hence, the process often requires not only product and business management representation but also architects and R&D management to be involved.

9.2.3 Bottom-up Innovation

One source of innovative new features that traditionally has often been ignored is the many ideas that employees of the company have as they work with customers, deployed systems and product development. This source of ideas has traditionally been ignored because of the exclusive nature of the release content management process. As there was way more potential release content than what could be built by the R&D organization, these ideas tended to, at best, be discussed at the water cooler or over lunch breaks, but never actually brought into the process for serious consideration.

The fact, however, remains that frontline people working directly with the customers and deployed systems often have the deepest insight into the actual issues and concerns and consequently are a great source of ideas for innovative features. Of course, these ideas often are very different in nature as compared to the earlier categories and can even be plain disruptive. Consequently, also in this category, some, many or most of the proposed feature ideas may not deliver the value that was expected.

In an R&D environment where any feature that makes it on the feature backlog is automatically and unquestionably built, including feature ideas originating from bottom-up innovation is extremely unlikely because of their (often) atypical nature and the lack of political clout of the frontline staff often proposing the feature ideas. However, if we start to treat the feature backlog as a prioritized collection of potential features, it becomes easier to also include bottom-up innovation in the backlog.

Experience shows that broadening the base used for creating the front end of the feature funnel is very effective in bringing a more diverse and innovative feature portfolio to the market that goes beyond the obvious. In addition to better serving customers, this also builds the innovative brand of the company.

9.2.4 Prioritizing the Feature Backlog

So far, we have discussed three sources of new features, i.e. customers, business strategy and bottom-up innovation. The challenge, of course, is that we can only have a single feature backlog, which means that the features from the different categories need to be combined in a single, prioritized feature backlog. Although we have already discussed prioritization within each category, the process is more complicated in this case as the features tend to be very different in nature and source of origin. Hence, prioritization becomes more of a comparing apples and oranges situation rather than anything else.

Although prioritization of three different categories of features is challenging, it doesn't free us of the obligation to do so anyway, so there are a few basic rules that are important to adhere to. First, although the relative importance of and investment in each category differs for each company, there should be features from all categories in the backlog and reasonably dispersed. Second, some companies that we work with use different techniques to describe the value of features. Although we discuss this in more detail in the next section, it is important to the describe what the expected impact of the feature will be on the system behavior and the customer behavior. This impact forms the basis for the value that the feature represents to the company.

The challenge in feature value modeling is that customer features can easily be described as more valuable than anything else as there are customers asking for these features, so obviously it is relevant for them. Here it is important to keep in mind that a feature that satisfies the needs of one customer is not necessarily terribly valuable. It for sure is less valuable than a feature that delivers value for all customers of the product.

Concluding, the fact remains that there is a significant amount of opinion-based and subjective prioritization of features. However, by explicitly modeling the feature value, the advantage is that when, in later stages, a slice of the feature is deployed and the intended value is not realized, it immediately allows the organization to investigate and potentially abandon the feature. It is important to note that in cases where the value provided by a feature is focused on improving system quality, e.g. performance, throughput or reliability, the expected behavior is concerned with the product itself and needs to be defined in those terms. This requires the team to associate a business value with the improvement of specific quality attributes of the system.

Finally, some companies, when starting with this approach, handle most features in the traditional model and apply the HYPEX principles only to some highly selected features. One question that often comes up is how to select a relevant feature to start out with. In our experience with various companies, the most relevant features to start experimenting with often have one of three characteristics:

> **Large gap**: One category is selecting a feature that already is implemented in the system but where there exists an uncharacteristically large gap between what was informally expected in terms of system or customer behavior and what actually happened in reality. This gap will confound the R&D team and this will provide a rich source of hypotheses concerning the explanations of the gap and proposals of what to do about it.

> **New domain**: Especially for strategic features, but also in other categories a second class of features suitable for experimentation is where the R&D team is asked to develop new functionality in an area where there is little previous experience. As the team finds it hard to predict the impact this new functionality will have on customers and deployed systems, adopting a more experimental approach may be very helpful to rapidly learn more about the new domain.

> **Multiple alternatives**: Finally, even in areas where the R&D team routinely develops new functionality, there will be requests for new features where multiple alternatives towards realizing the feature exist and where the team has no good mechanisms to compare the implementations relative to each other. One approach can be to adopt an experimental approach and try out skeleton implementations of the most promising alternatives and to use the outcomes to learn about the strengths and weaknesses of each alternative.

9.3   DEFINE EXPECTED BEHAVIOR

Once the organization has established a prioritized feature backlog, the process of selecting a feature is trivial: just pick the highest priority feature. In the HYPEX model, the next step is to define the expected change in behavior in the systems deployed in the field or in the behavior of the customers. If the feature is considered to be important, there should, of course, be a change in the behavior of either system or customer as there is no reason to build the feature in the first place.

It is important to connect the change in behavior, which is often expressed in operational and relatively easy to measure parameters, to the realized business value. This may require a model describing how the delta in the parameters leads to business value for the company or its customers. In our experience with the companies that we collaborated with around these questions, actually making the expected change in behavior explicit and relating it to business value is not often done. Especially when starting with this activity, it tends to lead to serious discussions where even product managers and others supporting a feature may still have very different expectations about the expected change in behavior and the associated business value.

Defining a value definition for a feature can, fundamentally, be conducted in one of two fashions. The first is to relate the feature to an overall value definition for the product or system. This value definition is then used to illustrate how the feature will, or is intended to, improve the overall value definition by some measurable amount. In the case where the number of stakeholders is very high and there is no clear overall value definition, a feature-specific value definition can be defined. The latter is, of course, easier for most systems, but has as a disadvantage that improvements provided by one feature can be negated by other new features being added to the system. Hence, the bottom-up approach requires some level of governance to make sure that the sum of the parts indeed increases as each individual feature drives its own value definition.

There are numerous aspects to measure about a deployed software system and its users and it is not feasible to provide a comprehensive overview. Instead, we discuss a number of examples of parameters that are often used to describe expected behavior. This list is by no means complete, but rather gives an indication of the ways companies reason about expected behavior:

Frequency of use: A first metric, in surprisingly little use in industry, is the frequency of use of customer-facing features. As we indicated at the start of this chapter, there is significant evidence that a significant percentage of features present in a system are never or hardly ever used. Hence, a metric that tracks the frequency of use for a feature is a powerful starting point. An expected behavior definition can be concerned with the frequency of use for a newly deployed feature. Thus, how often is the feature assumed to be used by customers?

Relative frequency of use: A second metric is more concerned with the use frequency for a feature as compared to other features of a system. As feature use, in most systems, follows a power function, many features are not providing the necessary business value. However, when a system has many users, the number of uses of an individual feature may still be high. However, it still may represent a small fraction of all the feature uses and this information gives an insight into the relative importance of a feature versus others. An alternative use for this metric is for the situation where an old and a new version of a feature are compared. One question could be to determine the frequency of use for people that are presented with the old version of the feature versus the frequency of use for people that are presented with the new version. This provides valuable information on the relative improvement provided by a new implementation of a feature.

Improved conversion rate: One of the metrics that fits on the system level is the conversion rate. Especially web and mobile commerce sites use this metric. The metric measures the percentage of users that complete a value generating transaction out of the total number of users. For an e-commerce site, this is concerned with the number of people that visit the website versus the number of people that actually buy something. Driving up the conversion rate is a surefire way to increase revenue.

Time for task execution: Especially for online tasks that require interaction with humans, a metric used to measure efficiency is the time required by the user to complete a task. Similar to the frequency of use, the metric can be used to compare different tasks implemented in the system or to compare old and new implementations of the same task. This metric is predominantly focused on business and administrative systems where the goal is to achieve efficiency. Shorter task execution will lead to higher efficiency for users.

Automation of a task: In systems where certain tasks are partially or completely automated, one metric to consider is the frequency with which customers make changes to the default process. As, especially in partially automated tasks, the user still is the final responsible one, he or she will make changes to the automated tasks if the outcomes are not in line with expectations. The less frequently the user adjusts the (partially) automated tasks, the better the automation level of a task is.

Improved system characteristics: The final category of parameters to measure is concerned with the non-functional aspects of the system, such as response time, throughput, mean time between failures, memory usage, etc. Some of these parameters are directly concerned with user experience, such as responsiveness, while others are predominantly concerned with driving down the cost of owning and operating the system, such as memory and bandwidth usage. Many of these parameters are used to measure the impact of features added to the system, but also to maintain an overall baseline of system behavior. In the latter capacity, worrying trends in some of the system parameters can be identified early and corrective actions can be proposed and implemented in the system.

9.4 IMPLEMENTATION AND INSTRUMENTATION OF CODE

Once the feature has been selected and the expected behavior defined, we enter the next step in HYPEX model: realizing the feature. At this point, we need to introduce the concept of the minimal viable feature (MVF). Traditionally, especially academia but also product management tends to treat features as atomic entities. This means that a feature is either part of the system or it is not. In industrial practice, however, it easily shows that the situation is far from that simple. Features can be partially implemented by supporting only certain stakeholders, implementing a limited set of use cases that are part of the feature, such as excluding exceptional situations, providing minimal user interface support as well as several other approaches. The fact that features are not atomic, but actually consist of some or several parts that can be implemented independently, provides us with a great opportunity to build the feature in a sequential manner. The advantage of this is, obviously, that the R&D effort required to build the feature can also be allocated in a sequential fashion, rather than being allocated in coarse-grained chunks.

The rationale behind the MVF is that employing a continuous feedback loop during development allows for adjustment of the feature implementation during the development process. This allows the R&D team to adjust the implementation based on the measures that come back from the field. It may also result in the feature being abandoned as the expected effects are not realized or, vice versa, the R&D team may decide to double down on it and expand the feature implementation as it delivers even more value than expected.

The process of building the MVF starts with product management and the R&D team jointly agreeing on the part of the feature that is likely to deliver the most value. This can be a quite difficult endeavor as a feature is intended as a logical unit and the different parts will be connected. In addition, members of the team may have very different ideas about what will bring the most value to the system or the user. Finally, the challenge often is to find a way to scale the feature down to a sufficiently small part, ideally 10-20% of the overall feature functionality. If the slice becomes too thick, the benefits of the model are diminished for two reasons. First, the R&D effort is still spent in large chunks and the feedback will not improve the accuracy of the development process. Second, when too much of the feature is built in one iteration, it is harder to interpret the data collected from the system in the field. When multiple aspects of the feature are built, it becomes difficult to determine which parts are causing the effects observed in the data.

In addition to building the code for the MVF, the system also needs to be instrumented in such a way that the metrics underlying the expected behavior can be collected. Although over time the system will collect most of the relevant metrics already, especially when adopting the HYPEX approach, many features will require additional instrumentation for data collection as well.

The technicalities of the instrumentation of code are often not very complicated as it's basically inserting small snippets of code that send off a small packet of data recording the event. At the same time, the analysis of the data and the ability to draw statistically relevant conclusions can be much more challenging. For instance, when measuring whether a system improved its performance, one has to take into account the normal variation in system performance due to different context and circumstances. This requires the data relevant for the feature to be collected well before the actual deployment of the feature in order to establish the normal variation of performance as well as for establishing patterns that follow daily, weekly or monthly cycles. Once a baseline is established, the feature can be deployed and the effect measured.

Even if an effect of a feature deployment is identified, it may still require further analysis as one-off external events may disrupt the data. For instance, while working with one case company, we experienced a significant delta in the data after deployment of a feature. Later analysis, however, unveiled that the world championship in football was causing the effect, rather than the feature itself. In addition, assuming that multiple R&D teams are working on adding different features to the system, the consequence is that any effects in the data can be caused by features deployed by other teams rather than by the R&D team itself. All these challenges require a careful and vigilant approach to the data collected and its analysis. Although this may seem obvious in theory, it is quite challenging for teams as experience shows that many features do not really cause any effect and consequently are actually not adding value to the system. Also, as the size of the effect may need to be significant to overcome the statistical noise, it can be quite frustrating for teams. Of course, one can wonder whether features that barely make it out of the statistical noise should be added to the system, but for many organizations, especially initially, it will lead to significant discussion in and between teams.

In the previous section, we presented a number of typical measures that are used in systems. Rather than repeating those, it is important to point out the time dimension of data collection. We already discussed statistical relevance of data and this often requires a sizable amount of data. Especially for systems with relatively few users or deployments, this may require that significant amounts of calendar time are required before conclusions can be drawn. This may complicate the use of data-driven techniques such as HYPEX outside the realm of Web 2.0 applications with millions of users. However, our experience shows that it is quite feasible to deploy these techniques in a wide variety of industries while delivering on the earlier discussed benefits.

9.5 GAP ANALYSIS

Once the MVF is deployed and statistically relevant data have been collected and analyzed, it is time to compare the actual behavior with the expected behavior to determine if the current implementation is sufficient to achieve the expected behavior. Although there might be cases where already the first MVF delivers the expected outcomes, in most situations there will be a gap.

The analysis needs to consider four different categories in order to fully cover all effects of the deployed MVF:

Expected positive effects: The feature was selected for development because there was a positive effect that the company was looking to achieve. So, the first action in the analysis is to determine to what extent the positive effects that were expected are actually realized. Without these benefits, obviously there is no need to develop the feature or even keep it present in the system.

Expected negative effects: Although perhaps surprising, most features will be positive for some metrics, but have negative effects on others. As maintaining properties of a system is a balancing act, it is acceptable, though not desired, for features to also negatively affect some properties. As part of the modeling of the expected behavior of the system or its users, the expected negative effects on the system are captured and incorporated in the overall assessment of the value of the feature.

Unexpected positive effects: In addition to the expected effects, one has to realize that there are likely effects that were not anticipated when modeling the expected behavior. It is important to explicitly investigate unexpected effects as these will influence the actual value of the feature. These effects are, obviously, unrelated to the actual metrics modeling the expected behavior, but have implications on other parts of the system. The unexpected positive effects will affect the value model for the feature and make it more relevant to keep in the system and may even cause increased investment.

Unexpected negative effects: Finally, there often also are unexpected negative effects associated with introducing a feature. An obvious example is performance which is, with additional functionality added to the system, almost always affected negatively. Similar to unexpected positive effects, negative effects also affect the value function of the feature and may cause the feature to be canceled in its entirety if the unexpected effects cause the value function to go negative.

The gap analysis will have one of three potential outcomes, i.e. the team can decide to conclude to declare the feature finished, the team can decide that the feature will be abandoned or the decision is to take the feature through another iteration of the HYPEX model. The main driver for this decision making process is twofold. First is the size of the gap between the expected and actual behavior. Second is the impact of the unexpected effects.

If there is a small gap between expected and actual behavior and there are no or minimal unexpected effects, the likely decision is to conclude development of the feature. It is important to realize that this decision can be reached well before the feature has been built in its entirety. In traditional development approaches, the whole feature, in all its aspects, is developed top to bottom. However, when using the HYPEX model, development ends when the expected value is reached. If it turns out that the value is delivered after having built 20% or 60% of the feature and the expected upside of building more is low, the R&D resources can be used more profitably on other features.

At the other extreme, it may turn out that none or very little of the expected behavior is realized. In addition or alternatively, there may be significant unexpected negative effects and few positive ones. In this case, the feature should be abandoned. This decision can be reached even if the actual behavior is approximating the expected behavior. We have experienced cases where the actual behavior did come close to what was expected, but there were such negative implications that were unexpected that the feature was dropped.

The final outcome is where the team decides that another iteration of the HYPEX loop is required. Often this is decided where there is a significant, but not dramatic, gap between the actual and expected behavior. This gap can surface in two ways. First, the MVF does result in a measurable deviation from the baseline, but there still is a significant gap between actual and expected behavior. Second, it may be that even the first slice of the feature already gives major positive benefits exceeding even the expected behavior. In this case, the team may realize that they have hit gold and rather than stopping development as the expected behavior is reached, the decision is to continue investing in the feature in order to maximize the delivered value. As the latter situations are relatively rare, we focus on the first type of gap. Finally, there is one more case to consider: the MVF may not have any noticeable effect on the system or its users after having been deployed but the company considers the functionality of strategic importance. Rather than abandoning the feature, the team may then decide to continue to iterate and learn more to explain the lack of effect.

9.6 DEVELOP AND TEST HYPOTHESES

When the decision is to run another iteration of the HYPEX loop, the first discussion that needs to be had is around the explanation of the gap between expected and actual behavior. Why does it exist in the first place? Although there will be a tendency to fall back into the traditional, opinion-based approach and to agree on the most likely explanation, it is important to treat any explanation of the gap as a hypothesis, rather than as a fact. Rather than seeking consensus on the most likely explanation, it is important to generate multiple hypotheses that might explain the gap. Once the team has exhausted the set of hypotheses that it can come up with, the next step is to assess each hypothesis and rank it on a priority list ranging from most likely to least likely. Once the hypotheses have been prioritized, the team selects the most promising one to experiment with.

In general, there are two main categories of hypotheses. The first category is concerned with the extent to which the feature has been implemented. Often, members of the team will consider the part of the feature implemented to be insufficient for the system or the user to experience the expected behaviour. When a hypothesis of this category is considered to be the most promising, the decision typically is to extend the MVF implementation with an additional slice of functionality. The second category of hypotheses focuses on the lack of understanding by the team of the user or the system. These hypotheses focus on the way the feature is realised and expect that an alternative implementation of the same feature will yield a different outcome. When a hypothesis of this category is considered to be the most promising, the existing MVF will be removed from the system and alternative MVF will be developed and deployed.

Especially in the case when there are major unexpected effects, the team will focus on other hypotheses and typically learn quite a bit about the relations between different parts of the system and the impact of new functionality on the behaviour of the system and its users. These cases, however, require a reformulation of the expected behaviour to include the unexpected positive and negative effects. This improved formulation of expected behaviour may then give rise to additional hypotheses outside the original scope of the feature.

Independent of the selected hypothesis, it is important to measure the effect of the action taken. A technique often used in this context is A/B or split testing. This type of testing can be performed either sequentially or in parallel. In the sequential version, the original implementation is considered to be the A version. The team then implements the additional slice of the feature or the alternative implementation and considers this to be the B version. After development, the B version is deployed, replacing the A version. The data collected while version A was deployed are now used as a baseline and the data collected after deploying version B are used to determine if the hypothesis was supported or not. In the cases of parallel A/B testing, both the A and the B alternatives are present in the system and for each feature instantiation, for each user or for each system a version is randomly selected and used. In this case, the data concerning version A and B are collected simultaneously which avoids some of validity challenges associated with sequential A/B testing.

Once the data have been collected and the selected hypothesis either supported or falsified, the team is back at the gap analysis stage. However, it now has more information and knowledge available and can use this to make a more informed decision.

9.7 ITERATION

As described, the HYPEX model is concerned with iteratively generating and testing hypotheses with the intent of closing the gap between expected and actual behavior, reducing the initially unintended negative effects and, where possible, maximizing the unintended positive effects. The focus has to remain on the value that a feature brings to the system, its users and the company so it is important to keep the focus on that, rather than on specific metrics of the system. As the HYPEX model emphasizes the generation of multiple hypotheses and subsequent prioritization and selection of these, continuous iteration between hypotheses and analysis is important.

Finally, although this book is not about data analytics and specific techniques for that, it is important to realise that achieving and maintaining quality of the data is quite challenging and that there are many complications that teams will experience when employing evidence-based development. Also, achieving measurable effects of feature implementations that exceed the random noise in a statistical analysis is surprisingly difficult.

The aforementioned, however, reinforces the importance of the model. If an R&D team is building a feature that has no measurable effect on the system performance of the user behaviour, should the team be spending its time on that? Or could it be that other R&D activities would potentially lead to a higher return on investment? The answer is obviously that the team should focus elsewhere.

The HYPEX model allows for a major improvement in the effectiveness of R&D by faster feedback loops and data-driven, rather than opinion-based, decision making. As we shared in the introduction, there is ample room for improvement as we consider that more than half of all the features in a typical system are never or hardly ever used and consequently are a complete waste of R&D effort.

9.8 EXAMPLE

To illustrate the concepts introduced in this chapter, we provide a simple example using a driving assistance function in a car. The driving assistance uses route planning to help the driver reach the desired destination. As the driver is driving, the system provides visual instructions concerning the route to follow. The company has instrumented the system to record the number of times the user deviates from the indicated route. This metric is used as an indicator of the number of times a driver takes the wrong action. One important success metric for the system is to have as few wrong actions taken by drivers as possible.

Based on customer feedback, the company has decided to implement a new feature to provide verbal instructions in addition to the visual interface. The verbal instructions feature has been prioritized and an R&D team has been assigned. The first step that the team took was to find the first slice to build and it settled on initially just providing a gong sound when an action was to be taken. During repeated iterations, the feature evolved to verbal support where the system tells the driver when to take action.

The success metric has been steadily improving but recently has plateaued and different efforts by the team have not resulted in measurable improvements. Analysis of the data as well as interviews with users have resulted in a hypothesis about the time period between the verbal instruction and the moment the driver has to take the action.

The R&D team does not have reliable data to know how long before the driver is supposed to take action the verbal instruction should be given. Especially during city driving, but also on complicated highway intersections, providing verbal instructions at the wrong time may lead to drivers taking the wrong action. This has led to significant discussion in the team and it was decided to run an experiment in the field.

The value function is defined as the percentage of successfully followed verbal instructions. The range for the time between verbal instruction and driver action is set between 2 and 30 seconds with a random selection of the time for each verbal instruction that is given. The system already has functionality to determine that the driver has deviated from the intended route. The team has set up a centralized server to collect the data from all the systems in the field and every time a verbal instruction is given, a data packet with the selected time period and the success or failure of the driver action is sent to the server.

When initially deploying the new version of the system software with the experiment embedded, it turns out that the data show two peaks in the value function, around 5 seconds and around 20 seconds, but the failure rate stays too high. The R&D team decides to bring the feature back to the R&D loop for further development. Careful analysis of the contextual data shows that the team has missed an important variable: the system should distinguish between city driving and highway driving as the 5-second interval leads to a high success rate in city driving whereas for highway driving the 20-second interval works better. Based on this insight, the R&D team extends the feature with functionality to determine city versus highway driving and decides to run a new experiment: in the case of city driving, the time interval is set between 1 and 10 seconds and for highway driving, it is set between 15 and 30 seconds.

The new software is deployed and the experiment shows that the optimal times is 6 seconds for city driving and 23 seconds for highway driving. The metric data show that the percentage of driving errors now is very low and the team decides the feature is done. The time intervals are hard-coded in the system and the final feature implementation is pushed to all systems in the field.

9.9   CONCLUSION

Traditional development approaches tend to treat requirements for new functionality of the system under development as given and will implement all functionality as specified. For feature development, this means that features are treated as atomic entities that will be implemented as specified with all aspects, use cases, exceptional states, etc.

At the same time, our research as well as that of others have found that for a typical system, more than half of all the features are never or hardly ever used. This means that, potentially, more than half of all the R&D effort invested in a system is wasted as it does not deliver any value to a customer or the company building the system.

In response to the aforementioned challenge, we introduced the HYPEX model in this chapter. HYPEX is a concatenation of the words "hypothesis" and "experiment". It is a process model that uses short feedback loops between systems deployed in the field and the R&D team to develop features in an iterative manner where the feature is broken down in a number of prioritized slices of functionality that can be realised sequentially. For each slice, the team predicts a certain value delivered to the system, the user or the company building the system and the data collected from the deployed system allow for validation or falsification of the hypothesized value.

The HYPEX process model allows to significantly improve the effectiveness of R&D in that it builds features only to the extent that value is realised. The model also supports the abandonment of features that do not deliver the expected value. Finally, it allows for significant investment in features that deliver unexpected positive effects.

The HYPEX model only focuses on adding features to existing systems already deployed in the field and it focuses exclusively on quantitative data collected from these systems concerning the behaviour of the system and its users. In that sense it addresses a relatively narrow scope. The next chapter provides a broader perspective on evidence-based development.

CHAPTER 10

Evidence-Driven Development

The era of big data that we are now at the forefront of has taught us a very important lesson: whatever our opinions and beliefs are, we need to constantly validate and verify these using data. It is not that our beliefs are wrong from the start. In many cases, these beliefs are based on experiences that are grounded in significant experience with the industry, the domain, the product and its customers and user. In a world where the rate of change and industrial revolutions is accelerating and creative destruction is prevalent, the challenge is that the things we learned and got to believe some years ago may no longer be true and relevant. This is fundamentally different for previous generations where the knowledge that one would acquire early in life, through schooling or otherwise, would remain valid for all or at least most of one's professional career.

In many ways it may seem surprising, but research in psychology, behavioral economics and related fields clearly shows that human decision making is far less rational and intentional than what we would like to believe as conscious human beings. Many of our decisions are taken subconsciously and immediately and we tend to rationalize these decisions afterwards. So, even though we think we make decisions in a rational, objective fashion, in the vast majority of cases, we make the decision immediately and subconsciously.

To exemplify the above, the book by Kahneman [29] provides an excellent treatise into the subject matter. He characterizes human thinking into two systems. The fast system makes decisions immediately and without any conscious thought based on all the experiences, knowledge and neural programming we have received. The slow system is where the fast system decides it encounters a new situation and it has no predefined response. The slow system is where one becomes aware of the situation, needs to model it, evaluate alternatives and then take a seemingly rational and objective decision. As humans, we spend up to 95% of our time in the fast system and only a small percentage of our time is spent in the slow system.

When it comes to the development and evolution of software-intensive systems, these research findings concerning human decision making have rather profound implications. It means that the vast majority of decisions made in an R&D organization are made subconsciously and with minimal awareness that a decision is being made. For the decisions where the engineer, architect or product manager is consciously aware that a decision needs to be made, the decision is mostly made based on previous experiences and the beliefs held by the person making the decision. It is important to realize that according to psychology research the human brain makes no difference between facts and beliefs. Consequently, once an architect or product manager holds a belief, it will be treated the same way as an irrefutable fact will be treated. Thus any decision taken by an individual will be based on facts and beliefs and questioning the beliefs is very difficult as we are wired to treat beliefs in the same way as facts.

In those cases where the scope and implications of a decision are such that a group of people needs to be involved, another dimension in decision making enters the equation: groupthink and group dynamics. Any arbitrary set of individuals thrown together will go through a process often referred to by Tuckman [48] as "forming, storming, norming and performing". During this process, the natural outcome is a level of cooperation and collaboration by mutual adjustment of personalities, opinions and beliefs. The latter part is important as these beliefs held by the group form the fundament of the group and constitutes the difference between a well-functioning team and a loose collection of individuals. This makes questioning these beliefs particularly difficult as it basically questions the identity of the group.

As group decision making is required predominantly in cases where it is difficult to evaluate the alternatives, the implications of the decision are significant and there is no obvious right answer; the group decision making process has a tendency to gravitate to the opinion held by most members of the group and led by the most vocal ones. As beliefs held by the group are again at the basis of the decision, there is a significant tendency to base decisions on beliefs rather than on available data and facts, especially when the data conflict with the held beliefs. History is rife with cases where teams and groups of people developed such strong belief systems that reality was just ignored in favor of the things the group wanted to be true. Business, of course, has a tendency to catch up with these groups over time, but for (sometimes extensive) periods the group can continue to operate until they are disrupted. We refer to these beliefs as shadow-beliefs, i.e. beliefs that are broadly held in a company, group or team even though these are no longer accurate.

Software-intensive systems companies, product management teams as well as R&D teams are as susceptible, if not more so, as other teams and groups in society. In fact, as software-intensive systems companies tend to employ many engineers and engineers tend to view the world through objective, formula-based and data-driven glasses, many in these companies have a significant blind spot for the fact that the majority of decision making inside these companies is irrational and belief based. As a consequence, engineers are not less, but even more susceptible to fall into the trap of shadow-beliefs.

In the previous chapter, we introduced the HYPEX model. This model focuses on the process of developing new features to be added to systems already deployed in the field. In addition, we focused on the stage in development where development of the feature has been initiated and not on the phases before the start of development or after the completion of the feature. Although HYPEX has proven to be an extremely useful model for the companies that have employed it, it is also clear that it only addresses one type of development and it focuses on only one phase in development. Finally, HYPEX is exclusively focused on quantitative data and ignores any potentially relevant sources of qualitative data. Hence, it is relatively narrow.

In this chapter, we present a much broader approach. We discuss evidence-based development for the development of all types of functionality and all development phases. In addition, we discuss the delicate interplay between qualitative and quantitative data and show that both types of data need each other in an effective, evidence-based organization.

The remainder of this chapter is organized as follows. In the next section, we present a conceptual framework in which we show the use of qualitative and quantitative data, cover more phases of development and allow for more types of development. Subsequently, we introduce the QCD model. The QCD model can be viewed as a major generalization of the HYPEX model and as such embodies many of the concepts introduced in the conceptual model. Then, we present an illustrative example of how a company may employ the QCD model to increase the effectiveness of development. Finally, we discuss the organizational implications of the model and conclude the chapter.

10.1   A CONCEPTUAL FRAMEWORK

The main tenet of this part of the book is that organizations and their people make too many and too important decisions based on beliefs rather than on actual data. This data can originate from customers, systems deployed in the field, publicly available data, competitor data as well as anecdotal and other types of data such as that collected from social networks. Although we have a tendency to focus on quantitative data in, preferably, very large quantities, our experience with the companies that we collaborate with is that companies evolve through several stages in their use and appreciation of data. Initially, companies that have seen the potential of "big data" tend to focus their energy on enabling the collecting of quantitative data without having a clearly understood goal as to the purpose of collecting this data. Once a significant amount of data has been collected, the next step tends to focus on deriving insight from the data and different forms of analysis are employed on the data providing more or less interesting results and knowledge.

Once the results come in and the company finally has quantitative data to base decision making on, the next step is concerned with the interpretation of the data. Interpretation is sometimes very easy, but in many cases it requires significant work to make sense of the data.

As an example to illustrate the aforementioned point, assume that a company has realised the challenges around the features that it continuously adds to its product that is deployed at customers in the field. Product management decides that they lack information about feature usage and the R&D team instruments the code with instrumentation that measures the number of times that features are activated. When the data comes back, it turns out that a new feature introduced several months ago and that sales and marketing have been using to drive sales is hardly ever used by customers. Clearly, this indicates a significant deviation from the expectations in the company. Even though it is very good for the company to know that a feature that it considered to be very valuable is hardly ever used by customers, it gives very little information about why the feature is not used by customers. Of course, many in the company have opinions and hypotheses as to why we're seeing this lack of feature use. And as we discussed in the HYPEX model, we can test these hypotheses. For instance, one hypothesis might be that customers are not aware of the feature. To test the hypothesis, the company may highlight the feature in its periodic communication to its existing users. Or change the menu structure of the product to make the feature more prominent. Another hypothesis might be that the feature is too complex for most users and we can conduct several user experience experiments. The fact of the matter, however, is that although we can take all these actions that result in additional data, there is another avenue of action available to us that companies need to resort to in order to make progress: the collection of qualitative data. Developers, product managers and user experience experts should connect with users and simply ask why these users are not using the feature. The answers may be very different from what one might expect. For instance, the feature may only be relevant for very advanced users that are passionate about the work automated and supported by the product. However, most of the user base just wants a simple solution that just works and that requires minimal interaction with and use of the system. Collecting qualitative data from a small subset of users will, undoubtedly, generate a very different understanding of the customer reality and the relative priority of the earlier generated hypotheses.

The above example is intended to show that although, with the focus on "big data", we tend to focus on quantitative data, we need to complement it with qualitative data that gives us an actual understanding of what the data actually mean. Quantitative data can give us an understanding of how the system behaves and what customers do, but we need to collect qualitative data in order to determine why people and systems behave in the way they do. Especially when we focus on humans, we need to be acutely aware of the gap between what customers say they want, do and expect to do in the future, and what really happens in reality. For all the reasons that we started this chapter with, there tends to be a sizable gap between what people say they want and do and their actual behavior.

There is an additional reason for our insistence on qualitative data complementing quantitative data. There are occasions where there is no quantitative data to be had. The creation or optimization of functionality moves through three main stages, i.e. pre-development, development and post-deployment. In each of these stages, data can and should be collected to ensure that the R&D efforts and the predicted value for customers is actually realized. However, during the pre-development stage there is no product or feature yet and consequently there is little to measure quantitatively. The only type of data that can be collected is qualitative data.

Our work on qualitative and quantitative data collection concerning the behavior of customers as well as systems has led us to the development of a conceptual model shown in figure 10.1. The three phases of development are shown in the figure on the top horizontal. On the left vertical, the type of data is indicated with purely qualitative and purely quantitative at the two extremes. The bottom horizontal indicates the amount of data available to the company. Finally, the right vertical indicates the awareness of the customer concerning the fact that data are collected concerning his or her opinions and behavior.

The diagonal line from lower left to upper right in figure 10.1 indicates the transition process during development. Before the start of development, the amount of information is low and mostly qualitative in nature. In addition, the customer is conscious of the fact that information is collected and may adjust opinions and espoused behaviour accordingly. As development proceeds through to later stages, the data become increasingly quantitative and the amount of data available increases. In addition, the customer tends to become less aware of the fact that his or her behavior is monitored and that data are collected. After deployment of the software, in the final stage, the data collected are almost exclusively quantitative in nature and the amounts can be staggering, e.g. tens of terabytes per day in some companies. In addition, as the customer is now using the system for its intended purpose there is little thought concerning the fact that data about his or her behavior still are collected. Different from earlier phases where we collected espoused behaviors (what customers say they do), we are now collecting actual behaviors (what customers actually do). As research has numerous examples of the gap between these two, it behooves product management and R&D organizations to carefully monitor the gap between espoused and actual behavior.

Where figure 10.1 provides an easy to understand model concerning the collection of data in the different phases of development, it provides little information on the practices and techniques used to actually collect this data. As development progresses from ideas and specifications to mockups and prototypes and finally to subsequent versions deployed, functionality, the ways to collect data concerning system and customer behaviour will change as well.

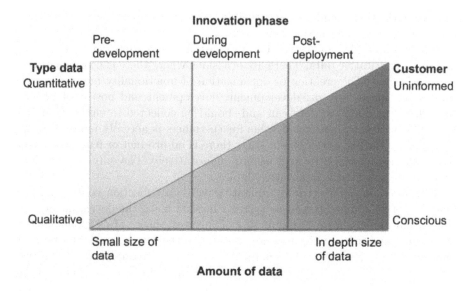

Figure 10.1 A conceptual model of customer data collection

In figure 10.2[1], we provide some techniques that we have identified in our research with a variety of companies [17]. As shown in the figure, in the early stages, the techniques are mostly, though not exclusively, qualitative in nature. Ethnographic studies and customer dialogues are often used to build deep understanding of and empathy with the customer by user researchers, designers and other roles in the company. In later stages, quantitative techniques such as A/B or split testing are frequently used to quantitatively assess the customer behavior as well as system behavior.

The final aspect that we have not yet covered in the conceptual model is the scope of the development addressed by the techniques. As shown in table 10.1, we identify three scopes of development. The first is the optimization of features already present in the system. Much of the R&D efforts in, for instance, e-commerce SaaS applications is concerned with reimplementing already present features with slightly different approaches, deploying these and comparing the customer behavior with the original implementation. This A/B or split testing is focused on optimizing the features already implemented in the system. The second scope of development is concerned with developing and adding new features to products already deployed with customers. With the advent of continuous deployment, this has become increasingly obvious but many traditional products, including telecom, automotive and healthcare systems, have been receiving software updates on a periodic, e.g. yearly, basis. As part of these periodic updates, new features have been deployed.

---

[1]Originally in [17]. Used with permission.

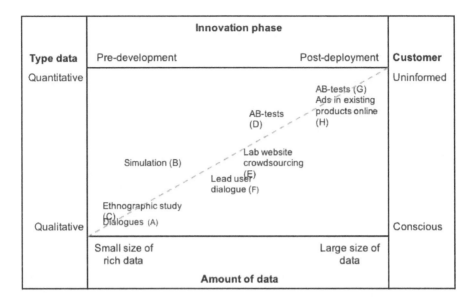

Figure 10.2 Types of customer feedback techniques

The final scope of development is the creation of entirely new products, either in the scope of the existing product portfolio or in a new product category.

The reason for explicitly recognizing different scopes of development is that the development approach as well as the techniques used for collecting data about customer and system behavior are quite different. For instance, BASES testing is a technique to test the marketable features of a new product against those of competing products. This technique is used before any development takes place, i.e. in the pre-development stage, and claims to be able to predict the success of new product ideas with a quite high degree of accuracy. Similarly, some companies use the concept of "feature alphas" to get early feedback on new features. The approach is to take a stable release of the product and add just the new feature to it and share it with some customers. This allows the company to get feedback on the feature from real customers without, typically, running into quality issues that complicate the collection of customer feedback when multiple features are in the main code line of the new release of the product.

In table 10.1, for each of the nine blocks, some techniques that typically are used in that phase and for the indicated scope of development are shown. There are many more customer feedback techniques available as well as different techniques for collecting system behavior, but the purpose of this section is not to be exhaustive, but rather to indicate the key principles and the conceptual model of evidence-based development.

Table 10.1 Techniques for different scopes and phases of development

	Pre-Development	During development	Post-deployment
Optimization	Ethnographic studies	Independently deployed extensions	A/B testing
New features	Solution jams	Feature Alpha, In-product survey	Instrumentation
New products	Advertising, Mockups, BASES testing	Product alpha, Labs website, In-product advertising	Surveys, Performance measurements

10.2 THE QCD METHOD

We introduced the conceptual model in the previous section to provide a context for presenting the QCD method [42]. QCD stands for qualitative/quantitative customer-driven development and it seeks to embody the aspects that we did not address in the HYPEX model discussed in the previous chapter. Specifically, there are three aspects that are important to realize for the QCD model:

> As the name indicates, QCD employs both qualitative and quantitative data for supporting product management and R&D decision making and development processes.

> Second, the model is not just applicable to new feature development, but it can also be used for optimizing features already present in the system as well as the development of entirely new products.

> Finally, the QCD model covers all phases of development, including the pre-development and post-deployment phases.

The fundamental concept on which QCD is based is the notion of fast feedback loops at all stages of development. For every potential work item, before development, during development and after commercial deployment, there is a constant experimentation and validation of delivered customer value that is pursued with the intent of, to the extent possible, making evidence-based rather than opinion-based decisions. In the remainder of the section, we first describe the underlying principles of QCD. Subsequently, we present the key elements of the model and finally we present the overall model.

10.3 REQUIREMENTS TO HYPOTHESES

The first principle underlying the QCD model is that we stop talking in terms of requirements. Instead, we discuss hypotheses about what might add customer value as an input to the QCD model. The reason for this shift was given in the introduction to this chapter: the majority of features in existing systems do not add value as they are not used in the field by customers. One of the main reasons why this occurs is lack of validation of the relevance and importance of requirements to customers. On the one hand, product management, based on discussions with customers and consequently frequently anecdotal evidence, prioritizes certain requirements. On the other hand, R&D takes in these requirements and treats these as immutable and a proper source of truth and realizes the requirement or feature top to bottom and delivers the functionality according to specification. During this process, there is very little, if any, interaction with customers and once the decision to build a feature has been made, it will be built, come hell or high water.

When prioritizing a feature to be realized by R&D, product management has a certain model to explain the value of the feature to the customer. This model can be very simple and only live in the head of the product manager, but often there is a written document capturing the expected value of the feature at some level of specificity. A problem that occurs in virtually all organizations where we conducted our research is that this initial prediction of customer value is never verified after the functionality has been deployed in the field. As a consequence, the organization does not learn about the accuracy of these predictions and consequently does not improve its ability to increase the accuracy. In earlier research, we have coined the term "Open Loop" to refer to this phenomenon [40] and it is one of the fundamental causes of the "featuristis" problem discussed in the introduction. The QCD model addresses this problem such that it provides support for (1) deciding if a product or feature should be built at all and (2) if there is justification for the product or feature, for deciding to what extent a product or feature should be built. Also the second part is of relevance as, despite the notion "minimal viable product" being widespread in the software engineering community, in most mature software engineering organizations, once the decision has been made that a product or feature should be built, it will be built to the full extent, including all the bells and whistles that the R&D organization can imagine. Doing this without evidence that there is value in building the full extent of the product or feature is a significant waste of R&D resources as the Pareto principle applies here as well: 20% of most products and features provide 80% of the value.

Based on our research, discussed in the previous paragraphs, we use the notion of hypotheses instead of requirements to describe the potential functionality content of a new product, the next release of software for an existing product or even for optimizing already realized features. Hence, we focus on identifying and prioritizing these hypotheses and recording these in a prioritized hypotheses backlog. Different from backlogs in agile development, this backlog does not contain requirements but rather hypotheses. Hence, it is not yet clear that the items in the backlog should indeed be built. In addition, the hypotheses backlog is prioritized, meaning that there is a clear ranking of more important and less important hypotheses. This means that the hypotheses backlog is not a bucket holding all the ideas that have ever been suggested in some unstructured fashion, but rather that all hypotheses (at least the top set that would fill a decent period of development) are prioritized in a clear order. In most companies, product management has one or several stashes of loose ideas that they can pull from if necessary. This, however, is very different from our prioritized hypotheses backlog.

Each element in the backlog, a hypothesis, contains a number of elements. First, the hypothesis, obviously, has a title and description. In addition, it has a description of the value this hypothesis will deliver to customers or other stakeholders. This description can, initially, be more qualitative in nature, but needs to become more quantitative over time. Depending on the organization, it may be required to provide clearer description of all the stakeholders as well as risks. Especially for companies where the product or system has multiple stakeholders, it is important to establish the benefits and consequences for each stakeholder. It is not unlikely that some new functionality will positively affect one stakeholder but negatively affect another. For later decisions, more in-depth understanding of the extent of benefits and negative consequences is quite important. In addition to the predicted value, there also is a required investment to be recorded. Each hypothesis requires a certain amount of R&D resources and potentially other resources to be realized. As the effectiveness of R&D is a function of the delivered value and the required R&D resources, both need to be captured. The final element is the evidence that confirms this value prediction. When a hypothesis is initially presented, there will be no or very little evidence, but the intent of the QCD model is to iteratively collect additional evidence over time.

The important part of the elements of the hypothesis is that there is a gradual progression and updating of each of the elements, especially the evidence as the hypothesis is taken through evaluation loops, but also the description of value as well the impact on various stakeholders. Traditional product management and requirements engineering approaches are typically waterfall-ish in nature in that there is a preparation phase followed by a decision point on what is "in" and what is "out". The QCD model is explicitly designed to be continuous in nature, potentially all the way to post-deployment optimization, with the goal of maximizing the value created in return to the R&D effort invested in the product or feature. This may mean that promising functionality may be developed and deployed and subsequently removed because the expected value is not realized and the negative consequences are larger than the cost of removing already realized functionality in a system.

Hypotheses can originate from many sources, but generally we can identify three main categories. The first category is the business strategy of the company. The product or product portfolio fits into a larger business strategy and in order to realize this strategy, new products and new functionality in existing products need to be created. The challenge is that in many companies the term "strategic investment" refers to R&D efforts that receive funding without proper justification of the value created. Although there may be cases where this is the only way forward, often it is a lack of discipline in modeling the predicted value and evaluating this. The second category of hypotheses is concerned with customer feedback. Whenever the company interacts with its customers, there will be suggestions, requests and even demands on new functionality to be added to existing systems or for new products, systems and solutions. In some companies, there is a tendency to use the "loudness" and importance of customers to influence the prioritization of features. This is especially because the company only has opinions to put against the demands from customers. With the QCD model, however, the company will collect data and evidence, which provides a much stronger fundament for discussions with customers. The final category is perhaps novel in many organizations: as the teams take hypotheses through QCD feedback loops, the collected data and insights do not only inform the specific hypothesis being tested, but also give rise to new hypotheses. These hypotheses can originate from anyone in the organization, not only product management, and often offer an incredibly valuable source of innovation for the company. The QCD model provides a structured and systematic way to capture, model and prioritize these ideas and allows the company to crowdsource innovations from its entire employee base, rather than just the product managers.

Finally, the hypotheses on the backlog need to be prioritized. The primary principle for prioritization needs to be the return on investment (RoI), i.e. the value expected to be delivered against the estimated R&D effort required to realize the value. However, there are other forces at work as well. One is the availability of resources. When the top hypotheses are concerned with new products and the primary resources available are R&D teams associated with existing products, these teams need to be given product-related hypotheses to validate. Similarly, when most of the highest prioritized hypotheses are early phase ideas, the staff required to collect more evidence will be product managers and user experience researchers. These resources may not be available to the extent required. One way to address this is to associate a description of the skill set required for the next step in evaluating the hypothesis with each hypothesis. That allows teams that are ready for the next work item to explore the backlog, starting from the highest prioritized hypotheses, until the team finds a hypothesis for which it has the required skill set.

10.4 HYPOTHESIS TESTING TECHNIQUES

As it is with every hypothesis, at some point someone wants to test it in order to determine whether it holds or not. In traditional scientific approaches, experiments are designed to give an absolute answer where the scientist can state the validity of the hypothesis with very high certainty. In the QCD model, we use the concept of accumulating evidence as our goal is to decrease the cost of each experiment where we can. In addition, our focus is less on validity but rather on the value that the idea underlying the hypothesis would deliver to customers. Hence, rather than a hypothesis being selected and tested all the way, we take a step-wise approach where we determine how we can collect more information about the likely value delivered by the hypothesis in a small, low-effort fashion.

To evaluate and take a next step in accumulating evidence, the team owning the hypothesis selects a hypothesis testing technique. The best technique depends on the circumstances, but by and large we can put the hypothesis testing techniques into four categories organized according to two dimensions. The first dimension is stakeholder versus system. For most systems, there are multiple stakeholders, including the user (the individual actually using the system) and the customer (the individual or organization paying for the system). Although these may be the same individual in B2C markets, for many companies these are different parties. In addition, there may be other stakeholders such as installers, companies providing operational maintenance, integrators, etc. Especially in B2B markets, companies operate in a business network that contains multiple stakeholders. This means that any evaluation of hypotheses has to assess the implications for the most relevant stakeholders. It is quite typical that improvements for one stakeholder provide negative consequences for other stakeholders. For instance, when the company considers implementing improvements in the installation or operational maintenance, the customer will be happy because of the lower total cost of ownership for the system. However, the business ecosystem partners providing these installation or operational maintenance services will see a reduction in their revenue and may be less amused. A hypothesis testing technique focusing on the stakeholders needs to consider the diverse and frequently conflicting interests of different stakeholders.

The system in the first dimension is concerned with assessing the behavior of the system itself. Here we do not directly focus on the change in behavior of different stakeholders when evaluating the hypothesis, but rather we focus on the system itself. As the system provides value to its customers, users and other stakeholders, the hypothesis testing technique for this alternative will be concerned with whether the hypothesis actually improves the value delivered to all or some of its stakeholders.

The second dimension is concerned with qualitative versus quantitative hypothesis testing techniques. As the names indicate, some techniques focus on collecting hard, quantitative data that can be analyzed and subjected to statistical analysis techniques. Although we as engineers tend to have a preference for these kinds of techniques, it is important to realize that it is very easy to end up with large quantities of data where the actual semantics of the data is unclear. This can be due to a variety of sources, but our research has shown that it is quite important to complement quantitative data with qualitative data. Techniques focusing on qualitative data often involve more human effort as these techniques are typically concerned with immersion, sense-making and understanding. Whereas quantitative techniques allow us to assess hypotheses with statistically validated answers, qualitative techniques provide us with an-

Table 10.2 Examples of hypothesis testing techniques

Hypothesis Testing Techniques	Stakeholder	System
Qualitative	Observations and interviews, User forums, Mock-ups	Log analysis, Manual use case execution, Incident report analysis
Quantitative	Surveys, Usability tests, A/B testing	Benchmark testing, Software pre-release, System property tracking

swers to the "why" question and often provide the input to future hypotheses to be tested. Organizations developing software-intensive systems need to have a deep understanding of the domain and drivers of the stakeholder as well as the current and future developments. Here quantitative techniques help, but qualitative techniques provide significantly more understanding, depth and context.

In table 10.2, we provide an overview of the two dimensions as well as some example hypothesis testing techniques that can be used for each category. It is important to note that some techniques can be used in multiple contexts. For instance, A/B testing is often used to validate user behavior as well as system behavior.

As we discussed earlier in the chapter, there are three development phases to be considered when working with hypothesis testing techniques, i.e. pre-development, development and post-deployment. In addition to this, there are three potential system scopes that provide the context for the R&D team, i.e. feature optimization, new feature development in existing products and new product development.

Rather than providing an exhaustive overview of hypothesis testing techniques, we provide two examples and refer the reader to other literature for more information. Below, we discuss concept testing and A/B testing.

10.4.1 Concept Testing

Concept testing refers to hypothesis testing techniques that allow a product management and R&D team to assess the attractiveness of a new idea before starting any development. One instance of this notion is often deployed by start-up companies. When the company has an idea for a new product, the first thing it will do is book a domain and put up a website presenting the product as well as a mechanism for ordering the product. Then, it will buy some traffic, e.g. through Google Adwords or Facebook Adverts, and the company will collect data on the sales funnel. This may mean that there will be customers going as far as ordering the non-existing product and although it will be annoying for customers to find out that the product is not available at this point in time, if a sufficiently large percentage of potential customers go through the funnel and place an order, this is a very valuable signal that the product idea has potential and would warrant some development before testing again.

10.4.2 A/B Testing

One of the best known techniques in the Web 2.0/SaaS community is A/B or split testing. Here the customer base is split in as many alternatives as have been developed. Initially this often is only two, i.e. the original version of a feature or user interface and the alternative, but as the company grows in maturity, it will start to evaluate multiple alternatives in parallel. Each customer visiting the website is assigned one alternative and some relevant business metric is associated with the behaviour of each customer. For e-commerce sites, this is often related to conversion, i.e. the percentage of users visiting the website that actually orders something. For other types of systems, however, other factors may be more important. By running the experiment for a sufficiently long time to collect statistically relevant amounts of data for each category, the company can determine the alternative that is best for its customer base.

Although A/B testing may seem quite trivial in nature, realizing it in a variety of system types, collecting the relevant information and ensuring data quality can actually be quite challenging. For a variety of reasons, it may not be feasible to run parallel A/B tests, but rather the company needs to run sequential A/B tests. This means that the data for version A are collected first, then version B is deployed and data are collected for this version. This complicates the data analysis as other variables will have been affected as well and it requires careful experiment design to ensure sufficient data quality.

A final aspect to realize is that analysis of A/B testing data may also result in hypotheses concerning customer segmentation. When running an A/B test, the result may be inconclusive but in-depth analysis may show that the customer base can be segmented and that one segment should be served version A and the other segment version B. At this point, A/B testing is not just concerned with testing feature alternatives with a homogeneous customer base, but also with developing a segmentation of the customer base that allows for increased personalization of the service provided to customers. This will, of course, complicate the development of features deployed to all customer segments as the same feature may have positive outcomes for one segment but negative ones for others.

10.5 SCOPE OF DEVELOPMENT

Once a set of hypotheses to test is available and I have access to a set of hypothesis testing techniques, the next step is to consider the scope of development. We identify three scopes, i.e. new product development, new feature development (in already deployed products) and feature optimization (of already deployed features). In the sections below, we describe each of the scopes in more detail.

10.5.1 New Product Development

Although the development of entirely new products is not as common, when compared to the other scopes of development discussed below, depending on the industry, it does happen on a regular basis. The challenge with new product development is that there is very little context for conducting (especially quantitative) tests on the product concept itself. In most companies, a new product complements an existing product portfolio but differs from the existing products in one or some important ways. One typical reason is technological progress, often following Moore's law, which allows the same functionality in terms of data storage or processing for 50% of the original price after only 12 or 18 months. A second reason may be shifting customer and market priorities where the dimensions that earlier products were optimized for, e.g. product performance, have been deprioritized in favor of other aspects, e.g. installation, operating or troubleshooting cost. Although some of the aforementioned developments can be achieved by evolving existing products, there are times when portfolio management decides that a new product is in order.

The challenge with new product development is that, on the one hand, the R&D investment required is orders of magnitude higher than the other development scopes discussed below. On the other hand, it is typically much harder to get hard data on customer and system behavior through hypothesis testing techniques. Until there is a prototype to deploy at some lead customers that can be used for measuring real, rather than espoused, behavior, much of the work needs to be done based on the domain understanding of the R&D team and its ability to predict customer preferences and technological developments.

That said, over the last years and decades, several techniques have been developed to more accurately predict the success of new products. Some techniques present a description of a new product together with descriptions of competing products already on the market to customer panels to collect feedback on the relative preference of the new product over existing products. In addition, it often is quite feasible to create a prototype of the new product concept using the mechanics and electronics (assuming an embedded system) of existing products, assembled in a novel way as planned for the new products and with a mix of old and new software. Although R&D teams often will grumble about the inefficiency of this, confirming the foundational assumptions underlying the new product with the highest degree of confidence goes a long way to developing successful new products.

Once the basic mechanical, hardware and software architecture have been decided, it becomes more easy to create even more realistic prototypes to test with customers. At this point, it becomes much easier to validate hypotheses concerning the new product, even though it, of course, becomes much harder to make architectural changes.

In our research with dozens of companies, often lots of customer research is done before the decision to develop a new product is taken. The result of this process is a specification of the functionality of the new product. During the development of the product, the focus is on meeting the specification and all efforts are focused on establishing the match. Finally, during the latter stages of development and once the deployment of the product at customers has started, the focus shifts towards quality and identifying, prioritizing and removing defects that managed to get themselves inserted in the product. The challenge with this approach is that it makes two basic assumptions. First, it assumes that the work done before the start of product development has resulted in a product specification that accurately represents the customer and market. Second, it assumes that the customer and market preferences do not shift during the development process. As we already discussed in the previous chapters, we know that these assumptions are flawed. Hence, the product development team needs a relentless focus on continuous validation of hypotheses concerned with the product. Not only that, it also needs to periodically re-validate hypotheses to establish that customer preferences have not shifted. Finding the right balance between building the right product and building the product right is hard, but most teams err towards the latter and would benefit from focusing more on the former.

10.5.2   New Feature Development

During this part of the book, we have focused more on new feature development than on other scopes of development. The reason for doing this is that this is the most typical form of development in most companies. Especially in B2B markets, the typical model of operation is to get the "atoms" installed at the customer and to then use the "bits" to periodically deploy functionality that is intended to improve the performance of the deployed product in dimensions that the customer cares about. With the emergence of increasingly connected products and the concept of continuous deployment, new feature development will become even more important going into the future. Because of economic reasons, companies will seek to maximize the economic life of deployed mechanics and hardware by frequently deploying software that maximizes the value delivered by the deployed systems.

In the previous chapter, we presented the HYPEX model and this model is especially applicable during the development phase. However, it does not provide much guidance in the pre-development phase as the model starts with a prioritized feature backlog. Using hypothesis testing techniques to ensure the relevance and relative importance of features is particularly important as avoiding building a feature that is not prioritized by customers is by far the most promising improvement of R&D efficiency.

Especially during pre-development, most hypothesis testing techniques are qualitative in nature and focus on collecting input on what the customer says, i.e. espoused behavior. Although valuable, many companies would benefit from complementing these techniques with more quantitative techniques that measure actual behavior. For example, some companies put advertisements for new features in online products to measure customer interest by measuring the percentage of customers that clicks on the ad. Similarly, new features ideas can be added to menus in the user interface of the system. When a customer selects the option in a menu, he or she will be notified that this feature is "not activated" or "under development", while data are collected on the number of customers exploring the feature. Finally, some companies build mockups of new products and new features in existing products and study customers in user experience lab settings to verify that these customers actually select the features that are considered for development. This use of the user experience lab is different from its original use: rather than optimizing the user experience of features that already have been built or that are already decided upon, this use of the lab is to determine whether the feature should be built at all.

10.5.3   Feature Optimization

The final scope of development is feature optimization. The prevalence of this type of development depends heavily on the industry. For instance, in e-commerce systems, feature optimization consumes the vast majority of R&D effort. Adding new features to an existing e-commerce system will only complicate and clutter the user experience, which tends to be negative for conversion, the main metric tracked by companies in this industry. On the other hand, in embedded systems, including telecommunications, automotive and defense industries, feature optimization is almost unheard of and only engaged in if there are loud complaints from the customer base. In general, adding new products to the product portfolio as well as new features to existing products is viewed as a much more effective use of R&D resources.

Especially for companies that do not use feature optimization at all, this scope of development has significant promise and can provide a much higher degree of R&D effectiveness when used well. As each hypothesis has an expected value associated with its description, ensuring that this value is actually delivered is of critical importance. This requires data collection about feature use and other properties indicating customer and system behaviour. When, after deploying the first release of the feature, the realised value is not in line with the predicted value, investigation of the underlying reasons for this is of importance. Part of this is present in the HYPEX model, but HYPEX to a large extent focuses on the development phase and less on the post-deployment phase.

Unintended consequences of new features also require attention. These consequences may be positive or negative, but either way these tell us more about the system that we didn't know before as we would have modeled these implications if we had known about these. Hence one area of feature optimization efforts might be concerned with decreasing the negative consequences of a newly deployed feature while maximizing the positive consequences, even if these consequences were not identified from the beginning.

Finally, even if the value of a feature is realised at the time of deployment or after some feature optimization efforts and the unexpected consequences of the feature have been handled, the value of a deployed feature may still deteriorate over time. This can be due to changes in customer priorities or because of other features deployed later that affect the value as delivered by our feature. Feature optimization efforts may be dedicated to improving the delivered value by changing the feature implementation to decrease the negative consequences of feature interaction.

Although not commonly focused on, tracking the value delivered by features over time can also be used to determine when to remove a feature from the system. Although especially non-technical staff assumes that the lowest value that can be delivered through a feature is zero, the fact of the matter is that features can easily deliver negative value. When the negative value of a feature exceeds the cost of removing the feature, one should consider removing the feature from the system altogether.

10.6 BRINGING IT ALL TOGETHER: QCD

Up to now, we have mostly discussed the different elements of the QCD model, but not really provided a model to describe the process of using QCD. In figure 10.3[2], we present the overall QCD model with all its elements.

As the figure shows, the central element of the model is the prioritized hypotheses backlog. Whenever a product management or R&D team is available, it will select the highest priority hypothesis from the backlog for which it has the skills to take the next step. Once the team has selected a hypothesis, it determines what aspect of the hypothesis would benefit most from the collection of additional feedback. Based on the result, it selects a hypothesis testing technique. Depending on the technique, once the preparation or development work has been completed, the result is given to selected customers or deployed on selected products. Although, for example, traditional A/B testing uses the entire user base for its experiments, in the QCD model we use a more gradual approach where we first test with a limited set of customers or systems and only scale when it is clear that there are at least no negative consequences. Once the test is completed, the data are stored and analysed. Based on the analysis, the team may decide to abandon the feature, put it back in the hypothesis backlog at a lower or higher priority level, or, ideally, take the next iteration of hypothesis testing, preferably moving from pre-development to development or a later development stage or scaling the scope of deployment to a larger customer group or set of systems. This process we refer to as the

---

[2]Originally in [42]. Used with permission.

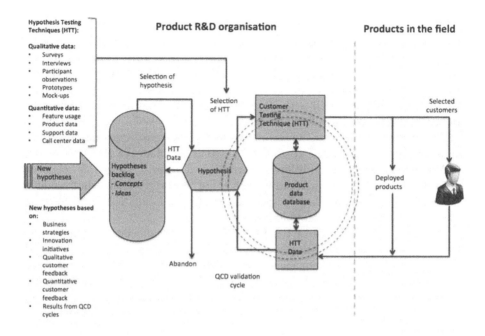

Figure 10.3 The QCD model

QCD validation cycle and it basically captures the work of a data-driven R&D organization.

10.7   EXAMPLE

To illustrate the notion of evidence-based development, we use an example from Viganbe, our case study company. One of the business units of the company is concerned with a B2B (business to business) market. Over the years, the company has established market leadership because of its outstanding product performance. Significant and consistent investment in research and development has, over time, resulted in a product portfolio that is superior to the competition in terms of product performance.

The strategy of focusing on the product performance has worked for well over a decade to maintain market leadership, but over the last few years a competitor has managed to displace Viganbe from the market leadership position, at least in terms of revenue and number of units sold. The initial response of the company was to double down on product performance and to catch up to this competitor, but more recently it has become clear that Viganbe's products still are market leading in terms of product performance and never lost that position. Nevertheless, this competitor has caught up and surpassed the company.

Senior management in the company is slowly waking up to the fact that the strategy that has made this product category so successful for the company is no longer working. Hence, it has asked a task force to investigate the root cause of the deterioration of the company's competitive position. The task force has interviewed several customers, both those that have left for the competitor and those still with Viganbe, and it has analyzed the competitor products. Based on this effort, the task force has reached a conclusion that is quite counter-intuitive to the company culture: the customers do not appreciate product performance to the same extent as what the R&D leadership of Viganbe believes. In addition, it turns out that areas viewed as relatively unimportant by the company are much more important than what Viganbe has realized up to now. These areas are: cost of installation, cost of operational maintenance and cost of troubleshooting.

Based on the analysis of the task force, it is clear that customers, over the last years, have shifted their priorities from the value created by product performance to the efficiencies created by lower cost. The current range of Viganbe products already exceeds the performance requirements from the customers and, at the same time, are significantly more costly to install, maintain and troubleshoot. Clearly, the company has fallen into a shadow-beliefs trap.

After the task force presented its findings, it was clear that the company needed to take some drastic action. However, management also realised that their basic beliefs and experiences were not accurate anymore and any decision making based on these would potentially be flawed. So, the company decided to adopt an evidence-based approach to addressing its challenges.

The goal the company set for itself was to reach parity with its competitors on the identified areas where improvement was required. This allowed it to define rather concrete and hard figures concerning the goals for new R&D efforts. Second, the entire R&D department was rallied and galvanized around the new goals and the new, evidence-based way of working and spent a full day in ideation efforts to create as many ideas as possible around lowering installation, operations and troubleshooting cost. Third, the R&D department was reorganized around cross-functional feature teams that contained all skills, ranging from product development to quality assurance, required to build new features and functionality end to end. Fourth, the company appointed change leaders to coach and mentor the R&D teams. Finally, the already ongoing effort towards continuous deployment was accelerated and rolled out to most of the customer base.

The new way of working followed the QCD process where teams select the most promising hypothesis from the backlog, collect data using a hypothesis testing technique and used the collected data to decide on abandoning or continuing with the feature as well as the relative priority of the feature as compared to other features. Once a team would reach the development stage, it would use continuous deployment to get its functionality out to some or several customers, together with instrumentation to measure, for instance, operational maintenance cost.

Over the course of a year, the company managed to reach parity with competitors concerning the key cost differentiators. As it had not completely ignored product performance in the meantime, it managed to also maintain product leadership. In the following years, this allowed the company to regain its competitive position and grow revenue and margins to regain its leadership in the market category.

10.8 CONCLUSION

As Kahneman [29] provided ample evidence for, many of our decisions are made instantaneously and rationalized only after the fact. For all the decisions where we accept that there is a need to think things through, we base our decision making on "what we know", i.e. the set of experiences, insights and beliefs that we have collected during our lives up to now. However, in fact, we base our decisions on what we think we know.

The human brain can not distinguish between facts, i.e. independently verified and broadly accepted, and beliefs, i.e. unverified but held true by the individual. Thus, in our minds, we treat both as identical. This in combination with "group-think" easily leads to a situation where the intra-company model of what delivers value to customers differs significantly from the reality of the customer base.

The root cause of the gap between intra-company models of customer value and actual customer value is caused by shadow-beliefs. Shadow-beliefs are beliefs that are held broadly across the company and that are considered to be true, but that in fact are not true. Group-think makes shadow beliefs incredibly difficult to identify and break and history is rife with examples of companies that completely lost connection with the market and where senior management operated based on a set of assumptions that had no bearing on the market.

The only reliable mechanism for decreasing the gap between models held by companies and the actual customer behavior and preferences is by frequent and relentless testing of the beliefs held by the company with customers. This validation has to take place in an objective, unbiased fashion in order to make sure that any gaps that surface are not glossed over but lead to investigation into the causes of the identified gap.

The main subject of this chapter has been to provide a conceptual model and a method to realize the adoption of evidence-based development throughout the development life-cycle and for all scopes of development. We recognize three scopes of development, i.e. optimization of already deployed features, new feature development in existing products and new product development. In addition, we identify three development phases, i.e. pre-development, development and post-deployment. For each scope and phase, there are several techniques available to collect data about customer and/or system behavior that allows for significantly improved accuracy of decisions made by R&D management and, consequently, improvement of the effectiveness of development.

The QCD method provides a systematic approach to conduct evidence-based development independent of development scope or phase. QCD has three main elements. First, rather than using the notion of requirements, it starts from hypotheses. Requirements are viewed as immutable and as chunks of requested functionality that need to be built. The notion of hypotheses allows us to treat each hypothesis as a potentially value-adding piece of functionality that needs to be proven through fast, iterative cycles. The second element is the notion of hypothesis testing techniques. There are many hypothesis testing techniques that can be organized into qualitative versus quantitative techniques and stakeholder-focused versus system-focused techniques. Each technique, when selected, is intended to collect additional evidence towards the value provided by the feature. The third and final element is the QCD process where teams select the highest priority feature that matches their skill set, select a hypothesis testing technique, collect data using the technique, analyze the results and decide on the fate of the hypothesis, i.e. abandon or keep, and its priority.

Although the conceptual model and the QCD method provide a structured and systematic approach to adopting evidence-based development, we do not provide mechanisms for addressing the adoption of evidence-based decision making across the company in areas not related to development. However, in our experience, the adoption of evidence-based decision making tends to spread from development to all other areas in the companies that we have worked with. And although the process is not always as fast and predictable as one would like, the company will move in this direction over time.

IV

Ecosystems

CHAPTER 11

The Stairway to Heaven: Ecosystems

No company, organization or even an individual is an island. Both as people and as organizations, we live in networks where we are connected to others. Through these connections, we interact and exchange, we collaborate and compete, we share and we learn. In fact, it is these networks that define any human endeavor, rather than the isolated actions of an individual or organization.

Even though we intuitively understand the importance of the networks that we operate in, many organizations have traditionally had a preference for operating independently, conducting all justifiable activities internally in the organization and keeping anyone who they are dependent on at arm's length through a strict, contractual interface. During the early 1900s, the large successful companies in the industrial revolution often built entire villages around their factories. Here they provided their workers and the families of these workers housing, schools, health care, shops and any other service that one could reasonably desire at that time and age. Of course, the reason for providing all this was that the governments of that time were unable or unaware of the need to provide this level of infrastructure. As these companies needed to attract the employment base, it was necessary to provide the infrastructure required to attract people. And it worked as even well into the second half of the 1900s, it was not unlikely for employees of these large, traditional companies to be the third or fourth generation of the family to work for the same company.

During the 1980s, the era of outsourcing started which focused on the notion of core competence. The basic premise is that any company that is successful has one or more core competencies where it is better than any other company and these core competencies are the reason for its success. In order to be more successful, the organization should focus its internal energy on the things that differentiate it and stop doing all the other things. Of course, the other things still need to be done, but these the company should outsource to other companies that, preferably, have the outsourced activity as their core competency.

The structural changes in the industry that followed from the focus on core competencies and outsourcing were dramatic and caused a major upheaval in the social contract between companies and workers. At the same time, however, it led to major improvements in the efficiency of the restructured companies, at the expense of increased dependency on other companies in their network that now conduct the non-core activities earlier conducted by the organization itself.

Although outsourcing has proven its value, the negotiation, monitoring and enforcement of contracts still is a human activity and this incurs significant cost. As a consequence, companies have a preference for doing business with companies of the same size as there will be comparable structures at the other end, the number of contracts to manage will be much lower and the level of trust is higher. During the last two decades, however, companies in, especially, the software-intensive systems industry have found ways to automate the process of creating contracts with partners in the same way as B2C companies found ways to largely automate the contracts and interaction processes with their customers. This led to the notion of crowdsourced software ecosystems. Pioneered to a significant extent by companies like Apple and Google in the iOS and Android mobile phone ecosystems, approaches were found for small development shops and individual developers to offer solutions to (often relatively small) customer segments. Here, Apple and Google provided the marketplace for customers and developers to find each other and, in the process, to vastly enrich the range of functionality provided to their customers through the use of external players.

The latter model of crowdsourced ecosystems drove two major innovations. First, as mentioned, it provides an effective way for organizations of vastly different size to effectively collaborate through standardized and automated means for contract creation, monitoring and enforcement. Second, and perhaps more important, the ecosystem partners are providing solutions that are awfully close to the core competencies of the companies providing the platform and marketplace. Hence, the core competency of these organizations may be as much in coordinating their ecosystem to their optimal advantage than it is to develop great products.

For the industry at large, our research shows that although the principles of core competencies, outsourcing and crowdsourced ecosystems are well understood, many companies are still quite poor at fully embracing these concepts. Many of the companies studied still have a preference to continue to do many things internally that should be outsourced and tend to manage their ecosystem partners during the selection, the execution and the conflict resolution stages, in a largely ad hoc and locally optimized fashion.

One of the reasons for the aforementioned challenge is that there are few really actionable models and frameworks for companies to use in determining the best course of action. Thus, every company has to build, over time, its own set of experiences and learn and structure its interactions with its ecosystem. There is little knowledge exchange beyond the vision level and, consequently, the operational level is ad hoc and executed based on the best efforts of the individuals responsible for the task.

This part of the book is concerned with software ecosystems and we present actionable models, insights and knowledge from different companies. In this chapter, we provide a broader conceptual basis into software ecosystems and define the third dimension of the Stairway to Heaven which is concerned with ecosystems.

11.1   SOFTWARE ECOSYSTEMS

The notion of ecosystems originates from biology. When studying different species, biologists realised that in order to understand the physiology and behaviour of a species, it was important to also understand what predators were hunting the species, what it ate and potentially hunted and what other species it may have symbiotic or competitive relationships with. In different attempts to recreate disappearing nature types, it is not sufficient to introduce one species, but rather it is necessary to introduce multiple species and to introduce them in a specific order. For example, in the eastern part of the Netherlands, traditionally there were large heather fields. During the 1970s, the fields were disappearing as local forests intruded on the heather fields. Although attempts were made to manually cut back the forest and to protect the heather fields, it turned out that in order to have a balanced ecosystem, something else was required: the reintroduction of roaming shepherds and their sheep. Permanently hosting sheep in the areas turned parts of the fields into grass areas and allowed the forest to expand elsewhere. So, the government reintroduced shepherds and herds of sheep that roamed the heather fields. The sheep ate the new growth that would become new trees and kept the heather healthy by eating from it. Similar examples exist in the US where several attempts are made to have the land at large farms return to the prairies that were there before the white man arrived. Again, to accomplish this, the careful and staged introduction of multiple species of plants and later animals is required. These attempts at creating sustainable ecosystems have led to a deepened understanding of the subject area.

In the early 1990s, Moore [35] applied the metaphor of ecosystems to the world of business. He defined a business ecosystem as an "economic community supported by a foundation of interacting organizations and individuals, which can also be perceived as organisms of the business world." Moore identified three important characteristics of business ecosystems. First, the organizations and individuals in the ecosystem have a symbiotic relationship with each other. This does not mean that all parties in the ecosystem have to have symbiotic relationships with each other, but rather that each party has some form of symbiotic relationship with some other party. The second characteristic is co-evolution. The ecosystem as a whole evolves and because of the symbiotic relationship, the parties evolve together. In fact, different business ecosystems in the same area compete with each other and one of the competitive differentiators is the speed and efficiency of co-evolution. A business ecosystem that more rapidly adopts innovations and novel best practices will, over time, outcompete other, more conservative business ecosystems.

The final characteristic of business ecosystems is that the parties share a platform. The term platform is highly overloaded with semantics, but we're basically referring to tools, services and technology that enhance the performance of the business ecosystem. The platform allows for efficiencies and performance levels that are difficult to match by even large individual companies.

Business ecosystems have a number of roles that are often, though not always, present. The first is the keystone firm. Although business ecosystems exist without a keystone firm, very often there is one, often large, company that owns the basic platform solution and that acts as a benevolent (or not so benevolent) dictator. The second role is that of the complementor. Members of this type provide extensions, services and other solutions that enhance the value of the basic platform and by that the value present in the overall ecosystem. The third role is the integrator. An integrator combines the basic platform with one or more offerings from complementors in product, system or solution that can be used as is by the final role, the customer. The customers in the ecosystem are, in the end, providing the funds that keep the ecosystem going. The role of the integrator can be adopted by the customer in B2C ecosystems. For instance, the user of an iPhone typically selects with applications he or she would like to have present on the device. In ecosystems where companies are the customers, the complexity of the final solution is often so high that an integrator can provide significant value by itself.

The benefits of operating in an ecosystem instead of acting as a standalone company towards a customer base are many, but tend to organize themselves in a few categories. First, an ecosystem can often provide a more attractive offering for new customers because of the wide range of functionality provided. Second, the ecosystem provides an increased "stickiness" for existing customers. Because of the complementors and integrators, just switching away from the basic platform provided by the keystone firm requires the customer overcoming a pretty big hurdle as the solution is not as standardized as solutions provided by individual companies. The third benefit, of great relevance to all roles in the business ecosystem, is the ability of ecosystem partners to share the cost of innovation. Because the several players can all contribute and perform their own innovations, the overall innovation output in the ecosystem can be very high compared to alternative constellations in the same industry.

Software ecosystems, the subject of this part of the book, are an instance of the business ecosystem concept. Similar to general business ecosystems, the aforementioned roles are present in software ecosystems. Also, the platform typically translates to a software platform. The complementors can exist inside the company building the software platform. In that case, we often refer to software product lines. Several software ecosystems originate from a software product line where the customer demand for functionality outstripped the company's ability to deliver on it and in response the company opened up part of the platform interface for third party developers, the complementors of software ecosystems.

Although several definitions of software ecosystems exist, we define it as "a business ecosystem consisting of a platform, a set of internal and external developers, a community of domain experts as well as integrators in service to a community and users that compose relevant solution elements to satisfy their needs." Software ecosystems have four important characteristics that are unique and relevant for understanding of the concept.

The first is the software platform. Typically provided by the keystone firm, the software platform provides the generic functionality in the domain that is required by all or most customers. Complementors provide solutions on top of the platform and use interfaces provided by the platform organization. Different from other industries, the complementors do not only live outside the company providing the platform, which can lead to interesting competitive situations between internal and third party solution providers.

The second characteristic is the constant evolution of the functionality in the ecosystem. Starting as novel and innovative and created by, perhaps, only a small complementor for a small customer segment, the functionality may become broadly adopted in the ecosystem and a differentiator for the complementor that drives its business growth. However as the functionality matures and the demand for the functionality broadens, the platform company will add the functionality to the platform, effectively removing the business for the complementor. Finally, as the platform incorporates functionality from many complementors, it tends to grow quite large and a process is required to remove matured functionality from the basic platform when it has outlived its usefulness.

The third characteristic, which has significant business implications in software ecosystems, is the extent to which different complementors can build on top of each other's contributions to the ecosystem. Whether this is supported is often determined by the nature of the ecosystem. In collaborative ecosystems, there are few restrictions and the culture of the ecosystem is such that everyone welcomes any investment in terms of time and energy that any party puts into the ecosystem. In competitive ecosystems, on the other hand, the complementors compete with each other and the platform provider competes with the complementors in subtle ways. In these ecosystems, the basic point for extension is the platform interface and other places to extend functionality, such as functionality by other complementors, is often actively discouraged or made impossible by the platform provider.

The final characteristic is concerned with composition and integration. As software is so malleable, composing and integrating solutions is on the one hand very easy and on the other hand difficult because of the challenges associated with quality assurance and backward compatibility.

In table 11.1, we provide a taxonomy of software ecosystems for the B2C domain. The taxonomy has two dimensions. The first dimension is concerned with the deployment infrastructure that platform solutions are rolled out in. In the B2C space, we can recognize desktop computers, web solutions and mobile solutions. The second dimension is concerned with the type of functionality. We identify three categories, i.e. operating systems, application domains and end-user programming. This leads to nine possibilities and in the figure we provide examples of each possibility. In the bottom row, we find the usual suspects when it comes to operating systems, ranging from Windows and Linux for the desktop computers to Android and iOS for mobile devices. For the web, things are a bit more complicated as the operating systems layer consists of components that are shared among multiple providers, but the market is still more fragmented in terms of real web operating systems. There are several players in the market that aim to take a share of it, such as Google with its App Engine and Microsoft with its Azure cloud platform. Ecosystems in the application layer are more concerned with smaller developer ecosystems organized around popular applications. For instance, according to some accounts there are more than 50.000 developers in just the US who build extensions to Microsoft Office. Similarly, companies like SalesForce, eBay and Amazon have strong developer networks enriching their base application. Finally, the end-user programming layer is concerned with providing configuration or programming environments for domain experts with little or no programming experience. Microsoft Excel, Mathematica and VHDL are good desktop examples. On the web, several experiments were conducted, including Microsoft PopFly, Google's mashup editor and Yahoo! Pipes, but none of these reached significant market adoption and were shut down. On the mobile devices, there is strong competition on the operating system level, but none of the applications reached a level of adoption and market capitalization that allowed for an ecosystem to develop around an application. The same is true for mobile end-user programming platforms.

Software ecosystems in the B2B space tend to be focused on successful and broadly deployed applications. For instance, SAP and SalesForce have rich developer networks around them that significantly improve the overall value of the ecosystem. From an evolutionary perspective, it is important to realize that the emergence of external developers often follows a pattern starting at the customers. Early on, the company providing a B2B software solution will also provide the integration of the solution with the other IT systems present at the customer. With a growing number of customers, however, the responsiveness of the company will decrease and customers start to take on the integration effort themselves. However, some customers will not have the IT skills inside the organization to conduct the integration themselves and instead invite 3rd parties to perform the integration in a consulting capacity. When some 3rd party company develops a brand around its skill set, it will

Table 11.1 Taxonomy of software ecosystems

category / platform	desktop	web	mobile
end-user program- ming	MS Excel, Mathematica, VHDL	Yahoo Pipes, Microsoft PopFly, Google mashup editor	none so far
application	MS Office	SalesForce, eBay, Amazon, Ning	none so far
operating system	MS Windows, Linux, Apple OSX	Google AppEngine, Yahoo developer, Coghead, Bungee Labs	Nokia S60, Palm, Android, iPhone

develop more and more integrations and it will start to see patterns between its customers. That allows it to start to develop reusable components that simplify integration. Although initially internally used by the 3rd party development company itself, over time these components become commercialized and offered to others in the ecosystem.

Successful software ecosystems provide an economic and technical environment that provides competitive advantages to all parties active in the ecosystem in their competition with others in other ecosystems or those that operate more independently. For keystone firms that provide the cornerstone for ecosystems, it is important to continuously monitor that all parties in the ecosystem manage to maintain an attractive position, in economic as well as other terms. If the keystone firm pulls too much value towards itself, it leaves too little for other players and these will then abandon the ecosystem. At the same time, leaving too much for others will not give the keystone firm the resources to develop and evolve its platform which will commoditize the platform and cause disruption of the platform and the keystone firm over time.

11.2 TOWARDS MANAGING COMPLEXITY

Before we dive into the third dimension of the Stairway to Heaven, ecosystems, we first have to introduce a conceptual model that we have coined the three layer product model (3LPM). As identified by Parnas [43] and Perry & Wolf [44] over two decades ago, architectures age and erode over time. This causes the cost of typical maintenance tasks to increase over time as the system is less and less suited to incorporate the most likely changes. Although many argue about the exact definition, researchers and practitioners agree that in large, long-lived software systems, the increasing complexity is the primary challenge.

For any system, there are two sources of complexity, i.e. the complexity of the problem domain and the complexity of the solution where architects and engineers add additional structure, design rules and design constraints in order to achieve the quality requirements of the system. During the evolution of the system, the solution complexity increases (even as the problem domain complexity remains constant) as new functionality does not match the original structure and no refactoring is performed, additional design rules and constraints are introduced and design rules and constraints no longer relevant for the system are not removed.

During the last decade, two additional complexity adding factors have appeared to the scene, i.e. the broad adoption of software platforms and the increasing awareness and experimentation with software ecosystems. Although platforms and clean interfaces provide a powerful decoupling mechanism, the fact remains that it results in previously unrelated development teams inside and outside the organization now are dependent on each other and need to coordinate their activities. In addition, the software artifacts that these teams work on now have dependencies on each other.

The aforementioned leads to increased complexity in at least four areas, i.e. design, ways of working, testing and release. Software dependent on other software communicates through interfaces. Independent of the quality of the interface design, the interfaces will evolve and as teams aim to maintain backward compatibility this results in more complex interfaces. This leads to more complicated interfaces, more interdependent ways of working, more elaborate and complex testing procedures and more difficult release processes to get software to customers.

Although many researchers and practitioners have expressed their concerns about complexity, it is often treated as an unavoidable fact of life, rather than as a manageable quality of a system. Consequently, existing approaches do not address the concerns related to different types of functionality and alternative approaches are required. Based on our research, however, we take the position that complexity is a manageable attribute of a system and that a significantly increased focus on simplicity is required. However, rather than addressing the full problem space of complexity, we focus on a specific challenge: the intermixing of different types of functionality with very different change frequencies.

In our research, e.g. [12, 14, 16], we have worked with dozens of companies and studied complexity of their software solutions and realized that the main reason why the complexity of systems increased over time: companies treat commoditized, differentiating and experimental functionality equally and without any differences. This causes several complexity increasing problems, including constantly increasing allocation of R&D resources to commoditized functionality, decreasing release frequency of new product updates and deteriorating architecture.

The companies that we have studied in our research have developed tactics and strategies to deal with some aspects of this problem. We have analyzed these tactics and strategies and combined these in a novel model, i.e. the three layer product model (3LPM). In the next sections, we first discuss the challenges experienced by the companies involved in our research. Subsequently, we introduce the three layer product model. Then, we discuss how the 3LPM addresses the identified challenges.

11.2.1 Complexity Problems During Evolution

As we discussed in the previous section, managing complexity and achieving a level of simplicity that is as close to the inherent complexity of the domain as possible is very important for the long-term viability of large-scale software. At the companies that we collaborate with in our research, we identified a number of behaviors and approaches that significantly complicated achieving this goal. Below we discuss these in more detail.

Lack of willingness to replace proprietary solutions with COTS or OSS solutions

In many of the companies we work with, engineering staff has a tendency to maintain investment in commoditizing components of the software, despite the fact that over time viable COTS and OSS solutions have become available. Often the functionality in these components at some point in time formed the basis for the success of the system and even though the functionality is no longer differentiating, the investment level in that part of the system has not been adjusted downward. This causes a significantly higher degree of complexity as the code results in a mix of different types of functionality that changed at significantly different rates.

Too low percentage of R&D resources spent on differentiating functionality

Due to the higher complexity of the software, companies often feel compelled to maintain investment levels on parts of the system that have commoditized and no longer represent differentiating functionality. This caused a situation that fewer and fewer of the R&D resources are spent on developing the competitiveness of the system. Most of the staff ends up working on maintaining and evolving "table stakes" functionality. Unfortunately, this problem exacerbates the complexity problem as the R&D resources working on commodity functionality add complexity due to the aging of the architecture, which makes it even harder to the folks building differentiating functionality to work efficiently.

Eroded product architecture, causing differentiating and commoditized functionality to be heavily intertwined

As the R&D organization does not distinguish between commoditized and differentiating functionality, these tend to become intertwined. Aggravating this is the lack of willingness to invest in architecture refactoring [32] as a mechanism to reduce complexity because the necessity to prepare the system for more easy inclusion of future differentiating functionality is not recognized. Hence, older and new functionality become mixed. The consequence is that the software architecture erodes over time, meaning that the structure of the system causes the typical changes to the system to affect multiple components in the system. This requires each team building the new functionality to know about the details of the entire design. As this becomes more and more difficult, teams will make changes with unintended consequences that result in errors that surface late in the development process and that are difficult to find and repair.

Product becomes increasingly unattractive for its customers
With the development staff spending more and more time on commoditized layers of the stack as well as bug fixing and preparing the product for release, the amount of new, differentiating functionality added in each product release is quite limited and decreasing. This causes the product to lose its appeal to customers. Of course, in the companies involved in the research, there were both internal and external customers. Internal customers used the products as platforms to build products, i.e. a traditional software product line approach, whereas external customers formed a software ecosystem around the platform and the products derived from it.

Concluding, this section clearly indicates the implications of unmanaged complexity and the consequences of not focusing on simplicity. Software companies need to find ways to maintain elegance and simplicity of the product architecture. This requires adopting an alternative approach to managing the evolution of the system.

11.3   THREE LAYER PRODUCT MODEL

The 3LPM is based on our experience with the companies involved specifically in this research as well as dozens of other companies that we have collaborated with around large-scale software development of long-lived systems. 3LPM organizes the product architecture in three layers and two interfaces. As commoditized, differentiating and experimental functionality should be kept in separate layers, interaction between layers occurs through interfaces. The lower interface is between the commoditized and differentiating functionality layers. In software product line literature, this interface is often positioned between the shared software assets and the products that make up the product line. The focus is on sharing the layer of commoditized functionality between as many products as possible, with the goal of achieving high R&D efficiency. The upper interface is between the differentiating and experimental functionality layers. In the software ecosystem community, this is the layer that is offered by a platform company to external developers that build applications, solutions or features on top of the functionality provided by the platform. However, software companies also use this layer internally to build experimental features for evaluation by customers. In practice, most of the innovation efforts concerning the system take place in this layer. In figure 11.1, the three layer product model is shown graphically.

Below, we discuss each of the layers in more detail, as well as, the two

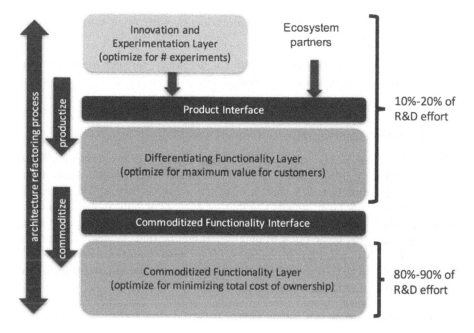

Figure 11.1 The three layer product model

interfaces. Subsequently, we discuss the productization, commoditization and architecture refactoring processes.

11.3.1 Commoditized Functionality Layer

The bottom layer of the system is concerned with the functionality that is necessary for the operation of the system but that is considered "table stakes" by customers. Often, the software in this layer is a combination of proprietary software, built over time by the company, and commercial and open-source software solutions. The focus of the team associated with this layer is (or should be) on minimizing total cost of ownership for the commodity layer. This requires the team to constantly analyze existing and new functionality with the intent of identifying lower cost ways to providing the same functionality. This typically includes the replacement of proprietary functionality with commercial components and the replacement of commercial, licensed software with open-source software.

The typical activities that take place in this layer are fourfold:

Incorporate functionality from the differentiating functionality layer into the commoditized functionality layer.

Replace proprietary software with commercial or open-source software components.

Replace commercial software components with open-source software components.

Incorporate new functionality that is necessary, but not differentiating, for the customer, in order to make it available for all users of the system at once.

11.3.2 Differentiating Functionality Layer

The second layer in the stack, as the name implies, is concerned with the functionality that differentiates the product from the competition. In addition, it contains the functionality that is of primary importance and relevance to the customer. This layer defines the market success or failure of the product. There are two parallel activities taking place. On the one hand, the team responsible for this layer takes in new functionality that, typically, originates from the Innovation and Experimentation layer with the intent of continuously adding new value to the system. On the other hand, the team partners with the commoditized functionality layer team on identifying chunks of functionality that are commoditizing and need to transition to the lower layer.

The activities that take place in this layer are threefold:

Selecting and incorporating new functionality initially innovated and experimented with in the higher layer.

Selecting and transitioning commoditizing functionality that needs to be pushed down to the next layer.

Reactively implementing new, differentiating functionality in response to customer requests or changes in business strategy.

11.3.3 Innovation and Experimentation Layer

Dividing the system in a commoditized and a differentiating layer is hard to do in practice, but is conceptually not overly complicated. We, however, identify a third layer in the model that is present implicitly but often not explicitly identified by industry or academia. This layer is concerned with innovative experiments, either with customers or internally, to identify functionality that provides significant value to customers and will be considered as differentiating the system from the competition.

Examples of functionality in this layer may be work done for a lead customer, a trial of a new product extension in a specific geographic market or an alternative implementation of already existing functionality with the intent of improving some of the quality attributes of that implementation.

There are three types of activities by the team responsible for this layer:

Developing hypotheses of future differentiating functionality by interacting with customers, analyzing competitive products, as well as brainstorming and other ideation techniques. Once candidates have been identified, it is important to experiment with these to, on the one hand, determine the relevance of the functionality to the broader population and on the other hand to determine the implementation complexity of the candidate functionality into the system.

Identifying new or evolving technologies that may be of relevance to the users of the system. Similar to the previous type, the team does not just identify new technologies, but also experiments with these. In the case of new technologies, the use cases for which the technology can possibly provide benefits or that become feasible due to the new technology need to be evaluated through experimentation with customers to determine whether there is sufficient benefit derived from the technology.

The third area is new customer facing innovations that potentially are not sufficiently important for any individual product, but that may provide a significant return when deployed for an entire ecosystem.

11.3.4 Productization and Commoditization Process

The layers of the 3LPM model have interfaces to achieve, decouple and maintain a level of complexity that minimizes the complexity added by the solution as it evolves over time, i.e. structure, design rules and design constraints. These interfaces are stable, but not static as these need to evolve when functionality transitions between layers. There are two operational processes that manage this transition, i.e. the productization and the commoditization process dealing with transitioning functionality between the top and middle layer and the middle and bottom layer, respectively.

The productization process is concerned with taking functionality into the differentiating functionality layer of the system. The typical pattern is to incorporate features that have been developed in the innovation and experimentation layer either by the company itself or by ecosystems partners. Although the name of the layer may indicate differently, at the point where a feature or set of features becomes relevant for productization, there already is a base of users that use the functionality and consequently the transition of functionality to the lower layer should occur in a way that impacts customers the least. The typical process is to let the original version and the new version in the differentiating functionality layer co-exist for a while, to let new customers use the new system version and to start transitioning existing users once the stability and scalability of the productized version is established.

The intent of the commoditization process is to decouple the differentiating functionality in the system from the commoditized functionality to the maximum extent possible to allow the differentiating functionality to evolve separately from and more rapidly than the commoditized functionality. The commoditization process also contains three main activities, i.e. selection and prioritization of functionality in the layer above that is commoditizing, the transition of the actual functionality to the commoditized functionality layer and replacing proprietary software with suitable commercial or open-source software solutions.

11.3.5 Architecture Refactoring Process

The productization and commoditization processes operationally deal with moving software downward in the system architecture over time. However, there is a third process that is required to make sure that the structure of the system does not deteriorate over time. This requires a level of investment in the proactive refactoring of the architecture of the system. The goals of the architecture refactoring process are threefold, i.e. minimize cost of evolution over time, manage interfaces and maintain end-to-end quality requirements.

11.4 VALIDATION

In the previous section, we have introduced the three layer product model as a means to differentiate the goals and metrics for different layers of the stack. We developed the model in response to our experiences at the several companies involved in the research as well as dozens of others. The problems discussed in the problem statement were derived from these companies. The three layer product model is a generalization of the strategies and tactics adopted by these companies.

As software systems still increase in size and complexity, it is critical to prioritize the focus on simplicity. For any system, there are two sources of complexity, i.e. the complexity of the problem domain and the complexity of the solution where architects and engineers add additional structure, design rules and design constraints in order to achieve the quality requirements of the system. During the evolution of the system, the solution complexity increases (even as the problem domain complexity remains constant) as new functionality does not match the original structure and no refactoring is performed, additional design rules and constraints are introduced and design rules and constraints no longer relevant for the system are not removed.

Although the complexity challenge of evolving systems has been studied extensively in the literature, the focus of the 3LPM is on an equally important problem: As systems evolve, their complexity increases because commoditized functionality, differentiation functionality and experimental functionality become intermixed causing complexity due to the different change frequency of the different types of functionality as well as the different economic drivers in each layer.

As a solution, the 3LPM defines three layers of functionality with clearly defined interfaces between these as well as three processes, i.e. a productization process, a commoditization process and an architecture refactoring process. TLPM can result in significantly increased simplicity of the evolving system resulting in higher productivity, increased lifetime of the system and increased quality.

11.5   ECOSYSTEM DIMENSION

Earlier in this chapter we introduced the notion of software ecosystems. Then we introduced the three layer product model. The reason for introducing the latter is because we have to introduce one more notion before discussing the ecosystem dimension of the Stairway to Heaven, i.e. the number of ecosystems that companies are involved in. Traditional thinking puts companies in one ecosystem. For instance, Microsoft is Windows, Google is Android, Apple is OS X, etc. However, when one starts to look in more detail, it turns out that companies are in multiple ecosystems. In general, we see that companies are in at least three ecosystems for every major business that they're in and these are organised according to the 3LPM:

> **Innovation ecosystem**: The innovation ecosystem is concerned with identifying new customer- and technology-driven opportunities that add value to customers. Innovation processes are concerned with identifying new ideas and then iteratively testing these to gather evidence concerning which are adding value and which do not. Innovation is highly suitable for collaboration with other players in the innovation ecosystem. These players can be complementors, integrators, customers or even complete outsiders that enter the ecosystem on the tail of some technology advancement that makes new innovations feasible for the ecosystem. This ecosystem is concerned with testing as many ideas as possible in order to find the few that add real, tangible value to customers. Consequently, the ecosystem helps both in generating more new ideas and in sharing the cost of innovation by doing part of the testing.

> **Differentiation ecosystem**: Once an innovation proves to be successful, it transitions to the differentiation ecosystem. This ecosystem is focused more on control, typically by the keystone firm, but even large companies need partners to successfully bring innovations to market. The focus in this ecosystem is to maximize the value for customers, so the company providing the differentiating functionality and its partners invests to maximize the value of the differentiation. This is important for economic terms, as a more elaborate differentiation can be monetized better, but also in terms of brand and market perception where a company that delivers a constant stream of valuable innovations is viewed as a better partner than a cost-focused commodities provider.

> **Commoditization ecosystem**: The final ecosystem is the commoditization ecosystem. Once functionality reaches this state, the focus is on delivering it at the lowest possible cost, to replace proprietary functionality with open-source or COTS software and, when feasible, to stop

supporting certain features. Here the ecosystem is concerned with simplifying and replacing functionality provided by the products in the portfolio. Consequently, the ecosystem partners in this ecosystem tend to have more of a supplier focus and the basic metric of success is reducing cost. Again, the nature and structure, in terms of partners, of this ecosystem is different from the other ecosystems.

Later in the book, we introduce the three layer ecosystem strategy model (TELESM). This model provides a more in-depth discussion of the topic, the different types of ecosystems and strategies that companies can adopt to strategically operate in these ecosystems. For now, however, we introduce the three ecosystem types as we need this concept as we introduce the third dimension of the Stairway to Heaven.

The Stairway to Heaven model, as presented in this book, consists of three dimensions. In the first part, we focused on the speed dimension. This dimension is focused on increasing the efficiency of software engineering, i.e. how to build things right. So, we focused on agile work practices, continuous integration and continuous deployment. In the second part of the book, we focused on evidence-based development. This is concerned with effectiveness of R&D, i.e. building the right thing. The focus is on ensuring that those activities that we allocate R&D resources to indeed deliver the highest return on investment and deliver the most value to customers. Even if we manage to focus our R&D resources on the most important topics, however, most companies still end up spending vast amounts of resources on work that is not differentiating and adding value to customers, but that needs to be done in order to deliver the product, solution or service. For example, when asking dozens of companies what percentage of resources is allocated to the commodity layer in 3LPM versus the other two layers, the responses ranged from 65% to 95%, with the majority being around 80%. This means that four out of every five people working in your organization are doing things that no customer cares about. It is just commodity and although it needs to work, your customers are not going to select your company over your competitors because of that functionality. Consequently, after focusing on efficiency and subsequently focusing on effectiveness, there is still a huge opportunity to free up R&D resources from commodity work and allocate these to value-adding activities. However, this requires a more strategic engagement with the ecosystems that the company is part of. So, the ecosystem dimension of the Stairway to Heaven is focused on efficacy, i.e. ensuring that the ecosystem engagement is such that the company's R&D resources are available for the most important work.

In figure 11.2, we show the five steps of the ecosystem dimension. These steps evolve from a company that is entirely internally focused and avoids relying on partners wherever possible to a company that explicitly and strategically engages all ecosystems it is part of in order to maximize its competitive position and the optimal allocation of its own R&D resources. Based on our

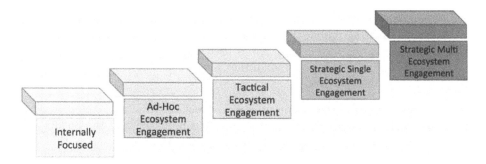

Figure 11.2 The ecosystem dimension of the Stairway to Heaven

research, we have identified that companies move through five steps. Below, we briefly present each of the stages:

Internally focused: The first and basic stage is where the company is exclusively internally focused. As no company is an island, the company, of course, has to interact with other companies, but the basic principle is that everything that can be done in house is done internally. The companies our company connects with are exclusively providing services that are hard or prohibitively expensive to provide by internal means. The relationship with these companies is at arm's length, cost and competition based and may be infused with low level distrust. The company has a very strong culture of internal versus external and everyone in the company behaves fundamentally differently towards colleagues as compared to suppliers. Of course, also this company needs customers and takes care of its customers, but the focus is more transactional than relationship based. To illustrate the point, at one of the companies that are involved in our research, one of the employees quipped: "If there was iron ore in the ground below our headquarter building, we would even have our own iron smelter."

Ad hoc ecosystem engagement: The next step on the ecosystem dimension of the Stairway to Heaven is where the company starts to engage the ecosystem in an ad hoc fashion. Often driven by some crisis or cost efficiency program, the company realizes that some issue or problem could be addressed by stopping to do something by itself and to give it to another organization. The purpose of the engagement almost always is cost reduction and the approach towards engaging one or more partners in the ecosystem is often more accidental than anything else. The trigger might be the need to reduce cost in order to preserve margins and when it turns out that an outside company can provide the same for significantly lower cost, deciding to outsource the work becomes so much of a no-brainer that it overcomes the cultural aversion to relying on outsiders. A second scenario that is quite typical in this context is where a western company seeks to establish itself in India or China. The regulations in those countries require a joint venture with a local company or individual and, suddenly, a company that is used to deciding everything by itself needs to find a modus operandi that is concerned with finding consensus with another partner.

Tactical ecosystem engagement: Once the first step towards relying on an outside company has been accomplished and the results are satisfactory, there is a shift in the culture where more areas that are contextual for a company are considered for outsourcing. The initial approach tends to be more tactical in nature, meaning that the selection of partners and collaboration with these partners is more structured than in the previous step, but still the engagement is tactical, rather than strategic in nature. This means that the interaction with ecosystem partners is more concerned with solving immediate problems than with a long-term partnership. Especially in the embedded systems companies that we collaborate with, there is a pattern where a lucrative deal with a new customer requires a level of customization of the software of the system being sold that can not be prioritized by R&D. In this case, the company brings in a software consultancy local to the customer in order to close the deal, but the selection of the partner is tactical and does not indicate any long-term relationship.

Strategic single ecosystem management: After bringing in tactical partners in multiple contexts and customer contracts, an awareness tends to develop in the company that there might be a better way to complement the work conducted by the company. The company realises that tactically selecting partners for short-term engagements easily leads to antagonistic relationships where the interests of the partner and of our company are at odds with each other. This leads to a desire for a more strategic model where one or more partners are involved with the company as part of a long-term relationship where co-evolution in the context of a symbiotic relationship can be realized. In this case, the companies also collaborate outside of individual contracts and perform joint strategy development, transition responsibility for certain types of functionality to each other and together look for ways to increase the overall value in the ecosystem. At this stage, the company has matured to the point that it can manage one ecosystem in a strategic fashion, but not all. Depending on the company, the ecosystem either is concerned with innovation or with commoditization.

Strategic multi-ecosystem management: The final stage is where the company has matured to the point that it can handle all its ecosystems in a strategic fashion. One of the interesting developments in this stage is that it may have relationships with the same partner in multiple ecosystems. And some of these relationships may be more competitive in nature whereas others are more collaborative. For instance, the two companies may work together collaboratively to explore some new innovation to validate the value that it brings to end-customers. However, once the orders for parts need to be placed, the partner has to compete with other suppliers on the same terms and following a specification that it may have helped develop. Although that may provide a benefit to the partner, it may still lose some business because of pricing or the demand for a dual supplier strategy by its client company. Managing these different interfaces and the different behaviors and attitudes that come with them is a sign of a mature company that can strategically manage multiple ecosystems and do so over time. Especially for cornerstone firms, there is a strategic need to "look after" the entire ecosystem in order to keep the other companies involved and engaged. This is a strategic challenge that often collides with the traditional, internally focused culture where the world is viewed through a win/lose lens rather than a win/win perspective. Again, managing this intra-company challenge is necessary to operate in a strategic fashion with a company's ecosystem.

In the following sections, we describe each step of the ecosystem dimension in more detail with the intent of providing sufficient information for the reader to place his or her company on one of the steps as well as to provide input on the best next steps to take in order to climb the stairs to the next level.

11.6   INTERNALLY FOCUSED

11.6.1   Definition

The first level on the ecosystem dimension of the Stairway to Heaven is the stage where the company is internally focused. In the introduction, we described the large successful companies from a century ago that did everything in-house including providing a school and hospital for their employees. Modern companies at this stage, of course, rely on the services that society has started to provide over the last 100 years. Also, activities that are clearly outside the core of the company, such as cleaning, cafeteria and security services, are typically provided by outside companies. However, everything that is concerned with R&D, manufacturing and distribution is as much as possible kept in-house in the company. Of course, the company operates in a value network and has suppliers and customers but it tries to maximize its scope of responsibility and treats the relationships that it needs to have more on an arm's length, formal and contracts-driven.

The innovation processes are predominantly driven by internal activities. Even though the company takes in innovation originating from the outside, the adoption tends to be combined with some soul searching as to why the company wasn't able to create this innovation inside the organization. Similarly, once functionality is commoditized, the company will wait longer than competitors to outsource it or to replace internal functionality with commercial or open-source solutions. One of the reasons is that by waiting, the company will ensure that the maturity of the outside solutions is so high, that it can rely on its preferred formal engagement model with suppliers rather than having to work more collaboratively to mature the alignment.

11.6.2 Drivers for Adoption

The main driver for this model is predominantly a mistrust of the outside world. Companies using this model tend to have been around for a while and have experienced success when the number and quality of potential partners was low. This means that early tries at collaboration have been largely unsuccessful whereas many things the company tried by itself did drive success and growth. This has built a culture where internal activities and people are trusted and the outside is viewed with suspicion, fueled by a past of bad experiences.

11.6.3 Ecosystem Principles

The ecosystem principles followed in this model are that one engages other companies in the value network if it is obvious that the company shouldn't do this itself. The engagement with the outside is almost exclusively in a value chain, meaning that it only engages with companies that have a supplier or a customer role and hardly ever with companies that could be partners. The interaction with suppliers and customers tends to be formal and contract based and centered around competition rather than focused on collaboration.

11.6.4 Implications

The implications of this model are that companies that are internally focused often have a challenge from a margins perspective. As the company keeps activities in house that it, if it had operated on higher levels of the ecosystem dimension, would have outsourced to partners in the ecosystem, it is quite natural that the activities will be performed by staff that is not world-class at the activity at hand or that operates at cost levels not justified by the commodity level of the activity. Especially for activities that are obvious in their commoditization, because of commercially available outside solutions, the company will at some point switch to these solutions. However, it will generally do this much later than its competitors and only when the perceived risk level is quite low and the level of standardization is quite high so that the transition does not require deep collaboration. As the company is spending a larger amount of its resources on commodity activities and it will be hard for it to operate these activities at efficiency levels on-par with the best-in-class dedicated companies, it is natural that the company will have lower margins than its competitors that have moved higher up the ecosystem dimension of the stairway to heaven.

11.6.5 Remaining Concerns

Companies have operated as internally focused organizations for centuries and many of them have done exceedingly well for decades at a time. However, with the increasing speed of evolution in industry, those companies that are not proactively adopting best practices in managing their organisation overall and research and development in particular are increasingly rapidly displaced by existing or new competitors that offer a superior solution to customers. This is best illustrated by the turnover rate of companies on the Fortune 500. The average tenure of companies was 95 years in the early 1900s. It had already dropped to 30 years in the 1980s. The most recent data, from 2015, showed that the average tenure of Fortune 500 companies has decreased to 12 years. Consequently, internally focused companies increase their risk of disruption as a competitor with novel, more ecosystem-centric practices is likely to offer the same solution to customers at a lower price or to offer an alternative solution that provides significant benefits to customers over existing offerings.

The main concern for companies that want to develop from this level is that it requires them to build a set of new skills that will be experienced as highly counter-cultural. These skills include the ability to collaborate with ecosystem partners in non-standardized areas where the partners have to collaboratively work their way forward to a solution. Also, the company needs to develop the skill to identify which functionality and part of its offering is differentiating and highly value adding and what is commodity and needs to be done by ecosystem partners.

11.7 AD HOC ECOSYSTEM ENGAGEMENT

11.7.1 Definition

Companies that are highly internally focused of course still hire people and some of these people may come from companies that more strongly rely on and collaborate with their ecosystem. These new hires as well as more enlightened employees in the company will, at times, feel that there is a significant opportunity to lower cost and increase speed by replacing some internal activity with an ecosystem partner than can provide the same or even a superior service. Those that challenge the internal corporate culture by insisting on engaging with the ecosystem to capitalize on this opportunity are helping the company reach the next stage of the ecosystem dimension of the stairway to heaven, i.e. ad hoc ecosystem engagement. At this level, the company does engage with the ecosystem but the engagement is ad hoc and driven in a bottom-up fashion by passionate individuals inside the organization. These individuals often have to overcome considerable internal resistance and have to perform significant amounts of additional work to successfully complete the ecosystem engagement. Although these ad hoc engagements with the ecosystem may seem small and insignificant, these are necessary as these activities are low-risk and help the company develop the capability to identify opportunity areas and to develop the collaboration skill that is required for the next steps.

11.7.2 Drivers for Adoption

The primary driver for engaging the ecosystem in an ad-hoc fashion originates on the fringes of the business of the company, rather than in its core. It often originates from an individual or small team being asked to address an area that is new to the company and it is clear that the company does not have the skills nor the ability to address this area at the competence level required. The point is that involving outside parties needs to be so blatantly obvious that it overcomes the internal culture of being internally oriented. At the same time, the area needs to be important, but not critical as the perceived risk needs to be low enough to allow the company to rely on outside partners. The balance between novelty, lack of internal skills and perceived risk will allow the company to explore relying on externals.

11.7.3 Ecosystem Principles

The main difference with the previous level is that the company is starting to rely on outside parties even in areas where it needs to collaborate in a more interactive fashion. Earlier, any reliance on outside parties was controlled by contracts, competition and formal relations. However, when entering a new area, a different mode of collaboration is required, one that is driven by joint exploratory work, experimentation and trust. The individuals involved in this setup will need to learn a new point of balance between contracts and formal agreements and inter-organizational collaboration in the true sense.

11.7.4 Implications

The ability of a company to move up the steps of the ecosystem dimension of the stairway to heaven is not only driven by the company culture, but also by the type of market and the type of product that the company provides. Some markets are highly stratified [18] meaning that the power in the business ecosystem is centralized in a few players and other ecosystem participants are operating on the whims of these few players. In these situations, the powerhouse companies, even when engaging with ecosystem partners, will be extremely careful to let go of control, even when entering in more collaborative modes operandi. In general, however, companies in more stratified markets will be more careful and slow in adopting ecosystem principles than companies in other markets.

The second factor that affects this is the type of product. If products are easy to copy and product development relies heavily on secrecy, adopting ecosystem principles is more difficult as even with non-disclosure agreements and contracts, companies will have a hard time trusting outsiders. However, if the differentiation is driven by hard to copy factors, such as integration skills for highly complex products, such as in telecommunications, or large scale manufacturing, such as in automotive, it is easier to collaborate with ecosystem partners.

For an organization that is starting to engage the ecosystem in an ad hoc fashion finding the right areas to engage and build expertise in working with the ecosystem is influenced by the factors described above.

11.7.5   Remaining Concerns

The organization has now taken the first steps in moving beyond the internal focus. However, its approach to engaging the ecosystem is still ad hoc and driven by individual initiative. These individuals and teams often need to overcome significant internal resistance in order to deliver on the potential of collaboration rather than doing things internally without considering alternatives. Consequently, the organization still does not decide more intentionally what to do internally and what to leave to its partners. In subsequent steps, the organization needs to become increasingly strategic about these types of decisions.

11.8   TACTICAL ECOSYSTEM ENGAGEMENT

11.8.1   Definition

The third step on the ecosystem dimension of the Stairway to Heaven is concerned with tactical engagement of the ecosystem. At this point, the organization has accepted that certain tasks, jobs or activities are better done by partners outside the walls of the company. Whenever a task of this kind is identified, the relevant team in the organization will reach out to the ecosystem and find one or a number of companies to partner with.

Although the notion of the ecosystem is accepted now and the company is starting to rely more on outside parties, the selection of the ecosystem partners is performed in a tactical fashion, rather than in a more strategic fashion. Because of this, the selection and collaboration with ecosystem partners is more transactional and less long term than what would be good for the company in many cases. However, it also fits the current culture of the organization, though changing, better than more inclusive, relationship-based long-term relationships.

11.8.2   Drivers for Adoption

The main driver for adoption is the evidence collected in the previous stage that there are significant benefits in collaborating with ecosystem partners rather than doing everything internally. That evidence, created in a sequence of ad hoc engagements, drives an awareness in the organization that for the right tasks, relying on the ecosystem partners is preferable over doing the same task internally. The drivers for the experienced benefits may include lower cost as well as faster realization and completion of the task and this is typically driven by the access to world-class expertise that is provided by partnering with an outside party.

As the evidence of the benefits develops, there will also be learning of things that did not go equally well or where the benefits were not realized to the expected level. Assuming early failures or below expectation outcomes did not kill the appetite in the company for this type of work, the company is also building up expertise on how to work with the ecosystem.

11.8.3 Ecosystem Principles

The key principle underlying the ecosystem engagement by the company in this stage is the desire to stay in control even when relying on ecosystem partners for certain tasks and engagements. The reliance on the ecosystem is experienced as a perceived lack of control and consequently, the company often develops mechanisms to compensate for that reduction of control perception. For ecosystem partners, this can feel asymmetrical in that the company is asking for large amounts of transparency and insight into the performance of its ecosystem partners but at the same time is very closed and secretive about its own actions and results.

11.8.4 Implications

The implication of this stage on the ecosystem dimension is primarily that the company is accepting as part of its culture and way of working that ecosystem partners provide real business value, because of cost, speed, access to competence or in some other way. This is of significant importance as in the previous level, any ecosystem engagement was driven by individuals who were fighting for acceptance of an ecosystem approach against the organization culture, processes, ways of working and structure.

11.8.5 Remaining Concerns

The primary remaining concern is that the company takes a tactical, rather than strategic, approach to engaging with ecosystem partners. Thus when the need appears, an ecosystem partner is selected to partner with based on availability for the specific task at hand. The company, however, does not drive long-term relations with these partners and is more focused on the transactional value that is created for both partners than on the long-term potential in terms of revenue, margin and more generally the societal benefit created.

11.9   STRATEGIC SINGLE ECOSYSTEM ENGAGEMENT

11.9.1   Definition

Earlier in the chapter, we introduced the notion of the three layer product model. The model is concerned with three layers focused on innovative and experimental functionality, differentiating functionality and commodity functionality. Each of these layers has, in principle, an ecosystem with a set of potential partners associated with it. Although we up to now have not differentiated between these ecosystems, it is necessary to distinguish between these ecosystems. This is because the fourth step on the ecosystem dimension of the Stairway to Heaven is where the company has started to manage one of its ecosystems in a strategic manner while still managing the other ecosystems still in a tactical way.

A company can be involved in multiple ecosystems but as a minimum, each product area is involved, consciously or not, in at least the aforementioned three. Starting to manage one of its ecosystems in a strategic, rather than tactical, fashion is an important step forward as it allows for much deeper partnerships between the company and its partners. Tactical partnership tends to be more focused on transactional collaboration which only works in more mature interfaces where standardization has already established a clear boundary between the company and its customers, complementors and suppliers. A more strategic partnership allows for deeper collaboration between the company and its ecosystem partners in areas where there is less standardization and an increased need for exploratory collaboration. This requires a higher level of trust and longer term focus as the measurable results from the engagement may take longer to establish.

11.9.2   Drivers for Adoption

The main starting point for adoption of this more strategic level of engagement is the identification of an innovation opportunity beyond the capability of the company itself when it is obvious that the company itself will not be able to capitalize on the opportunity by itself as it does not have all the skills and capabilities required. In that case, the company needs to reach out and build relationships with new or existing ecosystem partners. This type of relationship will be different from the engagement models that existed earlier and requires the company to engage differently as well, hence, the transition to a more strategic, long-term engagement.

Once the company has adopted the aforementioned behavior for new opportunity areas, it will start to engage in similar ways in areas that are not new but more established. Especially in areas where technological progress is very fast, working strategically with partners often has significant benefits as it allows for a more longitudinal approach.

11.9.3 Ecosystem Principles

The key ecosystem principle at this stage is the realisation that for at least one of the ecosystems the company is involved in, taking a more strategic and long-term focused perspective leads to better outcomes than a more tactical and transactional approach. The company now learns to distinguish between different engagement models for different ecosystems. In some of its ecosystems, the more tactical and often more competitive engagement model is more suitable whereas in other areas a more strategic and collaborative model is better.

11.9.4 Implications

The main implication is the increasing consciousness in the organization concerning the engagement model for different ecosystems. These models can be categorized along the tactical versus strategy dimension and along the competitive versus collaborative dimension. At this stage, the company is increasing its awareness of and ability to handle these different engagement models.

11.9.5 Remaining Concerns

Although the company has become more aware of the different engagement models, individuals in the organization are not all equally aware and able to act strategically. Also, as the company is, at this stage, only managing one ecosystem in a strategic fashion. The other ecosystems are still managed more in a tactical fashion and the interaction with ecosystem partners tend to be more in line with the old organizational culture of being internally focused. Although the company is already doing really well at this level in terms of ecosystem engagement, the next level is concerned with addressing all ecosystems in a strategic fashion.

11.10 STRATEGIC MULTI-ECOSYSTEM ENGAGEMENT

11.10.1 Definition

The final level of the ecosystem dimension of the Stairway to Heaven is where the company manages all its ecosystems in a strategic capacity, thus focused on the long-term benefit of the organization and in line with its strategy. Although this often means taking a longer term perspective, this does not have to be the case. Also, although several researchers in software ecosystem research tend to focus on collaborative strategies in software ecosystems, such as those in open-source software communities, Wikipedia and others, this is not at all required. Ecosystems can also take competitive approaches, where the platform or keystone company encourages competition between ecosystem partners in a Darwinian approach of letting the best application win. The mobile app ecosystems for iOS and Android are illustrative examples of competitive ecosystems. This level, consequently, is not concerned with long term or collaborative strategies, but rather with intentional decision making concerning the ecosystem engagement model in order to ensure optimal alignment with the business strategy and long-term benefits of the organization.

11.10.2 Drivers for Adoption

The main driver for adoption of this level is the growing realization in the organization that the strategic engagement that the company has realized in one ecosystem can and should be scaled to multiple, if not all, ecosystems that the company is involved in. Earlier in the chapter, we introduced the three layer product model. At this level, both the innovation ecosystem and the commodity ecosystem are managed strategically by the company. If the company developed a strategic engagement model for one of the ecosystems, it will not develop a strategic approach for the other one too as it has realized that there are significant economical and strategic benefits to doing so.

11.10.3 Ecosystem Principles

The key principle underlying this phase is that the company has a very well-developed understanding of what it is uniquely suited to do and what aspects are contextual to it. Those aspects that are contextual should be considered for offering to the ecosystem as part of its strategic goal to focus its own resources as extensively as possible on its differentiation. This notion often leads to a lean organization.

The second principle that is important is that the company works with the innovation ecosystem to find exciting and relevant new insights that, over time, provide significant value to customers. Once the customer relevance as well as the revenue potential is established, the next step has to be that the company takes more and more control of the innovation and either removes the ecosystem partners or reduces their role significantly. Finally, when the concept starts to commoditize, the company starts to explore collaboration with ecosystem partners, but now in the commodity ecosystem, to decrease the cost of ownership of the concept.

11.10.4 Implications

As the company is now fully strategic in all its ecosystem engagements, one implication may be that the decisions made by the company in terms of engaging its partners may not always be understood so easily by ecosystem partners that are at lower levels. For instance, especially in fast moving industries, it might be confusing for partners to see the company collaborate around an innovation, then pull it in house for a year or two and then start to collaborate around the same concept again. Alternatively, when the company employs both collaborative and competitive strategies, it may be complicated to understand the differences in behavior from the same company in different contexts.

11.10.5 Remaining Concerns

Even if the company reaches the highest level on this dimension on the Stairway to Heaven, there are still areas where organizations need to continue to learn. One area that remains difficult even at this level is the timing of the transition between innovation, differentiation and commoditization. When to move something between the different stages affects many aspects of product development as well as the engagement model with the ecosystem. Consequently, developing helpful guidelines in the company as the experience with this grows is important.

A second concern that often remains difficult is the decision to engage with a new ecosystem. For instance, at the time of this writing, the notion of Internet of Things is at the peak of the Gartner hype curve and it will affect many companies that we work with. The question is how a company should decide to start to invest in innovation around Internet of Things. The naive answer might be immediately, but the reality is that early, exploratory activities around this area have an opportunity cost as well: the time spent on exploring innovation related to Internet of Things can not be spent on other activities that may result in more revenue. For new innovation areas, the company will need to engage with other ecosystem partners but the timing as well as the engagement model remains a challenging matter.

Finally, similar to earlier topics, the decision on using a collaborative versus a competitive approach is not easy to take and is often influenced by the culture of the company and the industry in which it operates. For instance, in the automotive industry, the OEMs (the car brands) are the ones that have the power and typically take a competitive approach towards their suppliers. With the increasing rate of innovation and role of software, the competitive model where the supplier of a part was selected early in the development of a car model based on a fixed specification is increasingly difficult. With the growing role of software and the need to bring late innovations into cars close to the start of manufacturing, the engagement model between car manufacturers and their suppliers is changing. The fixed requirements are increasingly turning into a basic set of requirements followed by a growing number of requirement changes over the course of a project. The expectation is that, going forward, the model will have to become increasingly collaborative in order maintain the competitive position of car brands, especially in the coming age of autonomous vehicles that will increasingly be offered as a service instead of through car ownership.

11.11 CONCLUSION

The third and final dimension of the Stairway to Heaven is concerned with ecosystems. Rather than focusing on the intricate details of the technology required for successful ecosystem engagement, we focused on the notion of business ecosystems and their application to the software-intensive systems industry. The main challenge for many companies in industry is the whole notion of opening up towards the outside world. The steps outlined in this chapter highlight the transition of a company that is exceptionally internally focused to a company that is extremely externally focused and that clearly distinguishes between the work that the company is uniquely suitable for and that should be done internally and other work that can and perhaps should be done by ecosystem partners.

One of the models that we use to discuss the approach to software ecosystems is the three layer product model. This model distinguishes between the commodity layer of functionality, the layer of differentiating functionality and the layer of experimental and innovative functionality. The company has different ecosystems to deal with for each layer of the model as well as manage the transition of functionality between these layers. The three layer product model can be used as a conceptual model, but it can also be used as a physical software architecture with different teams, with different success metrics, associated with each layer.

Although software ecosystems have associated technical challenges, in our experience, the technical challenges of realizing a software ecosystem are often quite manageable whenever the company is clear on the business strategy. For instance, one of the alternatives discussed in the chapter is the notion of collaborative versus competitive ecosystems. Especially as a keystone company, one can decide to let third party complementors compete against each other with the intent of finding the most successful innovation to pull into the differentiation layer using a Darwinian process of natural selection.

In this chapter, we have introduced the notion of software ecosystems as well as the ecosystem dimension of the Stairway to Heaven. However, there are many aspects that benefit from a more elaborate discussion. In the next chapter, we present the TeLESM model to discuss the different strategies that companies can use to engage with their various ecosystems.

CHAPTER 12

Three Layer Ecosystem Strategy Model

Software ecosystems, as a concept, allow companies to focus their internal resources on the activities that are the most differentiating to their customers and to rely on the ecosystem for everything else. The organizational culture at most, especially older, companies often started as internally focused and over time the company learned to rely more on its partners. Initially, these kinds of engagements are more ad hoc and tactical in nature, but over time these become more and more strategic in nature.

Engaging with the ecosystem in a strategic fashion requires that the company employs strategies to engage with the ecosystem in a way that optimally aligns with the best interests of the company. These strategies can be more longer term based or focus more on shorter term results and, orthogonally, can be more collaborative in nature or focus on competition between different ecosystem partners in order to obtain the optimal outcome for customers.

Although we have earlier alluded to this, to the largest extent we have discussed the relationship between the organization and its ecosystem. In practice, however, the company is, for every business that it is in, not involved in one but in multiple ecosystems. In order to structure this, we have used the three layer product model (3LPM) as a basis. The 3LPM organizes the functionality present in a product or product portfolio in three categories, i.e. commodity functionality, differentiating functionality and innovative and experimental functionality.

In this chapter, we use the 3LPM to introduce the three ecosystems that each business of a company is part of, i.e. one for each layer of the model. Based on that, we discuss the challenges that companies are experiencing in each layer. Then, we describe for each layer what the ecosystem strategies are that companies can employ based on a model where we span up the space of alternatives. Based on these foundational elements, we introduce the three layer ecosystem strategy model (TeLESM) and discuss how the model is and can be used in practice, followed by conclusions.

12.1 THREE ECOSYSTEMS

There are three ecosystems for every major business that a company is in. These ecosystems are related to innovation, differentiation and commodity, respectively. Each of these ecosystems is different in nature and characteristics, has different participants and alternative mechanisms for engaging with the ecosystem. Below, we discuss each ecosystem in more detail.

12.2 INNOVATION ECOSYSTEM

The innovation ecosystem is concerned with identifying new functionality, concepts and ideas that may add value to customers. Consequently, this ecosystem is highly exploratory in nature and focused on trying things out with customers to identify the most promising innovations for further exploration and, eventually, transition to the differentiation ecosystem.

Although a wide variety of innovation frameworks exist, we use a simple framework that captures the basics of any innovation process, i.e. ideation, concept creation and evaluation. Ideation is concerned with creativity and capturing and describing new hypotheses about what might add value to customers. Concept creation is the process where selected ideas and hypotheses are turned into mock-ups and prototypes that embody and realize the original idea. The evaluation stage is concerned with using these mock-ups and prototypes for evaluation with customers or with systems in the field. Although we describe the process as being rather linear, the reality is that the process is highly iterative in nature. An idea may first be conceptualized as a mock-up and tested with some customers. Upon a successful (or at least sufficiently promising) outcome, the mock-up is further developed into a demo that can be more or less interactive. This demo is then again tested with customers. If this also proves to be successful, the demo can be evolved into a full prototype that can be used with deployed products or at the customer site for evaluation. Once this also proves to be successful both in terms of technical feasibility and customer value, the concept becomes a candidate for transitioning to the differentiation layer.

12.2.1 Drivers

The innovation ecosystem has a number of drivers that one needs to understand in order to realize the specific nature of the ecosystem:

Exploratory: The first and foremost aspect of the innovation ecosystem is that it is exploratory in nature in that it is about ideation, conceptualizing these ideas and testing these ideas with customers. The innovation ecosystem is concerned with evaluating as many ideas and concepts as possible as best practice has shown that in order to have a few successful innovations resulting from the process, the organization needs to evaluate many innovations.

Collaborative: The ecosystem engagement model for the innovation stage is highly collaborative. At this point, the focus is on jointly exploring new ideas and concepts by bringing together people, technologies and solutions to develop concepts out of ideas and to test these concepts with customers or with products in the field. Although some ideas can be developed and tested internally, many new ideas require partners in the ecosystem to realize and evaluate the concepts. Depending on the type of innovation that is being explored, the company may have to reach out to new partners in its ecosystem in order to be able to create a concept.

Risk prone: The third driver of the innovation ecosystem is that it is risk prone. During this stage we want to take risk and reach further than what we otherwise might want to do. Risk is to the largest extent driven by uncertainty, which may be related to technology and market risk, but may also include internal risks such as lack of coordination between functions that need to collaborate for realizing an innovation, lack of access to skills that are not prevalent in the organization or long lead times that cause the company to miss the market window. Although innovation is concerned with taking risk, the innovation process is to a large extent concerned with mitigating this risk by taking small, iterative steps where risks get assessed and mitigated. Although especially in technology companies, the technology risk is often viewed as the primary risk, research and empirical data show that almost always the primary risk is market risk, i.e. customers just don't care about an innovation that is considered to be fabulous inside the company. For large companies, the second risk, almost as high as the first, is that many innovations do not fit the current organization setup and consequently are unable to find a home to grow and develop. Although technology risk exists, it is rather seldom that a team of committed engineers is unable to create a technical solution when the specifications are clear.

Less control driven: The final driver for the innovation ecosystem is that the company is less concerned with control in this stage. Nor does it have to be the organization that initiates the innovation process. Innovative companies engage as easily on ideas that originate from the outside as ideas that come from inside the organization. Being agnostic to the origin of ideas is important as, to quote Bill Joy, no matter where you are, most of the smart people work somewhere else. Thus outside ideas should be selected and taken forward with the same selection criteria as internal ones. Although the notion of open innovation has reached buzzword status, the reality is that many companies are heavily prejudiced against ideas coming from the outside.

Finally, it is important to remember that one of the key reasons for engaging with the ecosystem for innovation is to share the cost of innovation. A company that is internally focused has to carry all the cost associated with ideation, concept creation and evaluation. Being able to share this cost with the rest of the ecosystem allows the company to explore many more ideas, even if this means giving up some level of control and, in some cases, having to share the spoils of successful innovations. Proponents of internal innovation often refer to some example of a profitable innovation that, if done purely internally, would have been much more lucrative for the company. This is a classical case of survivor bias as one tends to forget about all the other, unsuccessful, innovations that were evaluated together with ecosystem partners as well.

12.2.2 Characteristics

Because of the specific nature of the innovation ecosystem, the characteristics of the ecosystem are also different than the other ecosystems. Below, we discuss the different aspects of the ecosystem in more detail.

Who

As the ecosystem is predominantly concerned with identifying, developing and validating new concepts and technologies to deliver new value to customers, the participants in this ecosystem tend to be "downstream" from the company itself. Consequently, the typical partners are its customers and, where available, its customers' customers. Especially in the B2B space, the company's customers will have end customers as their customers. As innovation often requires a more vertical integration of all functionality by the innovating company, the company can achieve this by bypassing other players downstream from it in the value network or by partnering with them.

Another category of ecosystem partners in this context are complementors. In software ecosystems, these tend to be 3rd party developers. Different from the general perception that these tend to be individuals or small companies, it is important to realize that these can be very large companies as well that just happen to exist in adjacent businesses and that seek to integrate into this industry by exploiting the platform provided by our company.

Finally, one of the perhaps unexpected, but quite typical, innovation partners is the suppliers of the organization. Because our company is their customer, they also need to co-innovate with their customers. In order to evaluate and mature their innovation, partnering with our company and testing the resulting innovation with our customers allows for new valuable functionality or solutions. In addition, it builds a more collaborative approach between the supplier and the company which makes it harder to adopt a more competitive approach.

What

At its core, the innovation ecosystem is about the development of new functionality. However, the nature of innovation is such that many seemingly promising ideas fail to deliver on their potential after meeting the reality with customers. Hence, the goal of the innovation ecosystem is to test as many ideas with customers as possible with the intent of filling the pipeline of validated innovations for the differentiation ecosystem.

Many versions and alternatives of the innovation process exist, but at its core all these processes share three stages, i.e. ideation, concept development and validation. As the name indicates, ideation is concerned with new hypotheses about what might add value to customers. Concept creation is the development of an artifact that can be used for validation. Depending on the stage in the innovation process, this can be a mock-up, a demo or a prototype. The validation phase is where the artifact is tested with its target audience to determine its relevance for customers and to identify changes that would allow it to become more aligned with the customer needs. In software, the ideation, concept development and validation phases tend to be highly iterative with sometimes multiple cycles per day. For innovation that requires mechanics and electronics as well, the frequency and number of iterations tends to be much lower and the process much more linear. However, even here techniques are constantly developed to allow companies to iterate faster. For instance, 3D printing has allowed entire industries to speed up their experimentation with physical products.

Especially in B2B markets, customers tend to be very powerful and to have many improvement ideas concerning the products provided by the company. The challenge is that there always is a strong tendency in the company to respond to customers without too careful analysis of the overall implications, such as the opportunity cost of building the customer requested solution and consequently not building something else. Ideally, customer requests should be merged with all the other ideas that have surfaced in the company and be taken through the same innovation process. That should ensure that customer requests are first validated for broader relevance and avoids the company adding customer-unique solutions to its products.

Why

The primary reason for engaging the ecosystem for innovation is to share the cost of innovation as well as the risks associated with it. Sharing the cost is not intended to lower the cost of the innovation budget, but rather to allow the company to test significantly more ideas with customers than if it would focus on its internal innovation activities.

A second benefit of working with the innovation ecosystem is that the amount of ideas is much higher as ideas from partners are taken in as well. As diversity is a very important factor in innovation because it leads to more diverse or different ideas, it helps the company to focus its innovation efforts not just on its current main product categories, but also on new promising areas that are coming up that are outside or adjacent to the current business.

Partnering with others makes it easier to overcome the internal resistance of going beyond the current business.

When

Engaging the innovation ecosystem is often counter-cultural for companies that are on lower stages of the ecosystem dimension of the Stairway to Heaven. Often it requires specific triggers or drivers to make a company that would normally prefer to do things internally. Research by us and others highlight four main areas when it is especially suitable to engage ecosystem partners for collaborative innovation efforts:

> **High market uncertainty**: The first main reason for engaging with ecosystem partners is in those situations where the uncertainty concerning the market opportunity is very high. This typically concerns opportunities that are considered horizon 3 businesses in the McKinsey model [23]. As these opportunities tend to address new offerings to existing customers or offering existing systems to a new customer category, the uncertainty is high and companies look for ways to partner up to reduce the market risk while constraining investment in the innovation initiative.

> **Lacking skills**: The second reason, often related to the first one, is that the company lacks the skills for part of the innovation. It realizes that it needs the skills, but it does not have these skills available. Even if the company is willing to build the skill set, the delays tend to be such that it would invalidate the innovation as it misses the market window. In other cases, the skill set is not broadly applicable within the company and only applies to this innovation. In this case, there is no economic incentive to build the skill set in house and it makes more sense to partner.

> **Customer access**: A typical reason in especially B2B companies is the lack of access to end customers. The company has several business customers, but for many innovations it is the end customers that need to truly adopt an innovation before it becomes viable to convince the direct customers of the value of the innovation. In this case, the company partners with one or more of its customers to evaluate an innovation with end customers. That may well be the only way to get access to these customers.

> **Brand concerns**: The final reason is related to brand issues rather than technical or skill constraints. The company may not wish to associate its name and brand with an innovation until it has established how customers perceive the innovation. This can have a variety of reasons, but especially innovations concerning the business model and customer engagement model are often sensitive and may easily upset existing customer relations.

Although more mature companies will engage with their partners in the innovation ecosystem more easily, the points above are often triggers for less mature companies.

Mechanisms

The mechanisms that should be employed depend on the type of industry, customer and market. We distinguish between directed and undirected partner engagement. For instance, in markets where there are few, but large complementors, a direct engagement with a selected partner is often the best approach. Some mechanisms in this case may include customer involvement, such as in participatory design, or even conventional request for proposals.

In markets where there are many, small potential partners it is preferred to take an undirected approach. In an undirected approach, a variety of mechanisms has been developed over the last decades. When working directly with consumers, competitions can be quite effective to drive engagement and innovation. When looking for new or complementing functionality, events like entrepreneur days [19] to engage the relevant start-up communities can be an effective way to get new thinking into the company.

Concluding

The innovation ecosystem is critical for any company to ensure long-term survival. Although especially large mechanical and embedded systems companies have traditionally focused on internal technology-driven innovation, the rate of innovation and competition has reached levels that make this increasingly undesirable as it puts the company at risk of disruption. Effective engagement of the innovation ecosystem can take many different forms, but the focus should be on reducing the cost of innovation by collaborating and through this increase the amount of innovation efforts quite significantly. Accomplishing this requires the company to be curious, collaborative, daring to take risk and willing to let go of some control as the ideation, concept creation and validation is in progress. Once the innovation proves successful, we enter the differentiation ecosystem and then the drivers become different. This is the topic of the next section.

12.3   DIFFERENTIATION ECOSYSTEM

The differentiation ecosystem is concerned with maximizing the value of features that are considered differentiating to customers. Although other aspects such as brand will drive revenue, from a product, system and solutions perspective, the primary mechanism to drive revenue is to provide functionality that distinguishes the offering from competing ones. The purpose of the innovation ecosystem is to identify those ideas and concepts that provide significant value to customers and where the company can achieve a unique position in terms of product functionality. This differentiation will be temporary, ranging from a few years to a few days, depending on the industry as competitors will recognize the innovation and either copy it straight off or find ways to deliver similar functionality in alternative ways. When this happens, the functionality has commoditized and it transitions to the commoditized functionality ecosystem.

12.3.1 Drivers

The drivers in the differentiation ecosystem are fundamentally different from those in the innovation ecosystem, as we discuss below:

Competitive: The first main difference to the innovation ecosystem is that in the differentiation ecosystem, the functionality and features are driving the revenue and growth. Consequently, this is no longer concerned with exploration, but with using the functionality to compete. As one aspect of differentiation is exclusivity, the notion of collaboration in the innovation ecosystem shifts to competition in the differentiation ecosystem.

Internal: Although the company is happy to take ideas and concepts from the outside while innovating, when it comes to offering differentiating functionality to customers, the primary focus of the organization is to "own" all relevant aspects and not depend on the goodwill of others. The company can take innovation partners into the differentiation ecosystem with it, but it will want to ensure effective collaboration.

Effectiveness: At this stage, the company knows what functionality should be delivered, so the focus shifts from exploration to efficiency. Hence the focus is on maximizing the value delivered to customers against the most effective R&D investment.

Risk averse: In the innovation ecosystem, the company is happy to take risks as the consequences of failures are quite limited. Once functionality enters the differentiating functionality ecosystem, failures in delivering will affect the customer base and the risk appetite of the company will drop dramatically.

Control-driven: Finally, the company will seek to establish control to the level that it knows its customers will be served and that it can provide the solution with the differentiating functionality to all customers that it seeks to deliver to.

Concluding, the drivers in the differentiation ecosystem are quite different from the innovation ecosystem. Many companies fall into the trap of not intentionally managing the transition of functionality between layers. This easily leads to tension and misunderstanding in the organization.

12.3.2 Characteristics

The characteristics of the differentiation ecosystem are a result of the drivers for the ecosystem. In the sections below we provide an overview of the characteristics of this ecosystem.

Who

The differentiation ecosystem is much less open and collaborative and consequently the number of partners in the ecosystem tends to be less than in the innovation ecosystem. When successful innovations transition to the differentiating ecosystem, companies seriously reconsider the partners to ensure that the partners can deliver to customers reliably. For instance, when partnering with small start-up companies, it is quite important to confirm that this company would indeed be around for delivering its part of the innovation. A second factor in reconsidering partners is potential conflicts in other parts of the business as well as collaborations that the partner may have with competitors. The final factor is concerning the governance cost of partner networks. Each partner brings a certain amount of overhead with it; so limiting the number of partners brings benefits. Hence, when choosing between a new partner and an existing one, the company may choose to work with the existing partner even if the solution provided by it is less attractive.

Once the company has established the right set of partners, setting up the right contractual and control framework is of importance. As the company tends to focus more on control than collaboration, the trust established during the innovation phase needs to be complemented with legally enforceable means. Companies tend to start to treat their partners more as suppliers than partners during this stage.

What

The functionality that was transitioned from the innovation ecosystem is often quite basic at first and while in the differentiation ecosystem, the focus is on enriching the functionality, adding variants and, depending on the industry, customer specific extensions. In addition, as the functionality is now becoming broadly distributed, data collection around the usage and value delivered by the feature can start. This data can be used to further optimize the functionality.

Why

The focus in the ecosystem is on maximizing the customer value of functionality and the investments, both in internal R&D and the partner network is focused on this goal. The metrics for successful collaboration are expressed in these terms as well as the reliability of the provided solution. As the company is focused on providing highly differentiating and valuable functionality without increasing risk, these aspects are of primary concern.

When

As discussed earlier, the functionality enters the differentiation layer and associated ecosystem when the value of the functionality for customers has been established. Identifying the exact point of transition is not always trivial and in most companies that we work with this is a combination data-driven and experience- and opinion-based decision making.

Mechanisms

The dominant mechanisms used in this ecosystem focus on maximizing value of the differentiating functionality for customers and on ensuring control of required functionality. For maximizing value, the main approach used is evidence-based or data-driven development. As the data are now available, so the techniques used in the previous part can now be employed. For ensuring control, companies use a combination of patents, contracts and licensing agreements.

Concluding

The differentiating functionality ecosystem is focused on maximizing the value of functionality that has proven to be relevant for customers. As the functionality now is delivered to customers and used in live systems, the reliability of new functionality needs to be sufficiently high. This puts specific requirements on the ecosystem partners and consequently the composition of the ecosystem changes as functionality moves from the innovation to the differentiation ecosystem. The functionality will be part of this ecosystem for a limited amount of time, but during that time the functionality needs to be monetized and used to drive revenue and growth. Once it transitions, it becomes part of the commoditization ecosystem that we'll discuss next.

12.4 COMMODITIZATION ECOSYSTEM

The commoditized functionality in a product or product portfolio is concerned with functionality that is required for the product to function, but that is not differentiating from a competitive perspective. In other words, the functionality is necessary for the company to sell its products to customers, but customers will not select the company because of the commodity functionality. Consequently, the company wants to provide the functionality and provide it in a reliable fashion, but at the same time it wants to minimize the cost of providing the functionality as there is no differentiation in it. Consequently, the company will seek to collaborate with ecosystem partners in order to drive down the cost. In the remainder of the section, we discuss the drivers and characteristics of this ecosystem.

12.4.1 Drivers

The drivers in the commoditization ecosystem are again different from the drivers in the other ecosystems, though these can be viewed as a combination of those of the innovation ecosystem and of the differentiation ecosystem. Below we discuss the drivers in more detail.

Cost focus: The main driver of the ecosystem is the cost focus. As the functionality no longer is driving revenue and growth, but customers rely on the functionality to be present, the main focus now is to offer the functionality at the lowest possible cost. Several strategies for lowering the cost exist, including replacing the proprietary functionality with commercial or open-source components, outsourcing the maintenance and evolution of the functionality and several others. The key commonality between the strategies is the focus on reducing cost.

Collaborative: The first important driver is that the commodity ecosystem is collaborative in nature. This often requires a significant change in mindset for the company as the functionality has been treated as internal and something that needs to be protected. However, as the functionality is now a commodity, there is no need to protect it in the same way as competitors provide the same functionality. Hence, providing the functionality in partnership often provides benefits.

Risk averse: Although the drivers are focused on reducing cost, the fact remains that customers are relying on the commodity functionality. Consequently, the company cannot afford to lower the reliability and dependability of the functionality. So, even if functionality is outsourced or replaced, the quality level can not be compromised.

Less control-driven: Finally, due to the cost-focus and the fact that the functionality is now commodity, the focus is less concerned with control and the company will be willing to relinquish control to the point that the quality of the deployed functionality can be maintained. Therefore, companies collaborate with the open-source community to share functionality with the community and, in the process, reduce cost of maintenance.

Concluding, the drivers of the commoditized functionality ecosystem are a combination of the drivers for the innovation and differentiation ecosystems, but primarily focused at minimizing cost while maintaining quality.

12.4.2 Characteristics

Similar to the other ecosystems, the drivers of the commoditized functionality ecosystem define the characteristics of the ecosystem. Below, we discuss these in more detail.

Who

As the ecosystem is mostly concerned with functionality that is relatively mature, the partners in this ecosystem are those that can provide this mature functionality. Consequently, suppliers are a typical participant in this ecosystem. However, especially for the software in software-intensive systems, open-source communities are typical partners as well. Although suppliers and partners can be partnered with, similar to virtually any B2B relationship, engaging with the ecosystem is very different. It requires engagement with community members and understanding their drivers, norms and values. In these communities, the traditional economic incentives are not those that entice especially front line engineers. The community is much more driven by reputation and general societal benefit. Hence, any company engaging the community needs to understand this and act in accordance with the community.

What

The functionality in the commoditized functionality ecosystem has matured to the point that most or all of the competitors offer the functionality as part of their offerings. Often this has led to some suppliers providing generic solutions or an open-source community having formed providing the basic functionality. The balance is between reliability of the functionality in deployed products and driving cost reductions in the evolution and maintenance of the functionality.

Why

The basic rationale for functionality transitioning to the commodity ecosystem is to reduce cost. However, some companies can also use the commoditization of functionality as a strategic driver as well. By driving commoditization of functionality that some competitors are still positioning as differentiating, leading players in an industry can disempower competitors. Similarly, players having difficulty with providing true innovations often try to innovate in commoditizing functionality seeking to maintain a semblance of differentiation for customers in order to drive sales.

When

One of the difficult decisions for any company to make is to decide on the timing of transitioning functionality from the differentiating to the commodity ecosystem. As long as the company can convince customers that certain functionality indeed is differentiating, of course the functionality should be presented as differentiating. However, it doesn't need to be managed as differentiating from an R&D perspective. When to transition from an R&D perspective is mostly concerned with the amount of feature growth around when the functionality starts to taper off. Early on, there are many requests for variants and customer-specific extensions. Later on, the scope of the functionality is fully covered and competition will have caught up. Then the transition can take place.

Mechanisms

When functionality is differentiating, the number of variants and customer-specific extensions tends to grow as these provide value to customers and, consequently, the company. Often, there is some form of low-end, mid-range and high-end variant. The first mechanism that is often employed is to reduce the number of variants and customer-specific extensions. Once this has been accomplished, the next step is to identify a strategy for reducing the amount of R&D effort and cost associated with the functionality. Later in the chapter, we will provide a comprehensive overview of strategies, but a common strategy is that the interface of the functionality to the rest of the system needs to be simplified, enforced and standardized. This requires an investment in architecture refactoring activities. Once this has been accomplished the functionality can be replaced with commercial or open-source alternatives or outsourced to partners or internal groups in low-wage countries.

Concluding

The commodity ecosystem is where all functionality ends up that has evolved through the innovation and differentiation ecosystem. The challenge is that unless explicit effort is dedicated to freeing up resources allocated to commodity functionality, the amount of required R&D effort grows continuously. In the companies that we work with, on average 80% of R&D effort is spent on commodity functionality. This means that in a typical company, 4 out of 5 people are working on functionality that is required for the system to work but that does not provide any differentiating value to companies in relation to their customers and the competition.

12.5 CHALLENGES IN ECOSYSTEM ENGAGEMENT

In our research, we have studied the challenges that companies experience in the different ecosystems. Below we share the predominant ones for each ecosystem.

12.5.1 Innovation Ecosystem

The innovation ecosystem is collaborative and exploratory. Consequently, the company needs to work with partners and be as open to ideas originating from the outside. Although managing the innovation ecosystem in a strategic fashion is a great way for companies to increase the amount of innovation while managing cost, there are challenges that the companies that we collaborate with experience. Below, we discuss some of these challenges.

Efficient evaluation of innovation propositions and partners

The first and foremost challenge for companies is to evaluate proposals and innovation partners in an efficient way. As the amount of resources available for innovation are limited and constrained in most companies, the organization needs effective mechanisms to evaluate these. The problem is that especially for innovation, predicting success is particularly difficult as innovation is typically concerned with breaking or redefining certain rules that are held as true up to now. Hence, evaluating these initiatives quickly and efficiently while minimizing the number of false positives and false negatives remains a challenge for the companies that we worked with.

Lack of metrics that facilitate innovation selection and prioritization

The next challenge is that most companies use metrics, key performance indicators and dashboards to control most of their business. This leads to a situation where companies, of course, want to use the same for their innovation efforts. Although most companies will use some form of innovation funnel with ideation, concept creation and customer validation as at least some of the main activities, our companies were struggling with identifying an effective set of metrics that help manage innovation activities.

Managing limitations set by customer and technology maturity
One of the hardest challenges in the relation with customers is the maturity of the customers with respect to new innovations. Even if the company can see the writing on the wall and has identified the most promising approaches to innovate and transition from using old technology, engagement models and business models, the primary customers may not be ready to adopt these innovations. Similarly, new technologies that are slowly maturing need at some point to be adopted by the company in its existing products or new products, enabled by the new technology. The challenge is again identifying when to adopt the new technology. Too late will create an opportunity for competitors whereas moving too early will create the "bleeding edge" problem, where the company is spending resources on maturing the technology that will benefit its competitors as much as the company itself. Finding effective ways to decide when customers are ready for new innovations and when new technology is ready to be adopted by the company remains a difficult challenge by the companies that we work with.

High costs due to technology-driven innovation cultures
A more internal challenge is concerned with the company culture with respect to innovation. Especially traditionally technology-driven companies have a challenge in that they think they know what the customer wants and these companies tend to focus their resources on adopting new technologies and evolving their existing product portfolio as well as new products around these new technologies. Frequently, after significant amounts of investment, the company is finally ready to test its innovations with customers and finds that it has missed fundamental aspects of customer needs and hence the technology-driven innovation fails to deliver on the expectations.

Lack of continuous validation with customers
Even in companies with a more enlightened innovation culture where the organization realizes the importance of the customer in the innovation process, we see that the companies fail to continuously validate their work with customers. This is often exacerbated by working with ecosystem partners as the coordination effort and focus is directed towards managing the innovation partners rather than focusing on the customer and validating the innovations with the customer.

Adapting to new innovation and new business models
Although companies are quite mature adopting technology-driven innovations that improve existing products, innovations that fundamentally transform the perception of the product and the business model are extremely difficult to internalize and adopt against. For instance, product companies that turn their business into a services business struggle with the fundamental change that whereas the company sought to sell as many products as possible, in a service deployment, the deployed products become a cost factor instead of a revenue and profit driver. Hence, the company needs to shift its culture to deploying

as many services as possible with its customer base while using as few of its products as possible. These types of transitions are very difficult and most of the companies that we work with are struggling with these transitions.

12.5.2 Differentiation Ecosystem

The differentiation ecosystem is where the revenue and growth for the company needs to be generated, so the introduction of valuable functionality that differentiates the company from its competitors is of critical importance. At the same time, customers have little patience for quality issues, outages and other issues that diminish the functionality provided by the products. The companies we partner with experience some challenges concerning the differentiation ecosystem and we discuss these below.

Timing the introduction of new technology to customers
The first challenge that companies experience is the timing of the broad deployment of new technology in new and existing products. Although the same issue exists in innovation, the customers are much more forgiving concerning quality issues when new technology is introduced in supposedly mature products. Although several companies use the notion of technology readiness levels [52], the challenge is that this is a very slow process and the risk that a competitor introduces new technology enabling highly valuable use cases is significant.

Transitioning of new technology into core offerings
The approach most companies take is to deploy new technology in some products that are more peripheral to the company with the intent of adopting the technology also in the core product portfolio. The challenge is again one of timing and none of the companies that we collaborate with has a clearly defined and proven process for this decision.

The same challenge exists when scaling geographically for companies that serve different markets with products dedicated to the specific market. Often, the company first tests new functionality in a market close to the R&D function and then scales to other regions in the world. The timing and practicalities around this are still challenging.

Balancing differentiation and partner management
The companies have experienced challenges with introducing new, differentiating functionality and solutions that are infringing on the markets of current partners. As companies seek to use partners for multiple purposes, it is difficult to end the collaboration with a partner in one area without upsetting the relationship in other areas. Maintaining the balance between keeping the products sufficiently differentiating while at the same time not infringing too aggressively on the markets of current partners is a challenging proposition that companies struggle with.

Defining metrics to classify R&D investments
As mentioned earlier, companies spend, on average, 80% on commodity functionality and all companies we work with seek to find ways to increase in-

vestment in differentiating functionality. However, companies have difficulty defining broadly accepted metrics to measure the R&D investment in each category of functionality and this complicates the discussions about prioritization of R&D investment in the product portfolio.

12.5.3 Commoditization Ecosystem

The commoditization ecosystem is where companies tend to spend the majority of their R&D effort and consequently the challenges around this ecosystem are in some ways better understood and more practices are established. However, there are still challenges experienced by the companies that we work with.

Deciding when to stop supporting a specific feature or functionality

As the commoditization ecosystem is where all functionality ends up if you wait long enough, there is a constant pressure to invest in more R&D effort in this layer. The only way to decrease R&D effort is to stop supporting functionality and exclude it from the system. For all companies that we work with, this is a particularly difficult decision that is taken very, very seldom.

Product usage data

All companies that we work with have very little data available about how the product is used in the field and which features are used by customers. This lack of product usage data exacerbates the aforementioned problem as it results in difficulties in deciding when to stop supporting commoditized functionality.

Strategic R&D resource allocation culture

In most of the companies that we work with, the realization that certain functionality is commoditized and should not receive investment beyond the absolutely essential was not present. The companies struggled with establishing a culture and mind-set where resources are allocated to differentiating functionality, rather than to development and maintenance of commoditized functionality. There are many reasons, including the quality concerns that may exist concerning the functionality and the mistaken belief by some engineers that certain functionality still is differentiating.

12.6 ECOSYSTEM STRATEGIES

In this chapter, we have introduced the three ecosystems that every company is part of, as a minimum, and described the challenges that these companies experience. In this section, we introduce the strategies that companies can use to make more intentional decisions around these types of functionality.

12.6.1 Innovation Strategies

Innovation is the lifeblood of any company. Without a constant flow of innovations in the pipeline, companies sink into the morass of commodity and the only remaining differentiator will be price. Companies that focus on price differentiation need to focus their energy continuously on internal cost and driving internal efficiencies, often at the expense of the staff as salary cost is among the easiest to quantify and focus on as part of efficiency improvements.

Although many different models and frameworks for innovation exist, when analyzing these in more detail, we can identify at least three basic phases that exist in all these, i.e. ideation, concept creation and customer validation. Ideation is concerned with new ideas about what might add value to customers. In the terminology of the HYPEX model that we introduced earlier in the book, these are hypotheses that need to be tested. The second phase focuses on the creation of a testable demo or prototype that can be used for validation. What shape or form the demo or prototype takes depends on the scope of the innovation. This can range from a new feature in an existing product to entirely new product concepts in new markets. For a new software feature in an existing product, the concept can be a few lines of code. For a new product, it can require the development of mechanical, hardware and software components.The final phase of customer validation is concerned with validating the concept with customers with the intent of determining the customer interest and willingness to acquire and pay for the product as well as identifying adjustments that would need to be made in order to optimize the product for the customer base. The challenge in this phase is to generalize the feedback from a small group of customers to represent the entire addressable market. Finally, the process is iterative in that the customer validation can lead to new ideas expanding on the original idea, adjustments to the concept and further customer validations.

The level of collaboration in the innovation process differs widely, depending on the industry and company as well as the type of innovation. Some companies almost exclusively innovate internally and these companies tend to focus more on technology than on other dimensions of innovation. Other companies innovate especially with their customers and use this close customer interaction to build close and strategic relations with customers in addition to driving innovation. Another category of companies partners closely with suppliers to introduce new technological capabilities to the market before the competition. Finally, some companies rely significantly on others to do their innovation for them and then either buy their companies or find ways to copy successful innovations.

Companies can employ a number of strategies to engage with the innovation ecosystem. In the list below, we present a set of innovation strategies that companies can employ. This set is based on the research that we have performed with several companies in the Software Center.

Me-myself-I strategy: This internally focused innovation strategy conducts all innovation activities internally, ranging from ideation to market validation. The company may use very advanced techniques for idea selection, concept creation and validation, but these tend to be internal. Traditional large companies often had research labs that were focused on (typically technology oriented) innovations. The labs would work with product units to bring new innovations to market.

Be-my-friend strategy: This mostly internal strategy is concerned with selecting the most promising internal innovations but then finding partners to realize and validate the concept and bring it to market. The company tends to treat its partners in this model predominantly as suppliers that perform the activities in a contracted fashion. This allows the company to capitalize on successful innovations, even though this conversely means that it carries the cost of failed innovations as well.

Customer co-creation strategy: This collaborative strategy focuses on partners that are downstream in the value network from the company itself. Typically companies that consider themselves to be very customer-focused employ this strategy. The notion is to collaborate with customers to improve existing products or to create entirely new products. By partnering with some customers and then generalizing the results to the entire customer base, the company increases the likelihood of success of new innovations. From a financial perspective, the company is often able to negotiate that the IP for the innovation is owned by itself while the customer will have some form of usage right or reduced fee in return for its participation. This allows the company to fully monetize successful innovations with the customer base while sharing the cost of customer-driven innovations.

Supplier co-creation strategy: The opposite collaborative innovation strategy is concerned with suppliers as innovation partners. Often, this strategy is focused on new or improved technologies that allow for new use cases to be addressed or existing use cases to be improved upon. Especially companies that position themselves as technology leaders tend to employ this strategy. The company may negotiate temporary exclusivity on new innovations that get developed as part of the collaboration. Permanent exclusivity is often hard to negotiate as the main driver for suppliers to co-innovate is to serve their entire addressable market with these innovations.

Peer co-creation strategy: Although it is very difficult to collaborate with competitors, there are in especially large companies ways for different internal units to collaborate on innovation. Here the focus is creating new solutions that can be applied at problems at both units. Especially in cases where different units bring different expertise to the table, the result can include new products for the company that do not fit either of the units but that are logical outcomes of the innovation process.

Even though this is a company internal innovation activity, we consider this a collaborative innovation activity because these units often do not connect in order contexts.

Expert co-creation strategy: Over the last decade, some organizations have developed expert networks that can be accessed with innovation challenges. These experts may be asked to address a particularly challenging, often technical, problem that the company has not been able to address itself. In this network, the experts compete with each other to develop a solution that meets the criteria, but the company collaborates with the network as such.

Copycat strategy: One of the most frequently used external innovation strategies is the copycat strategy where the company copies innovations that competitors have validated with customers. Often, the company will give some twist to the innovation to make it at least feel different from the competitor offerings, but the differences often are rather superficial. A great example of this behavior can be found between the iOS and Android ecosystems where many ideas are exchanged and copied.

Cherry-picking strategy: In industries where many innovations are available, companies employ a cherry-picking strategy where they evaluate successful innovations for impact and then pick the most promising and successful ones for duplication in their own product portfolio.

Orchestration strategy: Especially in cases where new innovations require multiple partners from different industries to come together to deliver an innovation that is entirely novel, one powerful innovation company has to orchestrate the partners and the innovation in order to create, divide and maximize the value created by the innovation in order to capture a portion of it.

Supplier strategy: In this strategy, the company selects external partners for collaborative innovation with the intent to turn these partners into "supplier-like" relationships. The intent is to have these actors as suppliers in the future when the functionality transitions to the differentiation ecosystem. Treating innovation partners as suppliers already during the innovation phase allows the company to exercise more control and better ways to monetize successful innovations while sharing the cost of innovation through joint development.

Preferred partner strategy: A similar strategy to the previous one is to work with partners that are designated as preferred partners. This allows the company to create alliances with selected external stakeholders to increase control and, over time, have them become part of the differentiation ecosystem. As a preferred partner, this organization can be more easily convinced to sacrifice some short-term revenue or benefit for the relationship.

Acquisition strategy: The most externally oriented strategy is to rely on the ecosystem to innovate and evaluate lots of different concepts and to then buy those companies with proven innovations and integrate these into the company. Although this is often an expensive strategy as the successful companies will be priced very high, it frees the company from spending too much energy on innovation itself, allowing it to maximize the revenue growth and profit from the existing businesses.

In this section we have provided a brief but comprehensive overview of innovation strategies employed by the companies that we have worked with on these questions. The companies employ different internal, collaborative and external strategies for each of the innovation activities of ideation, concept creation and customer validation. Once some innovation has delivered sufficient evidence that there is broad interest in the market for the innovation, the functionality is transitioned to the differentiation ecosystem.

12.6.2 Differentiation Strategies

The differentiation ecosystem is a very different ecosystem in that the focus is on revenue and margin growth and this tends to drive the need for control by the key players in any industry. The strategies employed in this ecosystem reflect this as these are focused on maintaining control and focus on valuable innovations and less on exploring large numbers of concepts against a low cost.

Below, we discuss some strategies that the companies that we work with employ in this ecosystem. As will be clear, the number of strategies in this ecosystem is much smaller and predominantly internally focused.

Increase control strategy: In this strategy, the company seeks for successful solutions developed by external actors and for domains where significant revenue is generated. In the early stages of a new type of solution, often diverse and quite customer-specific realizations are created. When the first signs of consolidation appear, the company incorporates the functionality in their product offering to increase control over new functionality, and reduce complexity for customers. Especially companies that employ a group of third party developers tend to scan the solutions by these developers for particularly popular functionality for incorporation into the product platform.

Incremental change strategy: A second strategy employed by companies in their differentiation ecosystem is to provide a constant flow of small and continuous improvements to differentiating functionality to have the product advance in an evolutionary fashion. This strategy can be very effective to extend the life of differentiating functionality by constantly increasing and improving the differentiators.

Radical change strategy: Especially in industries where it is difficult to deploy new functionality continuously, some companies choose to distribute infrequent but significant improvements to differentiating functionality to attract new customer segments and/or new markets.

12.6.3 Commoditization Strategies

The commoditization ecosystem is where functionality that has lost its differentiation ends up. The ecosystem strategies here are much more concerned with removing cost out of the maintenance and evolution of commodity functionality. Below we discuss the predominant strategies employed by the companies in our research.

COTS adoption strategy: The most obvious strategy in this ecosystem is to replace internally developed commoditized functionality with commercial off-the-shelf products. This typically requires the company to conduct some internal activities to reduce the number of variants of the functionality, standardize the interfaces and align these with the interfaces provided by the COTS component. Once this has been accomplished, the company can replace the proprietary functionality with the COTS component. Although this strategy incurs license fees, it frees the company from allocating its own R&D resources to the functionality.

OSS integration strategy: A similar strategy to the previous one is to replace proprietary functionality with an open-source component instead of a COTS component. Although the principle is the same, there is no license fee, although the license associated with the OSS component needs to be evaluated and there is an expectation from the community that especially companies using the component spend some effort on providing development effort that benefits the community as a whole. Once the open source component has been adopted, additional commoditizing functionality that fits the component could be integrated into the OSS component. This, however, requires the approval of the key decision makers in the community and that requires the company to build good relationships with the community. However, if this is in place, there is a fabulous partnership potential where the company transitions commoditizing functionality to the OSS component and no longer needs to fund maintenance and evolution cost and the community receives mature, valuable functionality that has been developed by professional developers.

OSS creation strategy: An even more ambitious approach is to initiate a new OSS community around some functionality that is a commodity but for which no component exists. The most promising approach often is to partner with competitors in the same domain in order to jointly develop a stack that all partners share in maintaining and evolving. Relying on an arbitrary group of developers and hoping that they will contribute to the community without some incentive is particularly naive and will not happen, except for very unlikely situations.

Partnership strategy: Rather than creating an entire OSS community, one can also take a more closed and selective approach by approaching specific partners with the intent of creating an agreement and alliance to facilitate the sharing of source code between selected partners. In this case, the partners can be internal to the company, such as in the case of inner source, or between companies, by, for instance, shared supplier arrangements.

Rationalized in-sourcing strategy: One approach taken by some of our partner companies is to shift maintenance and evolution of commoditizing functionality to other units internal to the company but based in low-cost geographical locations. Due to the lower salary cost, the company can capitalize on the cost benefits without sacrificing anything to other partners.

Outsourcing strategy: If no internal units are available in low-cost geographies, one strategy is, of course, to outsource the maintenance and evolution to a consultancy who will manage the transition of development to one of its own low-cost sites and take responsibility for the evolution of the functionality.

Push-out strategy: The final strategy that is obvious in theory and almost impossible to implement in practice is to drop commoditized functionality by terminating maintenance and support and finally even removing the functionality from the code. The benefits of this are obvious: there is no management, investment or anything else required. The challenge is that companies don't know who is still using the functionality that they would like to end support for. The perceived risk is often so high that companies do not even dare to consider it. At the same time, general management is often not well versed in software and fails to realize that even commoditized functionality costs resources to maintain and evolve and is not free.

In this section we have introduced the innovation, differentiation and commoditization strategies used by our partner companies. These strategies form the basis of the TeLESM model that we will summarize in the next section.

12.7 TELESM

The three layer ecosystem strategy model combines the three layers in the Three Layer Product Model and the strategies for each of the ecosystems associated with these layers into a model where companies are supported to make more strategic decisions about which strategy to use and when to transition between layers.

12.7.1 Innovation Strategy Selection

The strategies for the innovation ecosystem broadly fall into internal, collaborative and external categories. The best strategy for a specific innovation tends to depend on the type of innovation. More technological innovations as well as those where the company is world leading by objective measures often gravitate towards internal strategies. Areas that are not particularly prioritized by the company but that are required by customers often are more external in nature and the innovation strategies tend to be external as well. The areas where the company is unable to conduct the innovation by itself but that still are highly prioritized are where the company often selects a collaborative strategy.

Although the above line of reasoning may seem obvious, our experience shows that companies often employ a small set of innovation strategies and tend to default to the same strategy independent of it being the best approach or not.

12.7.2 Transition to Differentiation Ecosystem

Once an innovation reaches a certain level of maturity and shows significant promise of delivering value to customers, there will be a point where the functionality should be transitioned to the differentiation ecosystem. Deciding on the timing of this transition is challenging as it brings together multiple factors. First, there often is a set of innovations that are reaching the required maturity and these need to be prioritized based on the biggest promise. Second, the R&D organisation responsible for differentiating functionality has limited capacity and consequently the prioritization may need to be based on the availability of resources. Third, especially for innovations that require partners to contribute to the delivery to the customer base, there is significant coordination required and these partners need to be able to deliver on the required scaling that happens when transitioning from innovation to differentiation. Again, this may affect the prioritization of the innovations to be transitioned. Finally, other functions in the company, such as marketing and sales, may have opinions on which innovations to promote in order to align optimally with their agendas.

12.7.3 Differentiation Strategy Selection

The selection of a differentiation strategy is less challenging as there are relatively few available. During this stage, the company is mostly concerned with ensuring that it has control of the differentiating functionality so it can monetize it with customers and to maximize the economic life of the differentiating functionality by continuous or step-wise improvement of functionality. This improvement is often concerned with adding variants and customer-specific extensions in order to maximize the availability and value of the functionality to the entire customer base.

12.7.4 Transition to Commodity Ecosystem

Similar to the transition between innovation and differentiation, the transition of functionality to the commodity ecosystem is difficult from a timing perspective. Most companies look to extend the life of differentiation functionality by iteratively adding smaller chunks of functionality. However, at some point the competition will have caught up and the company is better off focusing its R&D effort on new innovations that provide real differentiation to the product.

The timing of the transition can be influenced for other reasons than purely internal reasons. For instance, a market leader in an industry may decide to commoditize functionality early to create a disadvantage for less advanced competitors that would like to extend the lifetime of what they still view as differentiating functionality. Also, the company may market functionality as differentiating for a longer time while R&D has already transitioned it to commoditization. In this way, the company can squeeze the last revenue from the functionality while already cutting the R&D investments.

Concluding, the point at which a company transitions functionality to commodity status is influenced by many factors. However, it is important to note that in our research, it has become abundantly clear that companies in the vast majority of cases fail to transition functionality in time and continue to invest in features that have long commoditized in the minds of their customers. Hence, at least from an R&D perspective, transitioning early is preferable over transitioning late as customers will have already classified functionality as commodity, even if sales and marketing will try to convince customers otherwise for a while longer.

12.7.5 Commodity Strategy Selection

Once functionality is transitioned to the commodity ecosystem, it undergoes a number of changes. First, the number of variants needs to be reduced significantly as the value derived from differentiating between different variants is no longer there. For instance, many companies offer low-, medium- and high-end versions of certain functionality while it is differentiating. Once it becomes commoditized, it is no longer relevant to offer these alternatives as it will not generate revenue anyway. Hence, removing all except for the high-end or otherwise most appropriate version and giving it to all customers is perfectly acceptable. Second, customer-specific extensions need to be standardized and, where possible, incorporated into the generic implementation of the functionality.

Once these refactorings of the functionality have taken place, we are ready to select the optimal strategy. The strategy to select will depend on several factors. First, for functionality that is rather unique to the company and where few others will be offering commercial or open-source alternatives, keeping the functionality in the company but transitioning to low-wage geographies may be the best strategy. This strategy is also the preferred one in cases where the functionality, though commoditized, contains IP that the company does not want to give up or share with potential competitors. As an alternative, the company can sign binding contracts with outsourcing partners or other collaborators to take over the maintenance of the software but under confidentiality and without the ability to monetize the software in other ways.

In the majority of cases, the preferred approach is to replace proprietary functionality with commercial or open-source software components. This requires the company to re-architect the proprietary software into a component with clearly defined interfaces closely resembling the component it will be replaced with, but once completed, the company is free from the cost for maintenance and evolution of the functionality in return for a license fee or some level of contribution to the open-source community. Also, in the latter case, the company can work with the community to periodically transition additional functionality to the open-source component and associated community.

In more exceptional situations, the company may engage in the creation of a new open-source community. As we discussed under the related strategy, this requires the agreement of a set of partners and their willingness to contribute to the component. However, if successful, it can provide significant benefit to everyone involved. For instance, the Genivi alliance [5] is an illustrative example where the automotive industry partnered to create an open-source in-vehicle infotainment platform. Although not stated explicitly, this initiative is an attempt by the automotive industry to counter the pressures by Apple and Google to make cars little more than really expensive accessories to one's mobile phone and to be able to dictate more of the strategic direction of the infotainment systems in cars.

12.8 CONCLUSION

The three layer ecosystem strategy model (TeLESM) starts with identifying that for each product or product category in a company, there are three main ecosystems to consider. These ecosystems are the innovation ecosystem, the differentiation ecosystem and the commoditized functionality ecosystem. Each ecosystem has different drivers, different characteristics, different strategies and different rules for strategy selection.

The TeLESM model addresses several challenges that we have identified in our research with leading software-intensive systems companies around the world. For instance, companies, and especially their R&D departments, often have only the most basic awareness of the state of functionality and whether it is innovative, differentiating or commoditized. Consequently, all functionality is treated the same. Also, many companies tend to focus on "going it alone" and rely much less on the partners or potential partners in the different ecosystems of which they are a part. As a consequence, the number of innovations tested with customers is much lower than what it could have been. Similarly, the percentage of R&D spent on commodity functionality ranges in the 65% to 95% range. This is means that the majority of R&D staff is working on functionality that is commodity and does not drive differentiation nor the associated revenue, margins and growth. There are several other challenges that were discussed in the chapter.

The TeLESM model also stresses that functionality transitions between ecosystems and that these transitions need to be explicitly managed. In each ecosystem, the functionality needs to be treated differently and the drivers and behaviors associated with the functionality change. This has effects on the involved partners as the company may even decide to change partners when transitioning functionality between ecosystems or even drop all partners associated with the functionality and make everything internal.

Effective engagement of the ecosystems that the company is part of is of strategic importance for organizations. It can mean that the company can focus the majority of its resources on the things that it is uniquely suited to do and leave the rest to others. Although the TeLESM model provides an important approach to addressing this challenge, it has its limitations. The primary one is that it mostly focuses on extensions to an existing product (i.e. horizon 1) and provides much less explicit guidance for the other horizons in the 3 horizon model including the introduction of new products and new product categories. However, the same principles apply to these horizons and use cases.

CHAPTER 13

Implications of Software Ecosystems

The transition from product-focused and internally oriented company to a platform-focused and ecosystem-oriented company requires far more than a few changes to the innovation strategies or engaging with the open-source software community. In fact, this transition requires a fundamental revision of the basic idea behind or philosophy of the company. Although there are a multitude of implications associated with the transition to an ecosystem-oriented company, there are three ways in which this expresses itself in a particularly fundamental fashion.

First, the company moves from a single-sided market model where it focuses almost exclusively on the customer of its products to a multi-sided market where ecosystem partners as well as customers need to be prioritized. This requires, in some ways, a balancing act, but at the same time the fundamental reason for participating in an ecosystem is that it provides economic benefits because of the efficiencies provided by the ecosystem. So, even if the participation in the ecosystem requires a more balanced approach, it provides major benefits. Having said that, learning to balance the needs of customers, ecosystem partners and the company itself to ensure that everyone thrives in the ecosystem is a complex activity.

Second, the company needs to reconsider what it does internally versus what it relies on the ecosystem for. Whereas the company initially focuses almost exclusively on doing everything internally unless it is blatantly obvious that it should be outsourced, when transitioning towards an ecosystem-centric approach, the company needs to develop a new set of rules about how it decides between internal activities and activities requested from the ecosystem. In addition, it needs rules for determining when it transitions activities from outside to inside and out again over time.

Finally, the organization needs to implement all the non-obvious changes required to successfully engage the ecosystem. These include changes to the architecture of its product portfolio and platform. As the organization will be providing interfaces to outside partners, it needs to be very careful as to how to structure these as the cost of evolving these interfaces is much higher in this context then it was in the internal world. In addition, the ways of working, processes and tooling are likely to be affected by the transition to ecosystems as well. The alignment between the ecosystem strategy, architecture and ways of working and the internal ones needs to be carefully made as it is critical that these reinforce each other. In practice, it easily leads to a situation where these are at odds with each other.

Concluding, there are several significant implications of moving towards an ecosystem-centric business model that the company needs to become aware of, plan for and implement in the organization. In the remainder of the chapter, we discuss several aspects of moving towards ecosystems. In the next section, we introduce the notion of industry structures, analyze how different industries change industry structures over time and the implications of these changes for the ecosystem engagement model. Then, we introduce the ESAO model as a conceptual framework for aligning different internal and external aspects of an ecosystem. Subsequently, we move into the challenges that we have observed at companies working with software ecosystems. This is followed by a discussion of the software engineering implications and a conclusion.

13.1 INDUSTRY STRUCTURES

Different industries take different approaches to engaging with ecosystems and these approaches change over time. An illustrative example is the computer industry. In the 1970s and early 1980s, the computer industry was a vertically integrated industry where every manufacturer developed a complete vertical stack of chips, motherboard and computer hardware, operating system, software as well as the sales and distribution model. The result was an industry structure where companies like IBM, DEC, Wang and others worked hard at driving vertical integration and to differentiate between each other in different places in the stack.

While the large computer companies were fighting each other on the mainframe front, a new development emerged starting with embedded systems and computer enthusiast clubs. This resulted in the development of the personal computer and its broad adoption in the 1980s and 1990s. The structure of the industry changed fundamentally from a vertically structured industry to a horizontalized industry where a dominant design had been established and companies were competing in each horizontal layer of the industry.

In figure 13.1[1], we show the transition as it was originally captured by Intel's Andy Grove. The story is extremely compelling and simple. However, as identified by several authors, including Baldwin and Clark [9], industries

---

[1]Originally in [27]. Used with permission.

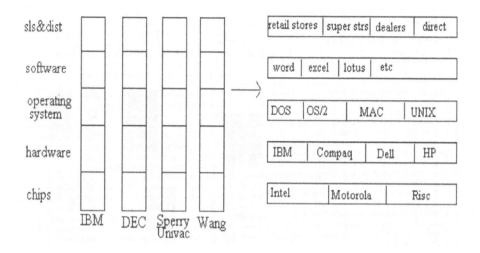

Figure 13.1   Transition of the computer industry between 1980 and 1995 per Andy Grove

do not naturally gravitate towards this point, but rather it depends on the type of industry, the underlying architecture and the business drivers.

In our research, we have identified that there are several industry structures between the fully vertical and fully horizontalized structures that one can identify and each of these has specific implications for the ecosystem in which the company operates. In the remainder of this section, we introduce these industry structures and discuss their ecosystem implications.

Our model is based on 5 "types" of industry structures. Figure 13.2[2] gives a simple visualization of the types using a rectangle to indicate the different approaches companies take in each industry structure. The marked segments represent the relative size of the stack that different companies contribute to the system. In the sections below, we describe each type of industry structure in more detail.

13.1.1   Vertically Integrated Firms

A company that is completely vertically integrated owns the entire process around its products, including the design, development and manufacturing as well as the delivery to the market. It also owns the specification, architecture and develops the software based on its customers' needs.

Characteristics: The architecture is controlled completely by the company; close customer contact; the company is responsible for all development.

---

[2]Originally in [27]. Used with permission.

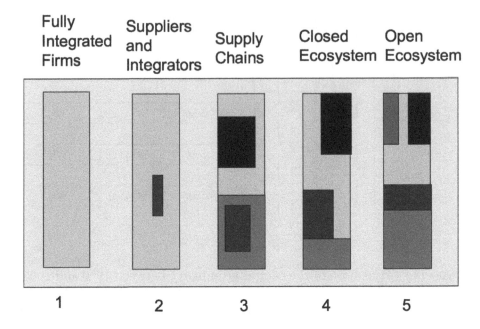

Figure 13.2 Model of industry structure types

Examples: The computer software industry in the 1970s. These days products with small dedicated software such as coffee machines, electric toothbrushes and electric razors.

13.1.2 System Integrators and Specialized Suppliers

This structure consists of system integrators that, similar to the previous type, take responsibility for the final product. The system integrators order standard or bespoke components from specialized suppliers to reduce their own development effort and/or when the knowledge is not available to develop that part of the product. The system integrator sets the requirements of the product and defines the high-level software architecture. It delivers the product to the market. The customer is typically not aware that part of the system is actually developed by a third party.

Characteristics: The overall architecture is controlled by the system integrator. Also, is the only party that is in close contact with the final customer. Although part of the functionality is provided by third parties (the specialized suppliers), the system integrator performs the final integration of the product.

Examples: Automotive companies use dozens or hundreds of suppliers but integrate the product and are the only brand visible to the customer.

13.1.3   Supply Chains

In the supply chain type, the product is developed by a group of mutually complementing companies, each with their own specialty. The difference with the previous type is that in this type, the system integrator does not own the product architecture. Instead, the product architecture is shared by the players and developed through close collaboration between the players. The software is frequently a layered stack of software, where each company in the supply chain adds the functionality related to its own specialty. However, the supplied software has to be tailored for each customer and integration may be done in stages. Because of the high degree of tailoring, software integration is likely to account for a substantial proportion of the development effort.

Characteristics: Although only the integrator has close contact with the final customer, the supply chain partners share control over the architecture. The functionality is developed by several parties; each party delivers specialized variants of products to the next party in the chain.

Examples: Digital televisions, mobile phone platforms, some automotive manufacturers.

13.1.4   Closed Ecosystem

When employing the closed ecosystem type, the product is developed by a group of companies and the product architecture is defined through standards. In a closed ecosystem there frequently is a dominant firm that defines the standards and controls the architecture, even if partners are offered the opportunity to influence architecture design decisions. The system platform is opened up, e.g. by offering an API or a domain-specific language, so that other parties can add functionality for their own use. Other parties could be the customers, the end-users or third party software vendors. The advantage for the leading firm is that it can offer a wider product line with less development effort and the customers or third parties can add functionality more easily.

Characteristics: Control over the architecture is owned by the dominant firm, acting as a (benevolent) dictator, that develops the platform. Third parties and customers can add functionality, based on close contact with the final customer. The overall functionality experienced by end customers is the result of contributions by several parties based on a common platform.

Examples: Microsoft Windows, eBay, SAP.

13.1.5   Open Ecosystem

In an open ecosystem, the role of standards increases even further. The architecture is rigorously defined through industry standards which may result in many of the components to be interchangeable. The standards are open, meaning that they are available for anybody to implement, well documented and largely unencumbered by intellectual property mechanisms. Open stan-

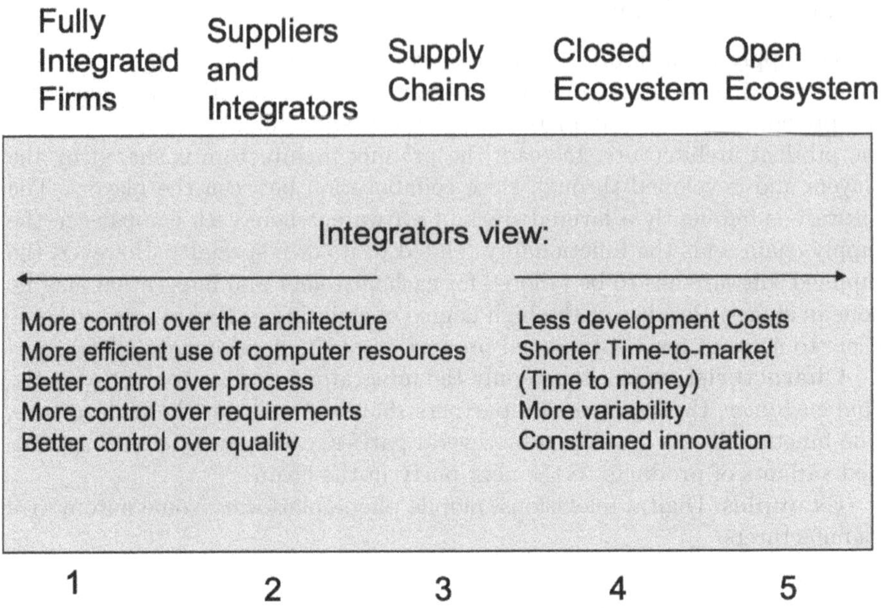

Fully Integrated Firms	Suppliers and Integrators	Supply Chains	Closed Ecosystem	Open Ecosystem

Integrators view:

←——————————————————————→

More control over the architecture	Less development Costs
More efficient use of computer resources	Shorter Time-to-market
Better control over process	(Time to money)
More control over requirements	More variability
Better control over quality	Constrained innovation

| 1 | 2 | 3 | 4 | 5 |

Figure 13.3 Forces of moving from one type to another

dards allow competition at the subsystem level, since suppliers can create competitive components. Hence the likelihood for one organization to become a dominant firm is reduced and power is shared more equally between the players involved in the ecosystem.

Characteristics: Control over the architecture defined through open industry standards. The integrator has close contact with the final customer and can combine a product based on interchangeable components. All parts of the system can developed by alternative parties and are interchangeable. Tailor-made solutions can be made by several parties for specific customer needs.

Examples: Eclipse Development Environment, Adobe Flash Platform.

13.1.6 When Industries Transition

The types discussed in the previous section categorize different approaches taken by companies in the software and embedded systems industries. However, over time the approach taken by a company or a company cluster evolves. Typically, an industry evolves from a vertically integrated to a more ecosystem-centric approach. However, there also are forces that cause companies to move towards a vertically integrated approach. In Figure 13.3[3] we show the forces that are driving companies to evolve over time.

The advantages of moving to a more ecosystem-centric approach are twofold. First, specialized firms are used to develop part of the system. In this way, the company does not have to carry the total development cost but instead is able to share the cost of development and innovation with others in the ecosystem. Second, assuming the architecture is designed or has evolved correctly, a richer variability can be offered at lower cost to the customers by using components from different suppliers or by offering third parties and customers the opportunity to develop the functionality they need.

On the other side, there are some disadvantages of moving to a more ecosystem-centric approach as well. First, the evolution of the architecture and the APIs shared with other ecosystem partners will be slower and more complicated since the industry structure is based upon the architecture. This has a tendency to concentrate innovation on the components in the architecture, rather than at the architecture overall. If the most promising innovations do not align with the architecture, this may constrain innovation and put the ecosystem at risk of disruption. Second, no matter how well the architecture is defined, system integration over organizational boundaries is more complicated and involved when compared to internal integration. This tends to increase uncertainty and time needed for system integration, especially the case in the Supply Chain model in which heterogeneous architectures have to be combined. Finally, the overall product quality is a combination of software from different vendors and failures often occur because of component interaction, unclearly documented APIs or unexpected use. Consequently, maintaining sufficient quality levels is a challenging activity that is complicated more and more as the ecosystem becomes more open.

13.2 ESAO MODEL

The industry structures discussed in the previous section cause companies to develop certain behavioral patterns as it comes to their strategies, ways of interacting with ecosystem partners and organizing themselves. These behavioral patterns easily become ingrained in the organization and as long as the business model and industry structure remain constant, these behaviors will serve the company well. The challenge is that with the increasing rate of change in the industry, the patterns and behaviors that make companies successful need to change at increasing rates as well. This requires companies to become more aware of and intentional towards their approach to interacting with their ecosystems as well as their internal approaches.

In our research with a variety of companies we observed that there are challenges associated with maintaining alignment between the different aspects of the business. This easily leads to misalignment between different parts of the

---

[3]Originally in [27]. Used with permission.

company that really should be aligned. Frequently, there is a trigger in one part of the company that leads to adaptation in that part, but this is not followed up with subsequent changes in other parts of the business.

In order to address this, we developed the ESAO model. In the remainder of this section, we first discuss the ESAO model. Then we exemplify the model by sharing some examples of transitions that companies went through as well as the sequence in which this happened. Finally, we describe different innovation strategies that the companies that we studied employed.

13.2.1 The ESAO Model

In order to align the ecosystem with the internal organization, we have developed the ESAO (Ecosystem, Strategy, Technology platform and Organizing) model [15]. This model consists of six interdependent and interconnected dimensions that are important to take into account for R&D. The six dimensions of the ESAO model concern both an internal company and an external company perspective. We first describe the internal perspective and subsequently discuss the ecosystem or external perspective.

The internal perspective consists of three main dimensions, i.e. strategy, architecture platform and organizing. Below, each of these dimensions is defined in more detail.

1. **Internal company strategy**: The strategy of the company lays down the basis for the future path of the firm concerning the business. In particular, the strategy is concerned with how the company generates revenue now and in the future. The company strategy is relevant for the internal prioritizations and decisions made within an organization and is closely related to the technology platform strategy. The internal business model development is part of the internal strategy. The business model defines how the firm creates and delivers value to customers and then converts payments received to profits.

2. **Internal architecture platform**: The architecture platform comprises the technical structure to build the technology platform as well as the technology choices. The company strategy defines which aspects of the business are prioritized and which can be deprioritized. This is important input for the architecture platform decisions as it allows effective management of future evolution cost.

3. **Internal organizing**: The ways of working, roles, responsibilities, processes and tools within R&D are important and closely related to the architecture and strategy of the firm.

External dimension: In the ESAO model, we use the same three dimensions discussed above for the external ecosystem.

1. **Ecosystem strategy**: The external strategy of a company is related to

the business and platform ecosystem of the firm and the strategic options that it has available in its current role in the ecosystem. Depending on the strategic choices made by the company, there are significant implications on the system and software development of the firm.

2. **Ecosystem architecture**: The ecosystem technological platform or architecture defines the strategy and interface between the internal technology platform and the solutions that are provided by ecosystem partners. In addition to the focus on interfaces, the focus is also on the technology strategy.

3. **Ecosystem organizing**: Deals with how firms work with their customers, suppliers, and ecosystem partners in terms of processes, tools used, ways of working, and ways of organizing the collaboration.

The EASO model has six main elements. These are not independent, but rather are interdependent and alignment between these needs to be maintained. In figure 13.4[4], the ESAO model and its six main parts are presented. Similar to the BAPO model [49], the ESAO model stresses the importance of aligning the business strategy, the architecture and technology choices and the way the company decides to organize itself. There are many examples of misalignment in the industry and it is not the purpose here to analyze these in detail. However, examples include misalignment between business strategy and existing software architecture. For instance, in one of our case study companies, the business decided to switch from a traditional license sales model to a dynamic and fine-grained subscription model for its products. The architecture of these products, however, was fundamentally unsuited for this new business model and due to the lack of alignment, the R&D organisation was unable to deliver on the business needs for a year after the business had announced the new model. Alignment challenges do not only take place between the three internal elements, but also inside of these. For instance, in many companies adopting agile development methods, the R&D teams adopted sprints and frequent delivery of new functionality for inclusion in the product, but the remainder of the delivery pipeline was fundamentally unsuited for anything but yearly release cycles in a waterfall style model.

The novel aspect of the ESAO model is the ecosystem dimension of strategy, architecture and organizing. Although many companies understand the importance of becoming a platform (rather than a product) company, the changes required to realize this have wide implications across virtually all aspects of the business. For instance, the intended ecosystem architecture, which includes the interfaces, but also the underlying design structures such as architectural styles and patterns, needs to be aligned with the intended business strategy defined for the ecosystem. Similarly, the ways of working, processes and tools for engaging the ecosystem need to be aligned as well. A typical

---

[4]Originally in [15]. Used with permission.

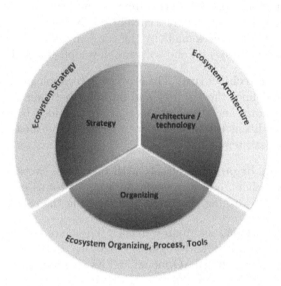

Figure 13.4 The ESAO model

example of an issue is the frequency and process for interface changes. These are relatively simple inside the boundaries of the organization, but require an elaborate deprecation process once outside developers are using the interfaces as well.

13.2.2 Triggers and Responses

To illustrate the EASO model, in this section we present three examples of companies that either due to changes in their business strategy or because of external triggers had to make changes that required adjustment in all six areas of the ESAO model.

The first company is a pure software company and a keystone player in its industry. Although the company had for many years successfully delivered a product to its market, during more recent years, it had started to notice that 3rd party developers had built solutions to extend the product with customer-specific functionality. This was initially met with a skeptical attitude, but over time the company started to realize that it would benefit from proactively engaging the developer community instead of fighting the development. Figure 13.5 described the sequence of steps that the company evolved through and table 13.1 summarizes the response by the company.

For the second company, the trigger was much more driven by changes in which its customers decided to engage with the company. The company is a tier-1 supplier to original equipment manufacturers (OEMs) and it had de-

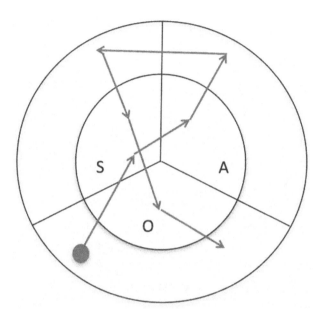

Figure 13.5 Case company A's ESAO journey

Table 13.1 ESAO responses at case company A

ESAO	Analysis
Ecosystem strategy	Adopting app store business mode
Ecosystem architecture	Introduce API and certification system
Ecosystem organizing	Proactively engage with developer community
Internal strategy	Focus changed on how to best serve customer segments
Internal architecture	Careful analysis concerning API & differentiation between certified and non-certified apps
Internal organizing	Unit responsible for 3rd party developers

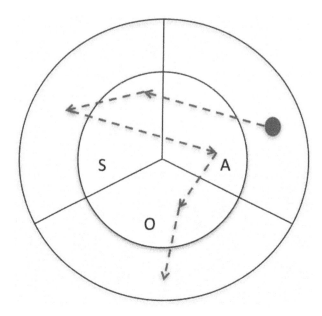

Figure 13.6 Case company B's ESAO journey

veloped turnkey solutions of one of the main subsystems for its customers for many years. Several of its customers, however, decided to revisit the engagement model. The reason was that the software in the subsystem was increasing in complexity and customers wanted to have more control over the software in the subsystem and to add their own software to the subsystem. In effect, the company was pushed back in the value chain from being a turnkey solution provider to component provider and integrator. In figure 13.6 and table 13.2, we summarize the implications of this change on the six ESAO elements.

The third company is a product business that has sold physical products including some hardware and software to its diverse customer base. It realized, however, that competition from Asia was causing significant price erosion in its main product categories. At the same time, its customers were expressing concerns about the cost of integrating its products into their larger installations. So, opposite from case company B, this company decided to forward integrate in the value network and to offer in a turnkey fashion to its customers. In figure 13.7 and table 13.3, we summarize the journey and implications that this company experienced during its transition.

Concluding, in this section, we exemplified the ESAO model using three case companies. We discussed the trigger and the responses by the company. Each shift, independent of where it starts, turned out to have implications on all six elements of the ESAO model. Although the model may seem trivial, in our collaboration with companies, we still experience many cases of misalign-

Table 13.2 ESAO responses at case company B

ESAO	Analysis
Ecosystem strategy	Shift from turnkey solution to component & integrator
Ecosystem architecture	Evolvement of modular architecture to allow for replacement of subsystems from other parties
Ecosystem organizing	Driving standardization efforts within their industry
Internal strategy	Change towards a 3-unit business model
Internal architecture	Careful analysis concerning API & differentiation between certified and non-certified apps
Internal organizing	Unit responsible for 3rd party developers

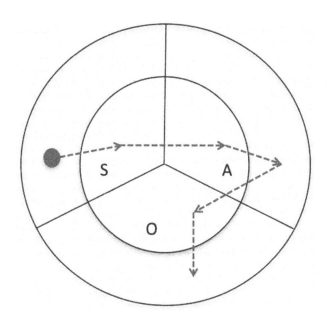

Figure 13.7 Case company C's ESAO journey

Table 13.3 ESAO responses at case company C

ESAO	Analysis
Ecosystem strategy	Shift towards turnkey solution provider; forward integrate
Ecosystem architecture	Adoption towards industry standards for integration and API for 3rd party developers to extend functionality
Ecosystem organizing	Simplify integration and decrease little interaction with others
Internal strategy	Adoption of a 2-business strategy
Internal architecture	Optimized for minimizing hardware resource cost but allowing extension through apps API
Internal organizing	Developed a governance mechanism to support R&D

ment. In our experience, the ESAO model provides a language and framework to discuss and explore implications that are taking place in the organization.

13.2.3 ESAO Innovation Strategies

When studying the innovation strategies employed by companies that were involved in our research around the ESAO model, we found that the companies employ one of four different innovation strategies.

The first dimension was concerned with innovation being predominantly internally driven or externally driven. In the internally-driven innovation strategy, the companies work with an innovation strategy in-house either based on technology-driven research or on customer input. With an externally driven innovation focus, firms rely on innovations that have been developed and proven on the market as a basis for the innovation strategy within the firm.

The second dimension was whether the companies employed a collaborative or a competitive approach to their innovation ecosystem. In contemporary literature, innovation ecosystems are primarily perceived as collaborative or open innovation approaches [4, 46]. Although open innovation research discusses different forms of openness, the main idea is to gain input or work jointly towards innovation and as such share the cost of innovation. However, from business ecosystems literature, it is clear that firms can have either a competitive or a collaborative approach [20] in how they work within their ecosystem. Based on these two dimensions, we define four different innovation ecosystem strategies for software-intensive firms. These strategies are summarized in table 13.4.

The strategies identified in the previous table each take a different approach to innovation. Below we describe each strategy in more detail:

1. **Benevolent orchestrator strategy**: This strategy focuses on inter-

Table 13.4 Innovation ecosystem strategies

Strategy	Collaborative	Competitive
Internally driven innovation	Benevolent orchestrator	Let them compete
Externally driven innovation	Thousand flowers	Play inside the box

nally driven innovation. Once the internal innovation is proven as a concept, the firm selects partners within its innovation ecosystem with whom it can share and collaborate in order to scale the innovation and test it with customers. The firm orchestrates the innovation, but works generously and collaboratively with its ecosystem in scaling the innovation towards customers. For example, one of the companies we worked with had a fragmented and complex ecosystem in which they were one of the players. The company therefore focused on internal innovation and, once proven, they went out to collaborate with selected partners to maintain their place in the ecosystem.

2. **Thousand flowers strategy**: This strategy focuses on a large set of customer-validated ideas and proven innovations from its ecosystem parties, i.e., thousand flowers. The firm selects only a few of these "flowers" or potential parties as collaborators for scaling innovation with their own customer base. The selection process of selecting a few of the flowers focuses on technology integration with the firm's internal R&D, as well as potential matches for suitable collaboration partners. A second company in our research was a market leader and keystone firm in their industry with few real competitors and chose to focus on external innovation to lower innovation costs and gain more input from their 3rd party developers and customers.

3. **Let them compete strategy**: This strategy is adopted by firms that primarily focus on internal innovation and is not open for innovation from its ecosystem parties. The ecosystem is mainly used for gaining insight in competition, new developments and trends. Once the firm has a customer-proven innovation, it reaches out towards external suppliers or developers to introduce the innovation, i.e. its product development ecosystem. The firm does this in a competitive fashion and lets ecosystem parties compete to get the best possible deal. One of our case study companies is one of the keystone players in a highly competitive market primarily driven by IP and therefore chose a competitive ecosystem strategy.

4. **Play inside the box strategy**: This strategy is performed by firms that are open for innovations from the ecosystem, but only when the ecosystem parties play by the rules, i.e., within the box, of the firm. These rules can be placed down in certification procedures, APIs, and

other contractual agreements like sharing revenue. The firm applies a competitive approach concerning innovation, but is able to take in new ideas and suggestions. One company in our research works in a highly competitive market driven by IP, but is one of the larger players. Therefore, they have chosen to work with a competitive innovation strategy based on their rules.

In our research it became clear that industries that are more driven by intellectual property and patents, are less open for a collaborative approach in ecosystem innovation and are more afraid for knowledge disclosure. These firms focus more on a competitive innovation ecosystem strategy. On the other hand, in industries where the first mover advantage is important, larger companies tend to be more collaborative and partner to identify innovations that have real market traction as early as possible.

The four different strategies discussed in table 13.4 also have implications for the elements discussed in the ESAO model. The innovation ecosystem strategy needs to be aligned with the internal R&D strategy, the technological platform or architecture choices as well as the way of working or organizing. From the case studies there are clear implications of the selected innovation ecosystem strategy for the internal choices.

As a final observation, especially the most internally focused case study companies had a tendency to open up to more external innovation impulses as they saw the value that ecosystem partners could provide. Interestingly, the companies started from collaborating in the operational ecosystem, then engaged with ecosystem partners in their product development ecosystem and over time brought partners into their innovation processes, creating an innovation ecosystem.

13.3 OBSERVED CHALLENGES

In our work with a host of different companies, we have collected a set of challenges that companies struggle with as they move towards more open ecosystems. The challenges can be organized according to the ESAO model, but we focus on the technical and organizational issues. In the sections below, we discuss several challenges that we have identified.

13.3.1 Software Architecture

Software architecture maintains the link between the business and the technology and platform and as such is critical to maintain agility and nimbleness in the organization. As discussed below, the companies involved in our research experienced a number of challenges around architecture.

Failing to keep it simple

We found that all companies in our research suffered from this problem, but especially companies with a significant portfolio of legacy products suffered from this. The key role of the software architect is to take the key software architecture design decisions that decompose the system into consistent parts that can continue to evolve in relative independence. However, no architectural decomposition is perfect and each has cross-cutting concerns as a consequence. These concerns cause additional dependencies between the components that need to be managed and add to the complexity of the system. Techniques exist to decrease the "tightness" of dependencies, such as factoring out the cross-cutting concerns and assigning them to a separate component or by introducing a level of indirection that allows for run-time management of version incompatibilities. In the initial design of the system, but especially during its evolution, achieving and maintaining the absolutely simplest architecture is frequently not sufficiently prioritized. In addition, although complexity can never be avoided completely for any nontrivial system, it can easily be exacerbated by architects and engineers in response to addressing symptoms rather than root causes, e.g. through overly elaborate version management solutions, heavy processes around interfaces or too effort-consuming continuous integration approaches.

Lockstep evolution

Some of our case study companies suffered from the lockstep evolution problem, i.e. all software assets have to move to the next iteration or release simultaneously otherwise the system or platform breaks down. When the system or platform can only evolve in a lockstep fashion, this is often caused by evolution of one asset having unpredictable effects on other, dependent assets. In the worst case, with the increasing amount of functionality in the assets, the cycle time at which the whole system is able to iterate may easily lengthen to the point where the product or platform turns from a competitive advantage to a liability. The root cause of the problem is the selection of interface techniques that do not sufficiently decouple components from each other. APIs may expose the internal design of the component or be too detailed that many change scenarios require changes to the API as well. The crosscutting concerns discussed under the previous point obviously exacerbate the lockstep evolution problem.

Insufficient quality attribute management

Even in a case where the functional aspect of the API has been designed properly, the quality attributes and the design decisions to achieve certain quality attributes may cause implicit inter-component dependencies. For instance, subsequent versions of a component, having different resource requirements and timing behavior, may cause other components to fail. Although quality attributes are inherently cross cutting, one can use mechanisms, such as containers, to minimize the impact of these kinds of changes. The case study companies developing embedded systems especially used solutions that bypassed the architectural design and principles. Often these solutions were introduced as a temporary, product-specific extension to solve a particular quality attribute problem but over time these solutions became part of the platform architecture as they were "sanctioned" as the exception tends to be turned into a rule.

Engineering processes

The processes used in R&D are critical for translating business and architectural intentions into realized solutions in the hands of customers. In an ecosystems context, these processes and the alignment between the internal processes and ecosystems processes are even more important. Below we discuss several challenges related to engineering processes identified during our research.

Insufficient pre-iteration cycle work

For some of the teams in one of the case companies that we studied, features that cross component boundaries were under-specified before the development cycle started and were "worked out" during the development. In practice, this requires close interaction between the involved teams and causes significant overhead that could easily be avoided by more upfront design and interface specification. A consequence of this approach is that it builds an "addiction" between teams in that there is a need for frequent (daily) developer-to-developer drops of code that is under development in order to avoid integration problems later on. This, in turn, often results in largely manual testing of new functionality because requirements solidify during the development cycle and automated tests could not be developed in time. Although this is a huge burden on internal development, it is virtually impossible in an ecosystem context. Hence proper focus has to be given to architecture work in order to avoid major disruptions in the interface with the ecosystem.

Unintended resource allocation

Resource allocation is a tool used by companies to align resources with the business strategy. In practice, however, at several of the case study companies, teams frequently assign part of their resources to other software components and their associated teams. The reason is that they are dependent on the other components to be able to get their own functionality developed and released. One can view this as a lack of road mapping activities and, in that sense, it supports the previous point. The consequence is again that the coordination costs between teams easily become excessive, resulting in a general perception in the organization that significant inefficiencies exist.

High and unpredictable product integration cost

A third problem, observed in all case study companies and to a significant extent caused by the earlier discussed problems, is that during product integration, incompatibilities between components are detected during system testing and quality attributes break down in end-to-end test scenarios. This causes a costly and unpredictable integration process that, being at the end of the development cycle, causes major difficulties at the affected companies. The adoption of continuous integration and continuous deployment is providing much of the solutions required to address this challenge, but especially in industries where mechanics and hardware play a significant role, the cost of integration, especially over organization boundaries, as we have in a software ecosystem context, remains a challenge.

Lack of process discipline

We found that some teams in our case study organizations suffer from a lack of process discipline. Although processes have been defined, we observed that engineers and teams sometimes simply ignore them. For example, in one organization, engineers in different teams worked out additional, detailed interfaces between their respective components, despite the fact that the designed architecture did not allow for any connections between these components. As a result, independent validation of the components became impossible. The architectural integrity was violated and during the evolution of the system, these implicit dependencies caused major inefficiencies in the development process. Although engineers and teams are aware of and understand the defined processes, the typical argument is that in this particular case the process is not applicable and that following the process would have negative consequences, e.g. cause delays. Once the difficulties begin to mount, this behavior is reinforced resulting in an increasingly lax process attitude.

Mismatched engineering processes

Another case is when the engineering processes are defined and followed, but the processes are simply not suitable for the type of system or platform and the organizational setup. For instance, processes relying on face-to-face communication or processes that assume interaction between teams during iterations cause significant inefficiencies in large R&D organizations and especially global organizations. For example in one case company, the delivery of the next version of a component to the integration team required verbal communication between the integration team and the component team who, after the company adopted global development, worked in a distributed setting with 12 hours time difference. The ability to have verbal communication was obviously highly impacted by the time difference.

Disconnected business and engineering processes

Finally, even when the proper engineering processes have been defined and used, the connection to business processes, especially product management, may be missing. Especially while implementing a new business strategy, not only the R&D organization, but also the rest of the organization has to change significantly. We found two major problems: (a) The business strategy is defined at a level of abstraction that still requires significant interpretation that cannot be performed by the R&D organization, especially with respect to prioritization and sequencing of functionality. (b) In the mature existing products, the product management has grown accustomed to defining the next release in terms of features to be added to the existing product. The new business strategy requires the definition of a completely new product or platform that has to be defined as an entirety and not as a delta of last year's product and the product management function is unable to provide necessary guidance. For instance, in one case company, a new platform that had been developed offered significant new business opportunities, but product management was unable or unwilling to exploit these for fundamentally new products.

13.3.2 R&D Organization

Although the notion of organization is not very popular in the software-intensive systems industry, it turns out that organizational structure and context are important for the architecture and the software process. Organizing the work in an R&D organization is challenging and this challenge is exacerbated when we enter a software ecosystem context. In our research, we have observed some challenges that we discuss below.

Globalization

Having software engineers located at different geographical locations or even crossing country boundaries has significant implications for the communication and collaboration of the engineer teams. Working geographically distributed increases the amount of time required to accomplish tasks due to cultural differences, time zone differences. Consequently, engineers need to spend more time in coordinating their work across the globe and have to shift their time for valuable work and global coordination, which makes development less efficient. Cultural and language differences are evident in globalization and cultural differences appear to lead to coordination difficulties and create obstacles to effective communication. For example, in one organization that we worked with, teams were geographically split, with the team lead architect and senior engineers located at the main site of the organization in Europe and the remaining engineers in a remote site in India. This required significant communication taking place over geographical boundaries resulting in very inefficient development processes as well as a demotivated team at the remote site, due to a lack of autonomy and responsibility of the remote site. In a software ecosystem context, it is virtually impossible to control the location and time zone of partners, which further increases the challenge in this area.

Tacit knowledge

Tacit knowledge is implicit and deeply rooted, and is an important aspect for working in global teams. Work practices, awareness of cultural differences as well as contextual awareness of a location can be defined as tacit knowledge of the local team members, which is difficult to share or transfer to remote teams or to ecosystem partners. Another aspect in which tacit knowledge is important to take into account is in organizational change processes. Tacit knowledge in this respect is a good match for the existing legacy of products and platforms. When a new business strategy is implemented, part of the existing tacit knowledge needs to be changed. However, as it is implicit knowledge it becomes difficult to implement the necessary changes. For example, in one case company, the culture allowed teams to add product-specific code in all areas of the architecture, which initially caused inefficiencies when the company transitioned to a product line approach. It took significant effort, especially by the lead architects, to convert the implicit, tacit assumptions into a formalized description of behavior, explain the negative consequences and to enforce a different approach to engineering.

Mismatch between architectural and organizational structure

One of the organizations transitioned from a product-centric to a product-line centric approach to software development. This requires a shared platform that is used by all business units. The organization, however, was unwilling to adjust the organizational structure and instead asked each business unit to contribute a part of the platform. Now each business unit had to prioritize between its own products and contributing to the shared platform and as a consequence the platform effort suffered greatly. Although the importance of aligning the organization with the architecture has been known for decades [24], in practice many organizations violate this principle constantly. In many ways, the ESAO model provides a framework for aligning architecture and organization, both inside the company and towards the ecosystem. Despite the conceptual frameworks, this remains a challenging topic for many companies involved in our research.

Coordination cost

A problem observed in all case study companies is that when decoupling between shared software assets is insufficiently achieved it leads excessive coordination cost between teams. One might expect that alignment is needed at the road mapping level and to a certain extent at the planning level. When teams need to closely cooperate during iteration planning and have a need to exchange intermediate developer releases between teams during iterations in order to guarantee interoperability, the coordination cost of shared asset teams is starting to significantly affect efficiency. In an ecosystem context, this becomes even more of a challenge as there are fewer mechanisms for coordination available and consequently it leads to even more complicated coordination challenges.

13.4 RECOMMENDATIONS

Our research in software ecosystems has led us to identify a number of key recommendations for companies that seek to develop and evolve their own software ecosystem. In this section, we describe the primary recommendations that we have identified as part of our research.

13.4.1 Customers First; Developers Second

Description

Successful ecosystems offer value to customers and achieve their first wave of success through customer adoption. Converting the application into a platform for external developers creates a second wave of success.

Rationale

There are two main reasons why ecosystems should focus on customers first and only then on 3rd party developers:

Developers are interested in reaching lots of customers, either for financial reasons or prestige. Technology is of secondary importance.

Customer success means the platform company has a durable competitive advantage that can be defended over time, increasing attractiveness for external developers.

Example
One illustrative example is Salesforce. From its founding in 1999 until 2004, the company solely focused on building its customer base. Once it had established a strong beachhead in the CRM market, it opened up its product for 3rd party developers.

Implications
This has the following implications for companies seeking to create and develop a software ecosystem approach:

Start from existing customer-rich product lines. These are the ticket to entry.

In order to reach customers, a multi-device approach where the same functionality can be reached independent of where I am as a user is crucial.

Customers' adoption of our core innovations is critical for developer involvement. Although companies aim to use the ecosystem as a means of sharing the cost of innovation, without customer adoption, the interest from 3rd party developers will be muted.

13.4.2 Platform Should Be in the Middle of Every Transaction

Description
The platform needs to be an integral part of every activity/transaction in the ecosystem. Although it is tempting to take an operating system-like approach where the ecosystem platform is agnostic to the applications running on top of it, this is the fastest way to disruption. The platform needs to be involved in each and every value creating activity or have proper control points.

Rationale
There are three main reasons why the platform needs to be involved:

The more activity occurs outside the core platform, the less the platform company is required; over time the competitive advantage erodes.

Exercising control over the transaction stream enables better security and trust from customers.

Monetization often applies use-based or transaction slice-based mechanisms.

Example

Facebook allows for 3rd party developers to host applications on top of its product. However, it requires that all applications use the login functionality provided by the company. This allows it to shut down any application that violates the rules that it sets for its ecosystem.

As a broader reflection, in our research we have found no examples of commercial software ecosystems where different 3rd party applications could use each others functionality to build even richer functionality. The rationale for commercial software ecosystem companies avoiding this is that it easily removes the platform from the value creation and transaction flow, which keystone players obviously want to avoid.

Implications

Depending on the industry that one is in, this has several implications for the keystone partner:

Minimize interaction outside (bypassing) platform and actively work to be the "conduit of choice".

Allow for storing application-specific data inside hosting platform in order to deepen the dependency on the platform.

Similarly, host 3rd party applications inside the platform in order to drive integration and inter-dependency.

Offer a set of "connecting services" that take the burden from developers in order to minimize the desire to build solutions outside the ecosystem platform.

Facilitate inclusion into the workflow in the product to minimize the need to replicate the workflow outside the platform.

13.4.3 Proactively Incorporate Functionality and Data Models

Description

Platform functionality commoditizes constantly and for the platform to continue to be differentiating, it needs to incorporate new functionality continuously. Similarly, platform functionality needs to be constantly pushing functionality down into the next computing platform layer. This is the basic premise for the three layer product model and TeLESM gives a framework for accomplishing this.

Rationale

The rationale for this recommendation has been discussed earlier in the book, but can be summarized as follows:

New computing platforms at higher abstraction levels are constantly created and the platform need "move up" in the stack or it loses its relevance over time.

Ignoring pushing functionality out will bloat the platform, bind more and more engineering staff to non-differentiating work and may disconnect the platform from the rest of the industry.

Example

The classic example in the software industry is the Microsoft Windows franchise. Since its inception, it has constantly been on the lookout for new functionality to include in the platform in order to increase its value to customers. This strategy led to near-monopoly status in the 1990s and clearly it was very successful. Being an operating system, Windows was less successful in pushing out functionality, but there are examples of functionality that have been incorporated in the PC hardware architecture and device drivers.

Implications

The constant and proactive incorporation of differentiating functionality leads to a number of implications:

Especially for application domain-driven ecosystems, the platform as provided to the ecosystem needs to include domain data models, functionality and user interface solutions. Simply providing a set of APIs is too simplistic and in practice the company should provide some form of "domain language" for 3rd party developers to operate in.

Constantly scan adoption of solutions developed by external developers and look for domains where significant revenue is generated. When the first signs of consolidation appear, incorporate the functionality (and possibly one of the companies) and nudge/drive other solutions out of the ecosystem.

Proactively re-architect the platform to align with maturing COTS solutions and swap when the cost of maintaining the internal component exceeds the cost of the external component.

Consider open-sourcing commoditized functionality to drive adoption of functionality and share maintenance cost. This correlates to one of the strategies in the TeLESM model.

13.4.4   Communicate Clear, Multi-year Road Maps

Description

The platform company needs to communicate clear, long-term road maps of functionality that it intends to release as part of the platform in upcoming releases. Customers and especially 3rd party developers need a clear and long-term perspective on the intent of the platform company.

Rationale

There are several compelling reasons for publishing road maps for the platform. Some of these include:

External developers can avoid entering into head-to-head competition with the platform company (where they tend to be at a disadvantage).

It warns external developers to leave an area of functionality that the platform intends to incorporate and to move upstream early, minimizing disruption for themselves, their customers and the overall ecosystem.

The platform company and external developers can align the release of new functionality to drive adoption of new solutions.

Example

Especially in the online platform business, companies like eBay and Salesforce publish road maps to their ecosystem partners. Even the highly secretive Apple will announce new features to their developers and work with them before the release of platforms to ensure alignment and synergy.

Implications

The implication of this recommendation is that the company will need to build new capabilities that it did not require as a standalone product company. This includes:

Develop internal capability for multi-year road mapping. In most companies, even if multi-year planning processes are used, these tend to restart from scratch every year. Once ecosystems partners are relying on the road map, this is no longer feasible and the company needs to actually plan multiple years ahead.

Publish an updated road map concerning data models, domain services, user experience solutions and compositionality with each release of the platform; guarantee that external communication is aligned with internal knowledge.

Actively work with developers in functionality areas that you intend to draw into the ecosystem platform. These collaborations can take multiple forms. One form is "acqui-hiring" where the company buys the 3rd party developer's company. Another form is where the platform company has decided to provide basic functionality in a domain and works with the 3rd party developers to provide specialized solutions on top of the basic functionality in specific niches and for specific customers.

13.4.5 Model Platform as the Next Computing Platform Abstraction Layer

Description

Especially for application-centric ecosystems, it is important to present the platform as a computing abstraction layer that hides the computing platforms below it.

Rationale

There are two main reasons why a platform should aim to present itself as a complete, encompassing structure:

> It enables the platform to be part of as many activities/transactions in the ecosystem as possible. The platform becomes the go-to place for anything related to the application domain addressed by the platform.

> It provides leverage over technology providers as the platform integrates the relevant solutions from other providers and presents one interface to customers. By doing so, it can freely exchange the technology providers with others if that provides benefits.

Example
One interesting example is the way in which Google Chrome seeks to position itself as the web computing platform that minimizes the ability of the underlying operating system to be differentiating. In that sense it aims to decrease the value of Microsoft Windows, OSX and Linux as desktop computing platforms. As a second example, although we have mentioned Salesforce before, the company explicitly positions itself as the CRM platform.

Implications
There are several implications to be considered as a consequence of this recommendation.

> The first is to use dominance in one device category, e.g. the desktop, to claim a similar dominance in other device categories. Especially application-domain platform companies should seek to establish themselves as channel-independent providers of domain functionality.

> Design the platform such that external developers only use the platform, no external technologies or solutions.

> Prioritize stability of the platform to the highest extent possible; platforms provide backward compatibility.

13.5 CONCLUSION

The goal of this chapter was to present the implications of adopting software ecosystems as a business strategy. The first challenge to that proposition was, of course, that companies in different industries have different starting points and opportunities to adopt software ecosystems. In order to shed light on this, we discussed a model presenting different industry structures. This model can help the company decide where its industry currently resides and what the implications on its ecosystem are.

We then discussed the ESAO model as a tool and framework to analyze the implications of adopting software ecosystems. The ESAO model has six main elements, divided in the internal strategy, architecture and organizing approach, and the external (or ecosystem) strategy, architecture and organizing approach. These six elements are orthogonal, but highly interdependent and the alignment between these needs to be maintained continuously. The ESAO model can be used as a framework to evaluate the implications of adopting an ecosystem approach as well as to guide the transition and evolution.

Finally, we discussed the challenges of software ecosystems and large-scale software engineering in an ecosystem context as well as provided a set of key recommendations that companies, based on our research, would benefit from at least seriously considering if not adopting outright.

Software ecosystems are a key technology for virtually any software-intensive systems industry and the ecosystem dimension of the Stairway to Heaven provides a systematic approach to incorporating it. This chapter provides tools, knowledge and recommendations for operating in a software ecosystem context.

V

Conclusion

CHAPTER 14

Conclusion

There are three focus areas that will define the nature of large-scale software and systems engineering in the coming decade and likely beyond. The focus areas are speed, data and ecosystems and the three dimensions of the Stairway to Heaven presented in earlier parts in this book have discussed each of these focus areas in detail. Each part provides tools and frameworks for addressing the respective dimension. Although we have largely presented these focus areas as orthogonal dimensions, the fact is that many connections exist between these and that they can not be treated as independent.

The primary relation in between the focus areas is synergy. The higher up one gets on one dimension, the more benefit other dimensions experience. For instance, the transition from continuous integration to continuous deployment shortens the feedback loop between development and customers with, typically, an order of magnitude. This enables the data dimension to transition to real-time data analytics, reporting and decision making as well. Rather than collecting data after the yearly release, continuous deployment allows the data dimension to improve its value as well. Often this leads to a significant investment in automation of the collection and analysis of data. This brings significant benefit in the third dimension, ecosystems, as it allows the company to automate certain parts of its engagement with ecosystems. Especially when a company has many third party developers, suppliers or other types of partners, automating manual processes is critical importance and instrumenting these automated processes is required to avoid excessive cost of managing the ecosystem partners. Hence, the same tools used to collect data and analyze customer behavior and the performance of systems deployed in the field can be used for instrumenting and automating the management of ecosystem partners as well.

In the remainder of this conclusion chapter, we first provide a summary of each dimension of the Stairway to Heaven and discuss the tools, mechanisms and frameworks that one can use to assess current state as well as techniques to transition from one step to the next. Then we discuss the interconnections and

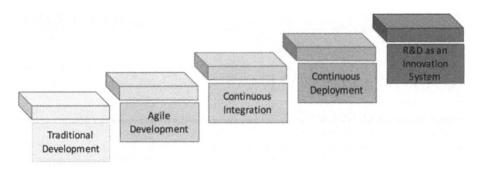

Figure 14.1 Stairway to Heaven: Speed dimension

synergy opportunities in more detail. We conclude the chapter by exploring what is on the horizon of software engineering.

14.1 SPEED

The Stairway to Heaven consists of three dimensions and its first dimension is speed. As shown in figure 14.1, the speed dimension defines the typical evolution that organizations evolve through as they adopt better software engineering practices. Starting from traditional waterfall development, the first step that companies take is to adopt agile development practices. Although several agile approaches exist, one common denominator is the notion of sprints of four weeks or less and delivering something of value to the customer at the end of every one of them.

Once the organization has adopted agile practices, the next step is to develop its continuous integration practices. The goal of continuous integration is to accomplish a situation where we always have a production quality version of the software available. Continuous integration causes the discussion in the company to change from "when can we ship" to "what needs to be in the release". As we can always ship the software, the question becomes whether we want to ship with or without certain features. Adopting continuous integration is not a binary step, but rather an iterative process incrementally aligning the test and verification system with a declared desired state.

To establish the current state, define the desired state and support the development of a plan transitioning from the current to the desired, we have developed the continuous integration improvement method (CITIM - Figure 14.2) which, as a main element, uses the continuous integration visualisation technique (CIVIT - Figure 14.3). CIVIT provides a powerful technique to create an end-to-end overview of all testing activities for a system or product, ranging from the individual engineer checking in code to the final acceptance testing at the customer. For each testing activity, the types of testing as well as the level of automation can be visualized.

Creating CIVIT visualizations has proven to be extremely helpful for com-

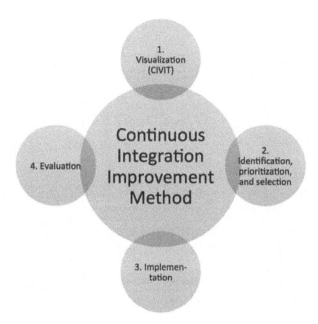

Figure 14.2   Continuous integration improvement method (CITIM)

panies during the adoption of continuous integration to create a common understanding of current state, desired state and prioritization of improvement
activities. Especially in large organizations, there is a significant lack of end-to-
end understanding of all testing and verification and validation activities that
take place in the company. This leads to several issues including inefficiency
due to duplication of testing efforts, slow feedback loops between development
and the rest of the organisation in case of errors and late discovery of issues
due to the setup of the testing process.

Once continuous integration is established, the next challenge to face is
the adoption of continuous deployment. In this book, we have discussed continuous deployment but do not provide specific tools as it largely focuses on
the acceleration and automation of existing deployment processes.

However, as we show in figure 14.4, in our experience with the Software
Center companies as well as many others, the typical pattern is that the continuous deployment loop is initially built up as a second iterative loop around
continuous integration. A separate release team is concerned with the deployment. This team makes use of some automated testing, but often has significant manual testing tasks to conduct as well before it considers performing
a deployment. In order to manage the deployment and the associated risk, it
maintains a deployment infrastructure with roll-back functionality. Although
one may expect that an approved deployment is just shipped out, in practice
even during continuous deployment, the team takes a staged deployment ap-

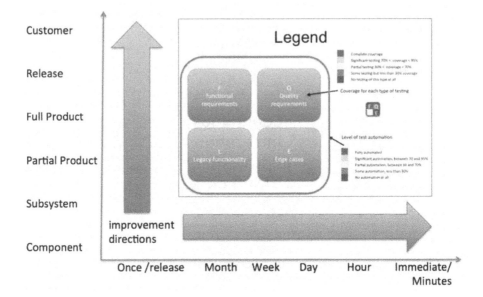

Figure 14.3 Continuous integration visualization technique (CIVIT)

proach and deploys in small batches and closely monitors the impact of the deployed software in order to identify issues that may require a roll-back.

Once the continuous deployment stage has been successfully implemented, the final step is to enable the data-driven approach to product development. In the final step, R&D becomes part of the innovation system of the company and facilitates experimentation with new features and products. Rather than the collection of data of basic system performance data, this requires a shift towards the instrumentation of systems with data collection focused on the delivery of customer value. Although the data dimension of the stairway to heaven is the primary dimension for this, it is important to realize that the speed dimension and the core R&D organization provides key enablers for the data and ecosystem dimensions of the Stairway to Heaven.

In our research, we have observed that the adoption of agile development and the relentless focus on delivering on the goals of the ongoing sprint naturally reduces a team's focus on architectural issues, defect management and other aspects that are less concerned with the immediate but are still critically important for the long-term health of the system. In response to this, organizations need to adopt mechanisms to explicitly and intentionally manage architecture, quality and prioritization of feature implementations.

In response to this challenge, we have discussed the ART framework. As shown in figure 14.5, the ART framework considers three main inputs for the overall backlog for the R&D organization around a product or product family. First, there are, of course, features representing new functionality that need

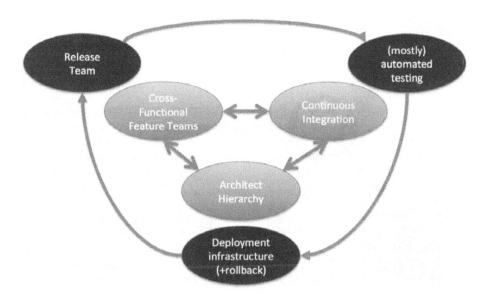

Figure 14.4 Continuous Deployment

to be added to the product. Second, there is a prioritized list of system defects which have slipped through the continuous integration system and that need to be addressed by a team specifically dedicated to addressing this specific defect. Finally, there is a prioritized list of architecture refactorings that needs to implemented in the system in order to maintain the architectural integrity and health. The work items need to be put in a single prioritized backlog by a governance team that balances the priorities of new features, defects and refactorings and assures an allocation that is in line with the business priorities.

The feature development in the ART framework can be conducted in different ways. As we have discussed in chapter 5, software development departments for products serving mass markets need to balance responsiveness to individual customer requests with the throughput of features that address the needs of all customers. In chapter 5, we presented a model for classifying features originating from individual customers as either customer unique or customer first. For the customer first features, we discuss an approach where customer-specific teams first build the feature for the requesting customer and then generalize the feature to suit the needs of the entire customer base. For customer unique features, we discuss the use of a professional services organization complementing the R&D organization that builds these features in a normal, commercial outsourced development setup. A professional services organization extending the product with customer-specific functionality has architectural implications that need to be considered. It may, however, provide a basis for evolving into a software ecosystem architecture as external

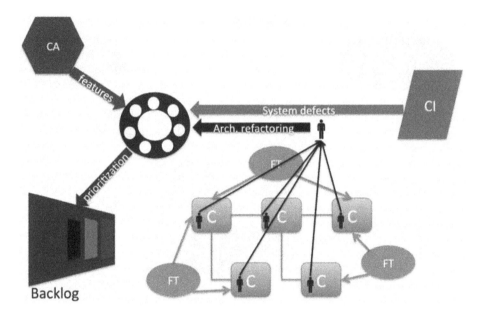

Backlog

Figure 14.5 The ART framework

developers are likely to require the same interfaces as an internal professional services organization would need.

14.2 DATA

The second dimension of the Stairway to Heaven model is concerned with effective use of data. As we show in Figure 14.6, there is a progression from the point where any attempts to work with data require a full manual and reactive approach to data to (at the other end) a state where the entire company is evidence driven and uses data for all decision making.

We have learned from the companies that we collaborate with that most companies collect copious amounts of data and yet find it exceedingly difficult to use that data to their benefit. This can be understood by the fact that collecting the data requires minimal changes to the organizational structure and ways of working where using the data requires, potentially, major changes. In table 14.1-data we provide an overview of the changes to collection, analysis, reporting and decision making as companies progress through the step of the data dimension. Starting from manual activities, the next step is to automate certain steps in often a rather static fashion. Although this provides value in and of itself we see that companies adopt a more dynamic form of automation where the automated activities are subject to a dynamic evolution process that, where possible, is automated as well.

As we seek to increase the value derived from all this data, we have pre-

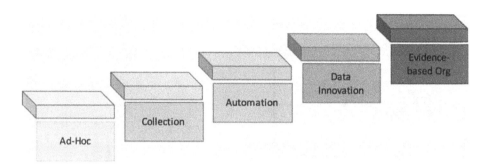

Figure 14.6 Stairway to Heaven: Data dimension

Table 14.1 From manual to automated; from static to dynamic

	Collection	Analysis	Reporting	Decision Making
Ad hoc	manual	manual	manual	manual
Collection	automated	manual	manual	manual
Automation	automated	automated	automated	supported
Data innovation	dynamic	dynamic	dynamic	supported
Evidence based company	dynamic	dynamic	dynamic	automated

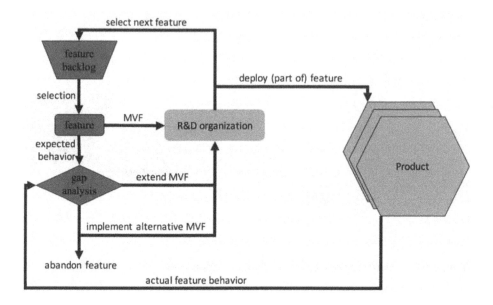

Figure 14.7 The HYPEX model

sented two models in earlier chapters. The first is the HYPEX model (shown in figure 14.7). HYPEX is mostly focused on the development of new features in existing products that already are deployed in the field. Using continuous deployment, the HYPEX model uses the data coming back from the deployed systems to determine if the feature is delivering on the predicted value.

The second model we introduce is the QCD model. The QCD model (figure 14.8) can be viewed as a generalisation of HYPEX and intends to support R&D teams to effectively manage data collected pre-development, during development and after deployment.

The challenge in most companies that we have worked with is that enormous amounts of data are collected in each of the stages of development. Some of this data are qualitative in nature, such as customer interviews, and other data are quantitative in nature, such as the number of trouble reports from the field. The challenge is that there is very limited exchange of data between the various groups collecting it. Consequently, there is no natural accumulation of data concerning new products or new features that companies can refer to in order to make informed decisions.

The QCD model provides a mechanism for managing each requirement, innovation idea, product concept, etc. as a hypothesis that needs to be tested. The testing is conducted using customer feedback techniques that in early stages tend to be qualitative in nature and turn towards quantitative data collection as we move towards later stages of development. One important aspect, however, is that each hypothesis can be abandoned when the data from the field do not warrant further investment in it.

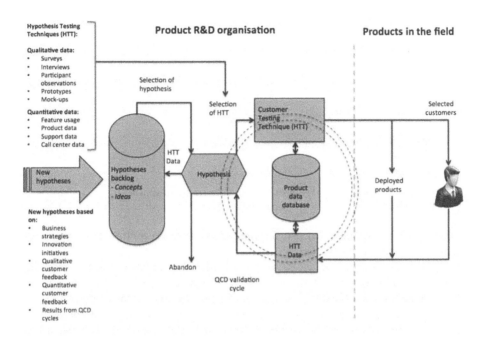

Figure 14.8 The QCD model

14.3 ECOSYSTEMS

The third dimension of the Stairway to Heaven is concerned with the ecosystem in which companies operate. As shown in figure 14.9, our research has shown that companies evolve from a point where they are internally focused and keeping the outside world at arm's length to a point where the ecosystem is engaged for everything for which the company itself is not uniquely suited and in line with its business strategy.

As a basis for our approach towards ecosystems, we use the three layer product model (3LPM). The 3LPM (figure 14.10) is a model that captures the evolution of functionality over time. The model is structured in three layers. The first layer represents the innovation and experimentation activities in the company. The goal of these activities is to identify functionality that may result in differentiation for the products of the company. Once differentiating functionality is identified, it is transitioned to the second layer where the R&D organization works on maximizing the differentiation of the identified functionality. This typically requires expanding on the functionality, adding variability for different customer segments, facilitating customer specific solutions, etc. Over time, however, the functionality will start to commoditize as competitors catch up and customers are less excited about the functionality. It will then transition to the bottom layer, which is concerned with commodity functionality. Each layer has its own optimization criteria, as shown in the

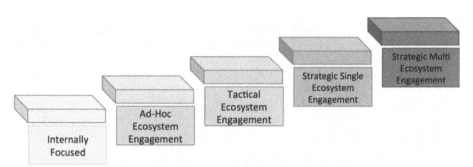

Figure 14.9 Stairway to Heaven: Ecosystem dimension

picture, and companies can use the model either as an architecture blueprint or as a conceptual model.

Based on the 3LPM, we developed TeLESM, the three layer ecosystem strategy model (figure 14.11). TeLESM starts from the notion that for a product or product family, companies do not engage with a single ecosystem, but with at least three ecosystems, i.e. one for each layer of the 3LPM. These ecosystems are quite different in nature and have different strategies and characteristics, such as drivers, partners and goals.

The innovation ecosystem is collaborative and concerned with exploration of the space of possible innovations and experimentation with these potential innovations to identify the ones that resonate with customers. The primary goal of the innovation ecosystem is to explore innovations that the company can not, or will be hard pressed to, deliver by itself and to share the cost of innovation.

Once functionality enters the differentiating functionality layer, the nature of the ecosystem engagement shifts to control driven and competitive. As differentiation drives pricing power, companies are extremely concerned about their control over the differentiating functionality and about leaking intellectual property to competitors. In addition, the new functionality now needs to work as customers will not accept low quality on new functionality. As a consequence, the partners in the differentiation ecosystem are controlled by the keystone player through contracts, service level agreements and other mechanisms.

Once the functionality starts to commoditize, it enters the commoditizing functionality ecosystem which is much more collaborative in its nature. The goal in this ecosystem is minimizing the total cost of ownership for the functionality and companies are willing to partner with anyone, including competitors, to achieve that goal.

As we show in figure 14.11, each ecosystem has different engagement strategies associated with it. These strategies can be more internally focused, but most have a strong collaborative nature and guide engagement with the ecosystem.

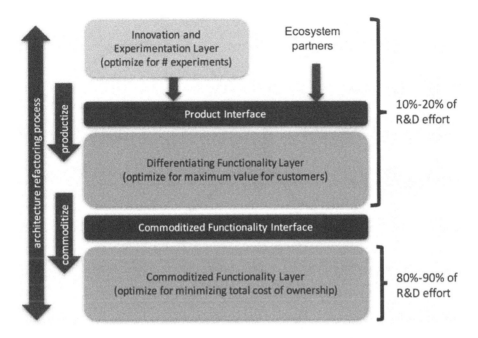

Figure 14.10 Three layer product model

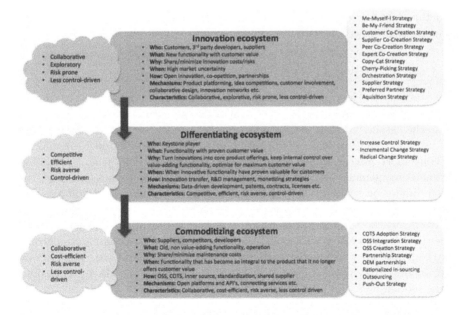

Figure 14.11 Three layer ecosystem strategy model

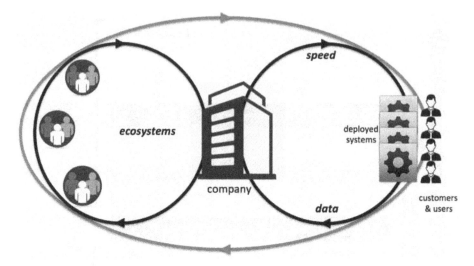

Figure 14.12 Stairway to Heaven overview

TeLESM provides a tangible tool for companies climbing the ecosystem dimension of the Stairway to Heaven as it provides a framework for strategic decision making for each ecosystem that the company is part of. The top level in this dimension is strategic multi-ecosystem engagement, which is translated into the company strategically managing its innovation, differentiation and commoditization ecosystems.

14.4 MAXIMIZING SYNERGY

The Stairway to Heaven model that we present in this book has three dimensions: speed, data and ecosystems. Companies can each of the dimensions and climb the associated stair and benefit greatly from it. For instance, companies can use the data dimension to improve the empirical basis for decision making without shortening feedback loops through continuous deployment or changing their engagement with their ecosystem. Similarly, companies can climb the speed dimension without using the data or their ecosystem. And doing so will significantly benefit the company.

However, the three dimensions are not fully orthogonal, but instead have synergistic relationships with each other. In our experience, companies become aware of and start to engage with the three dimensions in the sequence we have followed in the book. In figure 14.12, we visualize the three dimensions of the model.

The dimension that the companies that we work with start with is the speed dimension. The company adopts agile work practices, engages with continuous integration and, over time, transitions to continuous deployment with selected customers and, finally, all customers. Once the company starts to

transition to continuous deployment, the data dimension starts to be identified as a relevant dimension. This is caused by the shorter feedback loop
facilitated by continuous deployment, and product managers, architects and
engineers realize the opportunities with measuring system properties or customer behavior, rather than guessing. Consequently, companies start to engage
with the data in increasingly advanced ways and climb the stairs on the data
dimension. Once the company has dashboards in place and increasingly makes
data-driven decisions, it realizes that the same principles can be applied to the
ecosystem dimension. In response, the company starts to adopt more strategic
mechanisms for engaging its ecosystem partners and climbs the stairs on the
ecosystem dimension.

Concluding, although each dimension of the Stairway to Heaven can be
pursued independent of the others, in practice significant benefit can be accomplished by systematically engaging with all three dimensions and aligning
improvements implemented in each dimension with those in other dimensions.

14.5   HOW TO USE THE STAIRWAY TO HEAVEN

The Stairway to Heaven as presented in this book provides a framework
for strategic and systematic implementation of improvements in software-
intensive industries. Everyone knows that their company needs to improve
its system and software development practices, but in practice it proves to be
very difficult to prioritize and sequence the potential improvement activities.
The framework that we present in this book provides a set of tools, conceptual
models and techniques that practitioners can use.

To optimally use the Stairway to Heaven framework, one employs an iterative process of (1) assessing current state, (2) exploring, prioritizing and
planning improvements and (3) executing the improvement activities. In figure 14.13, we provide an example of an assessment of the speed dimension.
The assessment is conducted using a survey of employees and covers five dimensions and allows companies to compare themselves to others. It provides
insight into the areas where the company needs to focus its improvement
efforts.

In this book, we have provided several tools and techniques for assessing, planning and implementing improvements. In table 14.2, we provide an
overview of the tools and techniques presented in this book as well as the
chapter where the model or technique can be found.

The surveys have not been included in the book, but more information
can be found on the website (http://www.janbosch.com) or by contacting us.
We have conducted these surveys at several companies and we have learned
that each company requires some adjustments to the survey in order to optimally suit its purposes. Consequently, we prefer to work with companies and
practitioners directly when conducting these surveys. As the surveys are self-
assessments of the R&D organisation where every employee fills out an online

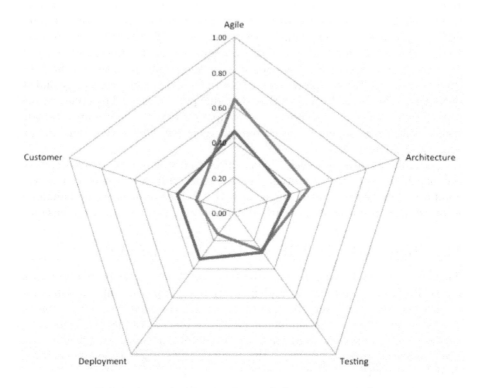

Figure 14.13 Example sssessment of speed dimension

Table 14.2 Overview of tools and techniques

Speed	CIVIT (Ch. 7), StH Speed survey	CIVIT (Ch. 7), ART mod (Ch. 6) , Customer tean model (Ch. 5)
Data	StH Data survey	HYPEX (Ch. 9), QC (Ch. 10)
Ecosystems	StH Ecosystem survey, ESAO model (Ch. 11), Industry structures model (Ch. 11)	TELESM (Ch. 12), Sof ware engineering implicatioı (Ch. 13)

survey, the cost and overhead for conducting a survey are reasonable and it can be implemented in a short time frame.

14.6 THE FUTURE

Although we believe that the three dimensions of speed, data and ecosystems will provide the key drivers for the software-intensive systems industry for at least the coming decade, there are new technologies and approaches on the horizon that will also influence the industry. In [13], we provide our perspective on the future of software engineering and we refer to that article for a more in-depth review. There, however, are three main developments that we believe are relevant for rounding off the discussion in this book.

First, companies will increasingly move from planning to experimentation. The increasing use of continuous deployment and the stream of data coming back from the field requires that companies transition from working with planned releases with detailed requirement specifications to a model where there is continuous experimentation with customers. The experimentation is concerned with optimizing features already implemented, developing new features in an iterative process or even building entirely new products.

There are two main reasons why the transition from planning to experimentation is critical. First, research shows that more than half of the features in a typical software-intensive system are never or hardly ever used. Using experimentation to test the relevance of new features for customers by building slices of features and measuring changes in customer or system behavior is a structured way to minimize the investment in features that add no value. Second, customer needs and desires change increasingly fast and companies that do not constantly test new ideas with customers are at risk of being disrupted by companies that identify shifts in customer preferences more readily.

The second trend is the adoption of machine learning and deep learning approaches where systems learn from data streams and feedback loops what behavior and patterns are relevant and which can be ignored. This allows companies to transition, for parts of the product functionality, from classical engineering to self-learning, autonomous systems or subsystems. Currently, machine learning applications are handled separately from traditional systems, but increasingly we will see hybrid systems that combine the best of both worlds.

Finally, organizations will increasingly abandon hierarchical organizational structures and adopt self-management practices. One of the main disadvantages of hierarchical management and decision making is the time required to make decisions. Especially in fast moving, highly complex environments, relying on a hierarchical model is a recipe for disaster as the quality and timing of management decisions becomes increasingly poor. The alternative is to decentralize management to the point that individuals and teams manage themselves. Again, agile teams today often have significant autonomy on how to conduct their work. As teams become increasingly cross-functional, self-management will increasingly be required to maintain competitiveness in a fast-paced world. The role of traditional management increasingly will be concerned with growing and steering the culture in the organization, resulting in individuals and teams making the right decisions despite the lack of traditional management hierarchies.

Concluding, to paraphrase Woody Allen, the future is where we spend the rest of our lives and for the software-intensive systems industries, the future looks incredibly exciting. The developments driving these industries will not only change the companies active in these industries but will change the very fabric of our society. Although some express concern about the speed of developments, the abuses of large-scale data and the demise of large internally focused companies to the benefit of ecosystem-centric companies, the fact remains that the quality of life in modern society is improving constantly and that this improvement is accelerating. Life has never been this good and it's only getting better! And software, in all its forms, is at the heart of all this. What a great era to be a professional working with this technology!

Bibliography

[1] Agile software development. https://en.wikipedia.org/wiki/Agile_software_development. Accessed: 2016-07-06.

[2] ISO/IEC 15504. https://en.wikipedia.org/wiki/ISO/IEC_15504. Accessed: 2016-07-06.

[3] Scaled agile framework. http://www.scaledagileframework.com/. Accessed: 2016-07-06.

[4] Ron Adner and Rahul Kapoor. Value creation in innovation ecosystems: How the structure of technological interdependence affects firm performance in new technology generations. *Strategic Management Journal*, 31(3):306–333, 2010.

[5] Genivi Alliance. Genivi alliance. http://www.genivi.org/. Accessed: 2016-07-06.

[6] M. Andreessen. Why software is eating the world. *The Wall Street Journal*, 2011-08-20:10–16, 2011.

[7] G. Kofi Annan. Reaching 50 million users. http://visual.ly/reaching-50-million-users. Accessed: 2016-07-06.

[8] Emil Backlund, Mikael Bolle, Matthias Tichy, Helena Holmström Olsson, and Jan Bosch. Automated user interaction analysis for workflow-based web portals. In *International Conference of Software Business*, pages 148–162. Springer, 2014.

[9] Carliss Young Baldwin and Kim B Clark. *Design Rules: The Power of Modularity*, volume 1. MIT Press, 2000.

[10] Jan Bosch. *Design and Use of Software Architectures: Adopting and Evolving a Product-Line Approach*. Pearson Education, 2000.

[11] Jan Bosch. Maturity and evolution in software product lines: Approaches, artefacts and organization. In *International Conference on Software Product Lines*, pages 257–271. Springer, 2002.

[12] Jan Bosch. From software product lines to software ecosystems. In *Proceedings of the 13th International Software Product Line Conference*, pages 111–119. Carnegie Mellon University, 2009.

[13] Jan Bosch. Speed, data, and ecosystems: The future of software engineering. *IEEE Software*, 33(1):82–88, 2016.

[14] Jan Bosch and Petra Bosch-Sijtsema. From integration to composition: On the impact of software product lines, global development and ecosystems. *Journal of Systems and Software*, 83(1):67–76, 2010.

[15] Jan Bosch and Petra Bosch-Sijtsema. ESAO: A holistic ecosystem-driven analysis model. In *International Conference of Software Business*, pages 179–193. Springer, 2014.

[16] Jan Bosch and Petra M Bosch-Sijtsema. Software product lines, global development and ecosystems: Collaboration in software engineering. In *Collaborative Software Engineering*, pages 77–92. Springer, 2010.

[17] Petra Bosch-Sijtsema and Jan Bosch. User involvement throughout the innovation process in high-tech industries. *Journal of Product Innovation Management*, 32(5):793–807, 2015.

[18] Petra M Bosch-Sijtsema and Jan Bosch. Plays nice with others? Multiple ecosystems, various roles and divergent engagement models. *Technology Analysis & Strategic Management*, 27(8):960–974, 2015.

[19] Petra M Bosch-Sijtsema and Theo JBM Postma. Cooperative innovation projects: Capabilities and governance mechanisms. *Journal of Product Innovation Management*, 26(1):58–70, 2009.

[20] Kevin Boudreau and Karim Lakhani. How to manage outside innovation. *MIT Sloan Management Review*, 50(4):69, 2009.

[21] Frederick P Brooks. The mythical man-month. *Essays on Software Engineering. Addison-Wesley Publishing Company*, 1975.

[22] Mary Beth Chrissis, Mike Konrad, and Sandra Shrum. *CMMI for Development: Guidelines for Process Integration and Product Improvement*. Pearson Education, 2011.

[23] Steve Coley. Three horizons model. http://www.mckinsey.com/business-functions/strategy-and-corporate-finance/our-insights/enduring-ideas-the-three-horizons-of-growth. Accessed: 2016-07-06.

[24] Melvin E Conway. How do committees invent. *Datamation*, 14(4):28–31, 1968.

[25] C. Ebert. Looking into the future. *Software, IEEE*, 32(6):92–97, November 2015.

[26] Christof Ebert and Capers Jones. Embedded software: Facts, figures, and future. *Computer*, 42(4):0042–52, 2009.

[27] Herman Hartmann, Tim Trew, and Jan Bosch. The changing industry structure of software development for consumer electronics and its consequences for software architectures. *Journal of Systems and Software*, 85(1):178–192, 2012.

[28] Anton Jansen and Jan Bosch. Software architecture as a set of architectural design decisions. In *5th Working IEEE/IFIP Conference on Software Architecture (WICSA'05)*, pages 109–120. IEEE, 2005.

[29] Daniel Kahneman. *Thinking, Fast and Slow*. Macmillan, 2011.

[30] Brett King. *Bank 2.0: How Customer Behaviour and Technology Will Change the Future of Financial Services*. Marshall Cavendish International Asia Pte Ltd, 2010.

[31] Mark W Maier, David Emery, and Rich Hilliard. ANSI/IEEE 1471 and Systems Engineering. *Systems Engineering*, 7(3):257–270, 2004.

[32] Antonio Martini and Jan Bosch. The danger of architectural technical debt: Contagious debt and vicious circles. In *Software Architecture (WICSA), 2015 12th Working IEEE/IFIP Conference on*, pages 1–10. IEEE, 2015.

[33] Antonio Martini, Jan Bosch, and Michel Chaudron. Architecture technical debt: Understanding causes and a qualitative model. In *2014 40th EUROMICRO Conference on Software Engineering and Advanced Applications*, pages 85–92. IEEE, 2014.

[34] Antonio Martini, Lars Pareto, and Jan Bosch. Towards introducing agile architecting in large companies: The caffea framework. In *International Conference on Agile Software Development*, pages 218–223. Springer, 2015.

[35] James F Moore. Predators and prey: A new ecology of competition. *Harvard Business Review*, 71(3):75–83, 1993.

[36] Dmitry Namiot and Manfred Sneps-Sneppe. On micro-services architecture. *International Journal of Open Information Technologies*, 2(9), 2014.

[37] Agneta Nilsson, Jan Bosch, and Christian Berger. The CIViT Model in a Nutshell: Visualizing Testing Activities to Support Continuous Integration. In *Continuous Software Engineering*, pages 97–106. Springer, 2014.

[38] Agneta Nilsson, Jan Bosch, and Christian Berger. Visualizing testing activities to support continuous integration: A multiple case study. In *International Conference on Agile Software Development*, pages 171–186. Springer, 2014.

[39] Helena Olsson, Anna Sandberg, Jan Bosch, and Hiva Alahyari. Scale and responsiveness in large-scale software development. *IEEE Software*, 31(5):87–93, 2014.

[40] Helena Holmström Olsson and Jan Bosch. From Opinions to Data-Driven Software R&D: A Multi-case Study on How to Close the "Open Loop" Problem. In *40th EUROMICRO Conference on Software Engineering and Advanced Applications*, pages 9–16. IEEE, 2014.

[41] Helena Holmström Olsson and Jan Bosch. The HYPEX Model: From Opinions to Data-Driven Software Development. In *Continuous Software Engineering*, pages 155–164. Springer, 2014.

[42] Helena Holmström Olsson and Jan Bosch. Towards continuous customer validation: A conceptual model for combining qualitative customer feedback with quantitative customer observation. In *International Conference of Software Business*, pages 154–166. Springer, 2015.

[43] David Lorge Parnas. Software aging. In *Proceedings of the 16th International Conference on Software Engineering*, pages 279–287. IEEE Computer Society Press, 1994.

[44] Dewayne E Perry and Alexander L Wolf. Foundations for the study of software architecture. *ACM SIGSOFT Software Engineering Notes*, 17(4):40–52, 1992.

[45] Eric Ries. *The Lean Startup: How Today's Entrepreneurs Use Continuous Innovation to Create Radically Successful Businesses*. Crown Books, 2011.

[46] René Rohrbeck, Katharina Hölzle, and Hans Georg Gemünden. Opening up for competitive advantage–How Deutsche Telekom creates an open innovation ecosystem. *R&D Management*, 39(4):420–430, 2009.

[47] CMMI Product Team. CMMI for Development, version 1.2. 2006.

[48] Bruce W Tuckman. Developmental sequence in small groups. *Psychological Bulletin*, 63(6):384, 1965.

[49] Frank Van Der Linden, Jan Bosch, Erik Kamsties, Kari Känsälä, and Henk Obbink. Software product family evaluation. In *International Conference on Software Product Lines*, pages 110–129. Springer, 2004.

[50] Eric Von Hippel. Lead users: A source of novel product concepts. *Management Science*, 32(7):791–805, 1986.

[51] Fred Wiersema and Michael Treacy. *The Discipline of Market Leaders*. Reading, MA: Addison-Wesley, 1996.

[52] Wikipedia. Technology readiness level. `https://en.wikipedia.org/wiki/Technology_readiness_level`. Accessed: 2016-07-06.

Index